JOEL BABB

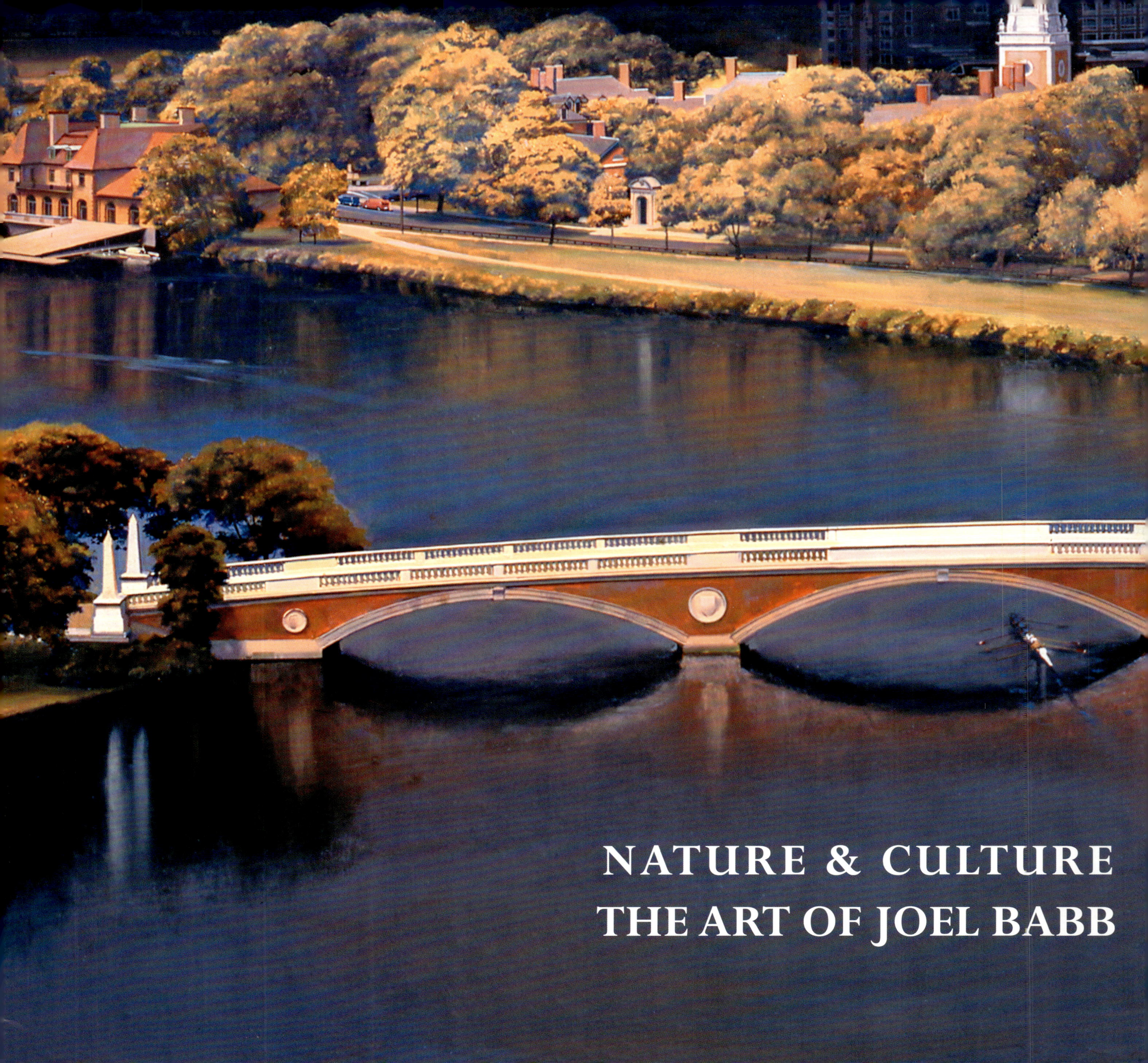
NATURE & CULTURE
THE ART OF JOEL BABB

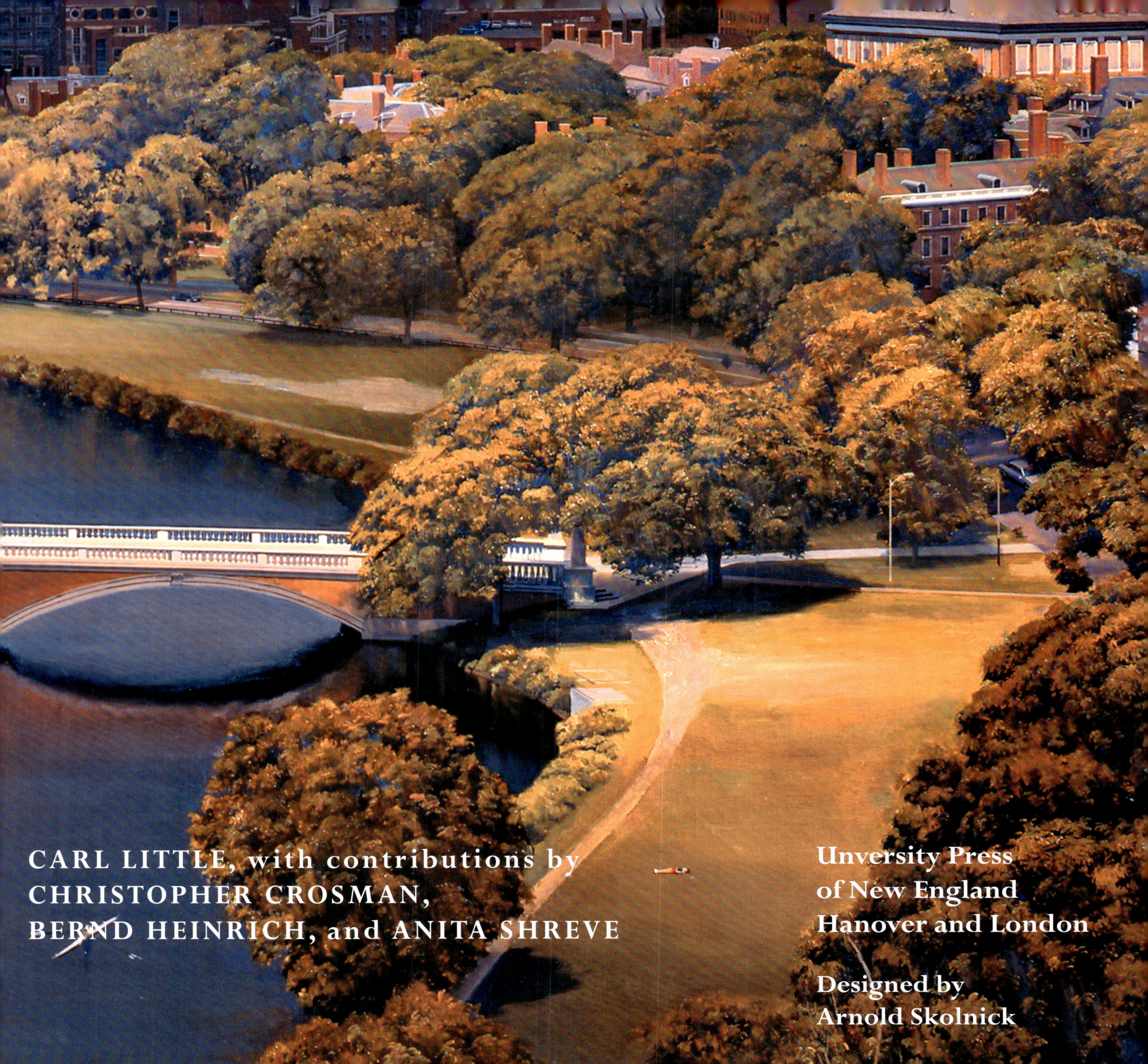

CARL LITTLE, with contributions by
CHRISTOPHER CROSMAN,
BERND HEINRICH, and ANITA SHREVE
Unversity Press
of New England
Hanover and London
Designed by
Arnold Skolnick

Published by
University Press of New England
1 Court Street
Lebanon, New Hamphire 03766

Produced by
Chameleon Books
31 Smith Road., P.O. Box 445
Chesterfield, Massachusetts 01012
413 296 8028
chambooks@earthlink.net

Designed by Arnold Skolnick
Copyedited by Jamie Nan Thaman

Printed in China

ISBN 978-1-61168-430-8

Library of Congress Cataloging-in-Publication Data

Little, Carl.
  Nature and culture : the art of Joel Babb / Carl Little, with
contributions by Christopher Crosman, Bernd Heinrich, and Anita Shreve.
  — 1st [edition].
    pages cm
  ISBN 978-1-61168-430-8 (cloth : alk. paper)
1. Babb, Joel, 1947—Criticism and interpretation. 2. Cities and
towns in art. 3. Realism in art–United States. I. Title.
  ND237.B125L58 2013
  759.13--dc23
                                        2012032030

For permission to reproduce any of the material in this book, contact Permissions,
University Press of New England, One Court Street, Suite 250, Lebanon NH 03766;
or visit www.upne.com

ACKNOWLEDGMENTS
The author wishes to thank Joel Babb for his aid and his art and for opening up the world of
perspective—and seeing. Thanks also to the Vose Galleries; to Frannie Babb for her hospitality
during winter visits to East Sumner; to Arnold Skolnick and his design chops; and to Martha
Hoppin for her editorial comments.

CONTENTS

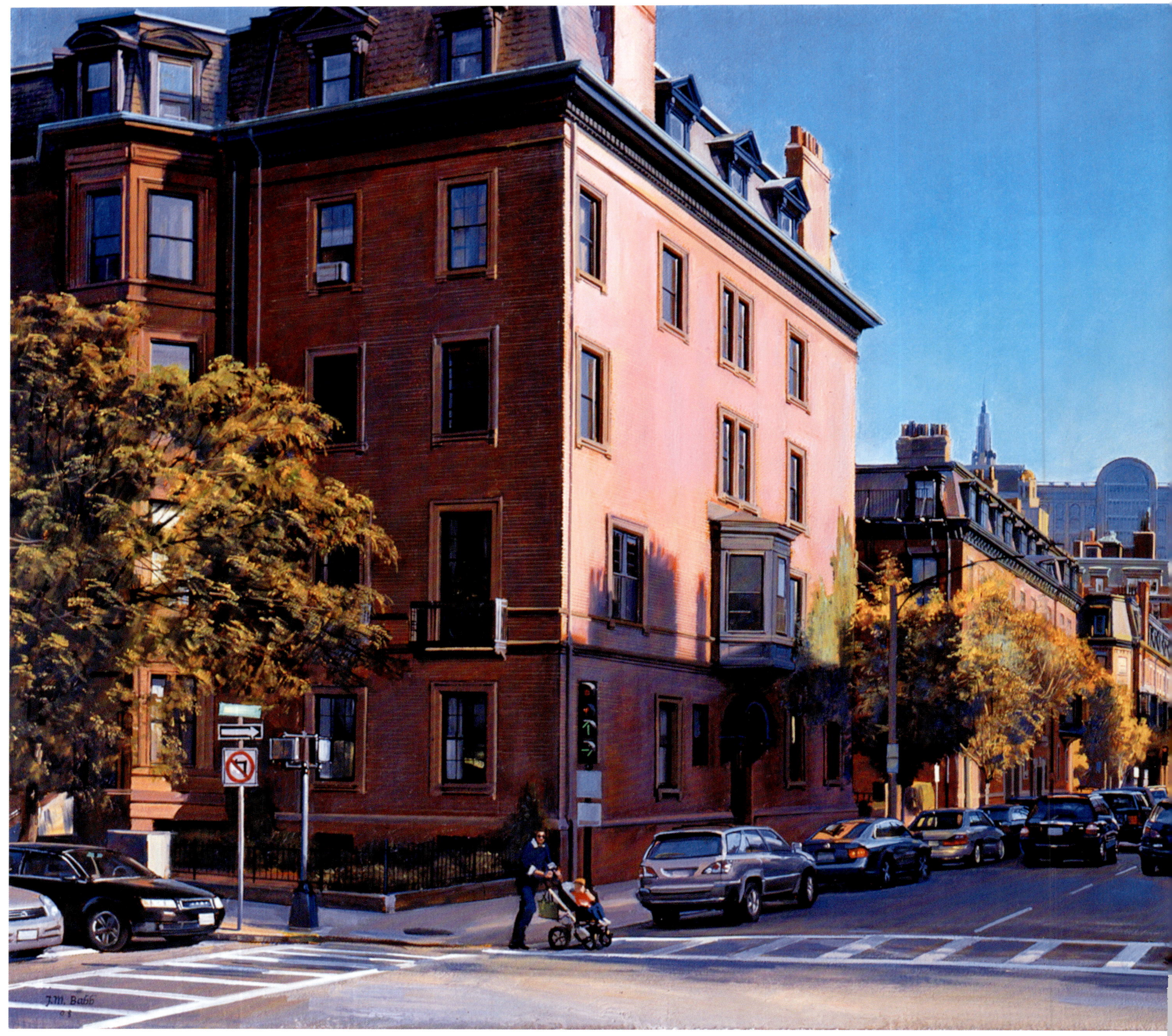

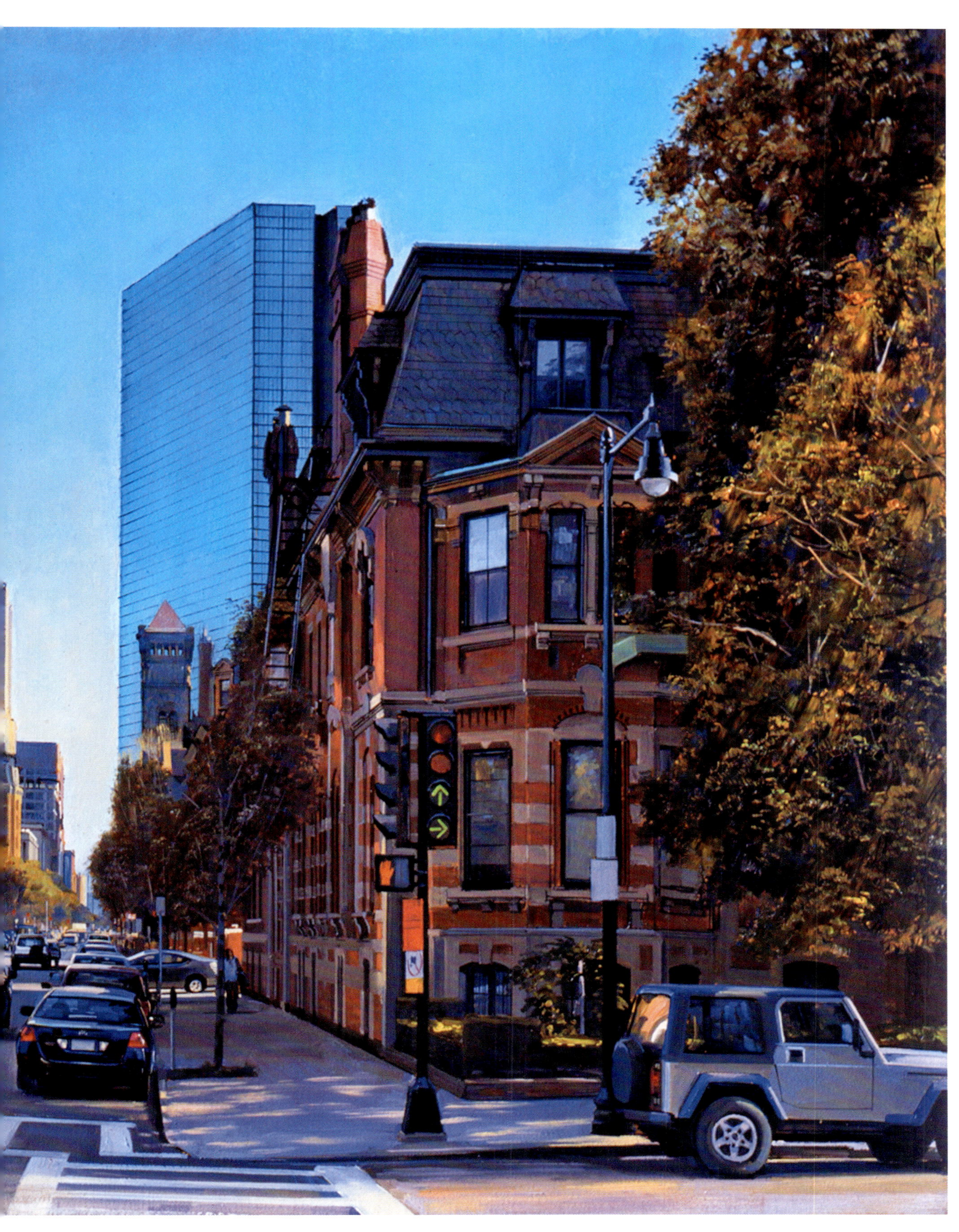

BEACON AND CLARENDON,
AFTERNOON LIGHT, 2008
OIL ON LINEN, 18 5/8 x 36 INCHES
PRIVATE COLLECTION

ONE HESITATES TO USE THE WORD AWESOME to describe the work of Joel Babb, but if we catch the word in its changing history from "inspiring fear" to the ubiquitous verbal tic it is today, we can apply its best-understood meaning—inspiring awe; jaw-droppingly amazing; and gobsmackingly astonishing—to the artist's cityscapes. Babb's finely detailed depictions of Boston, particularly those of the Back Bay extending from the Charles River to the John Hancock building, do for that city what Canaletto did for Venice. Beyond that first thrilling jolt that one is looking at something never seen before, there is the sensation of falling into the canvas with its three-dimensional and inexhaustible beauty. For those of us who live in Boston, it's almost impossible not to play the game, "That's my house (condo, apartment)!" Employing helicopters, cameras, and T squares, Joel Babb has, with his topographical but not quite photo-realistic cityscapes, allowed us to see something unique: not just the city as it precisely is, but rather the work of art that is Boston.

Equally arresting are Babb's cityscapes seen from street level: exacting views of the old Boston and the new colliding in such a way as to produce an almost electric tension. His painting *On Commonwealth Ave.,* for example, shows us varied architectural styles that are the essence of the Back Bay while sweeping in the present in the form of casual strollers in hooded sweatshirts and late model cars parked at the curb. In another, entitled *Beacon and Clarendon, Afternoon Light*, the nineteenth-century brick town houses of Clarendon are bathed in western light, in sharp contrast to the cool length of the John Hancock tower at the painting's vanishing point.

I never tire of walking the streets of the Back Bay. On each excursion, I see something I'm positive I've never seen before. A balustrade, an entire house, a twelve-over-twelve window. I've often said that the Back Bay of Boston is one of the few urban areas in America in which it is possible to walk for over an hour and not see anything ugly. It is an area of unique facades, varied textures, and the lovely Parisian boulevard that is Commonwealth. No house looks exactly like the other; each evokes a different feeling and history.

One summer, my husband John, who was in Maine at the time, was invited to a dinner party at which Joel Babb and his wife, Frannie, were guests. The host had in his living room several catalogs of Babb's work to peruse. After the dinner, John called me (in Boston) to enthuse over paintings he was sure would excite me. "You can find them on the Vose Galleries site," he urged.

I did as suggested, scrolling slowly through a collection I found both exquisite and intriguing. "How does he do that?" I kept asking myself. I stopped at the painting entitled *Beacon and Clarendon, Afternoon Light*. The principal structure is an unprepossessing brick town house bathed in extraordinary light juxtaposed with the pie-wedge of shiny cars making their way toward the sleek John Hancock tower. I looked at the painting again and had a moment of clarity.

"That's our house," I whispered to an empty room.

And it was. The house in which we had a condo. Babb had painted the bricks, the bay window, the sturdy arch over the front door and even lit lamps inside the six-over-six windows.

Awesome, I'm pretty sure I said.

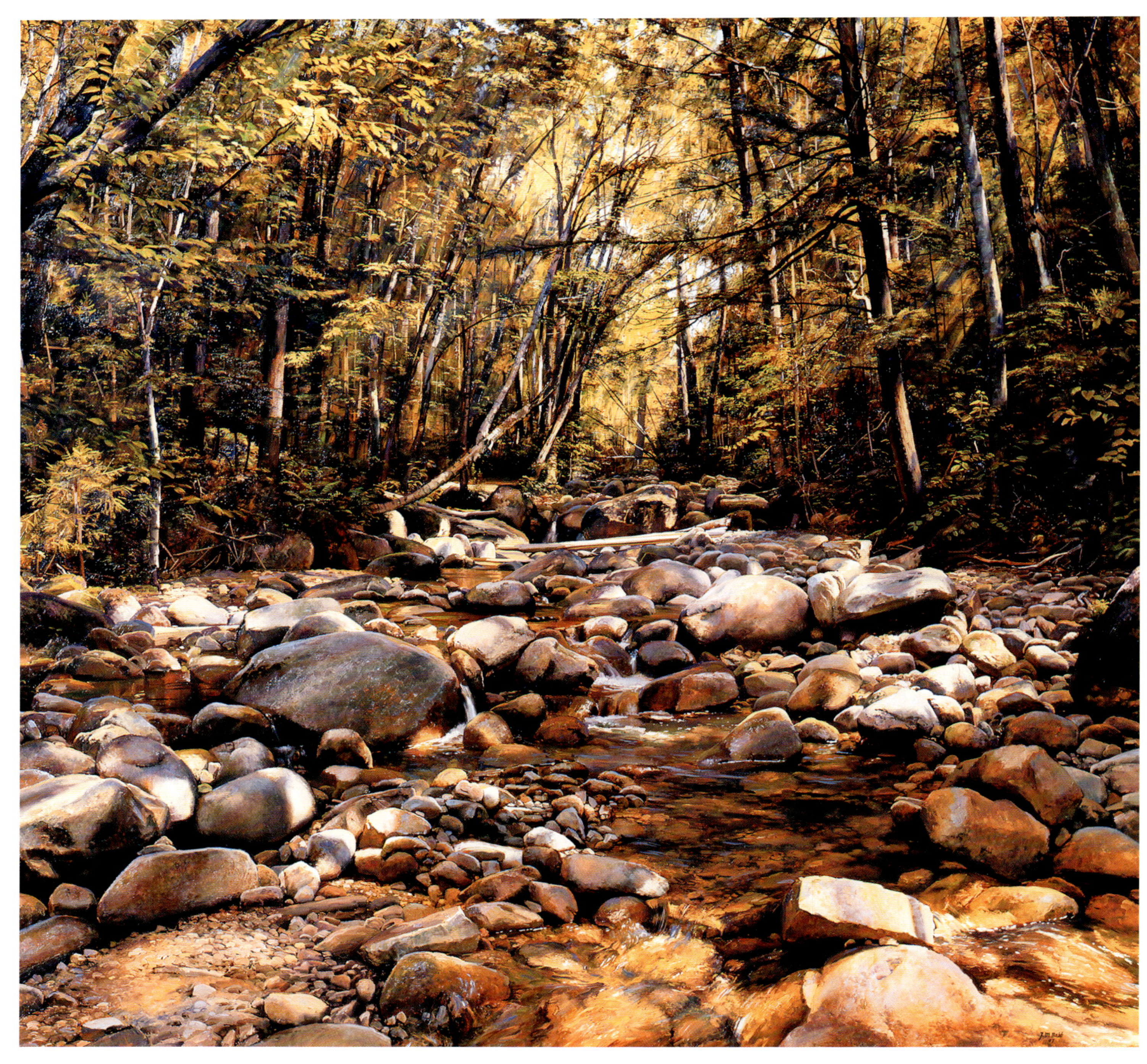

The Dappled Brook, 2007
Oil on linen, 48 x 51 inches
Private collection

INTRODUCTION

Christopher Crosman

That an artist would name his dog Ruskin (after the nineteenth-century
English critic John Ruskin, who championed Turner and other artists associated with
Ruskin's "truth to nature" aesthetic) suggests a certain self-deprecating wit and genial
affability. "Dogging" the artist, moreover, is his own good-natured awareness of the
conventional attitude holding that a realist painter in the early twenty-first century is
well outside the mainstream and hopelessly outdated. In fact, however, Joel Babb's
vision is very much of his own time, grounded in history and tradition but part of an
ongoing contemporary dialogue between nature and culture as seen in the work of
stylistically diverse and media-disparate contemporary artists, from Roxy Paine and
Ursula von Rydingsvard to Walton Ford and Tom Uttech to Bill Viola and James Turrell.

Babb's work verges on photographic verisimilitude and certainly has links to
Photo-Realism, a style that emerged during the mid-1960s and early 1970s in the work
of Richard Estes, Ralph Goings, Robert Bechtle, and Richard McClean, among others.
He freely acknowledges the importance of photography to his working process. But
crucially, Babb's work is not about the "camera eye," as it often seems to be in the work
of artists like Estes, where reflections, focal points, angles of vision, and lighting effects
complicate "reality" as opposed to clarifying it. Babb's precise and meticulous realism
is, at the end of the day, about clarity and discovery of the world that the human eye can
see but seldom does, at least not with the clarity and precision that Babb presents in his
paintings. And his work acknowledges and explores the mystery of perception, a process
that not even science understands fully—or, as he suggests, perhaps, less well than
philosophy and art are equipped to explore.

Trained in art history at Princeton, followed by travel in Europe, especially
Italy and northern Europe, Babb studied to become a professional artist in Boston,
notably at the School of the Museum of Fine Arts. At Princeton and in Boston, Babb
studied with several extraordinary mentors and teachers, including George Segal, the
well-known Pop sculptor of evocative urban settings haunted by ghostly white plaster
figures, and George Ortman, whose exacting geometric abstractions in the Bauhaus
tradition are latent in Babb's work even today. It was long hours in the museum galleries
as graduate student and teacher, however, that were central to his education and fundamental to his learning to look at masterworks, honing a catholic but exquisitely refined

visual literacy ranging from Canaletto to John Singer Sargent. Even before experiencing these rich and varied references and resources, Babb's midwestern upbringing must have surely effected a no-nonsense, pragmatic attitude toward painting as well as a prodigious work ethic. Perhaps only an artist raised in the suburbs of the American heartland (Lincoln, Nebraska) would complain about the lack of sidewalks in Rome (along with far too many people blocking his view of Roman monuments and architecture)!

Looking at his large aerial views of Boston, with their multiple vanishing points and vertigo-inducing perspectives, the viewer is suspended between heaven and earth. In our post September 11, 2001, era there is something poignantly unsettling about urban cityscapes and the view from tall buildings. But more reassuring is Babb's take on city life from on high: that there is an essential order, calm, and majesty present in the built environment and a profound continuity between past and present—Copley Square to the Prudential building—that might otherwise go unnoticed by street-level passersby in the modern, chaotic rush of city life.

In like manner, Babb's Maine landscapes—often large scale, with unexpected vertical or nearly square formats and high or absent horizon lines—place the viewer in unknown terrain, in locations that only intrepid, solitude-seeking backpackers and artists (at least those immune to black flies) tend to visit. Less disorienting than the cityscapes, Babb's paintings of the dense, tangled Maine woods and meandering brooks often have the same roseate underglow that infuse warmth into his red-brick tinged cityscapes. The warm or occasionally cool tonal ranges are a function of underpainting, or tinted grounds upon which additional layers of paint are painstakingly built up. Subtle color harmonies are tuned to the overall "key" of the painting. Indeed, as a colleague once remarked about the work of another well-known and oft-derided realist painter, Andrew Wyeth, Babb's brushwork is akin to the technique of a great pianist who seemingly pulls the notes from the piano rather than pressing or pushing down on the keys. And increasingly in his work, the overall surface dynamics of brush against canvas and painterly application emphasize the handwork that makes the image exist in the first place—the awareness that we are looking at a painting that is far from photographic and that contains far more to see and savor as a product of the human hand and eye than is offered by mechanical reproduction.

It is instructive, perhaps, to consider a much earlier city view that is also a landscape: Thomas Cole's *View of Boston,* 1839, is among the very first topographical depictions of that city, although to audiences of Cole's day the painting conveyed much more information. The viewer is placed on a foreground rise and looks toward the harbor and barely discernible low buildings clinging to the distant shoreline, a small but expanding settlement against the vastness of earth, sea, and sky. On a gentle rise at the left center, pointing above the horizon line and illuminated by a break in the cloud-filled sky, is a white steeple and church. The church, although distant, is placed at the viewer's eye level, reinforcing its prominence and spiritual nearness as the mental space between viewer and church collapses. Consistent, no doubt, with the city's own pious image of itself at the time, Cole here equates Boston with the celestial City of God, located on the newly cultivated fringes of the vast, beneficent American Eden. In a more secular vein, Joel Babb also deftly places his viewers between the here and the hereafter, between compression and expansion, between the particular and the universal, between nature and culture.

Nature and culture, vitality and power, are, after all, timeless subjects. As is Babb's insistence that looking hard—both close and distant—is powerful and vital and a gift. His and ours.

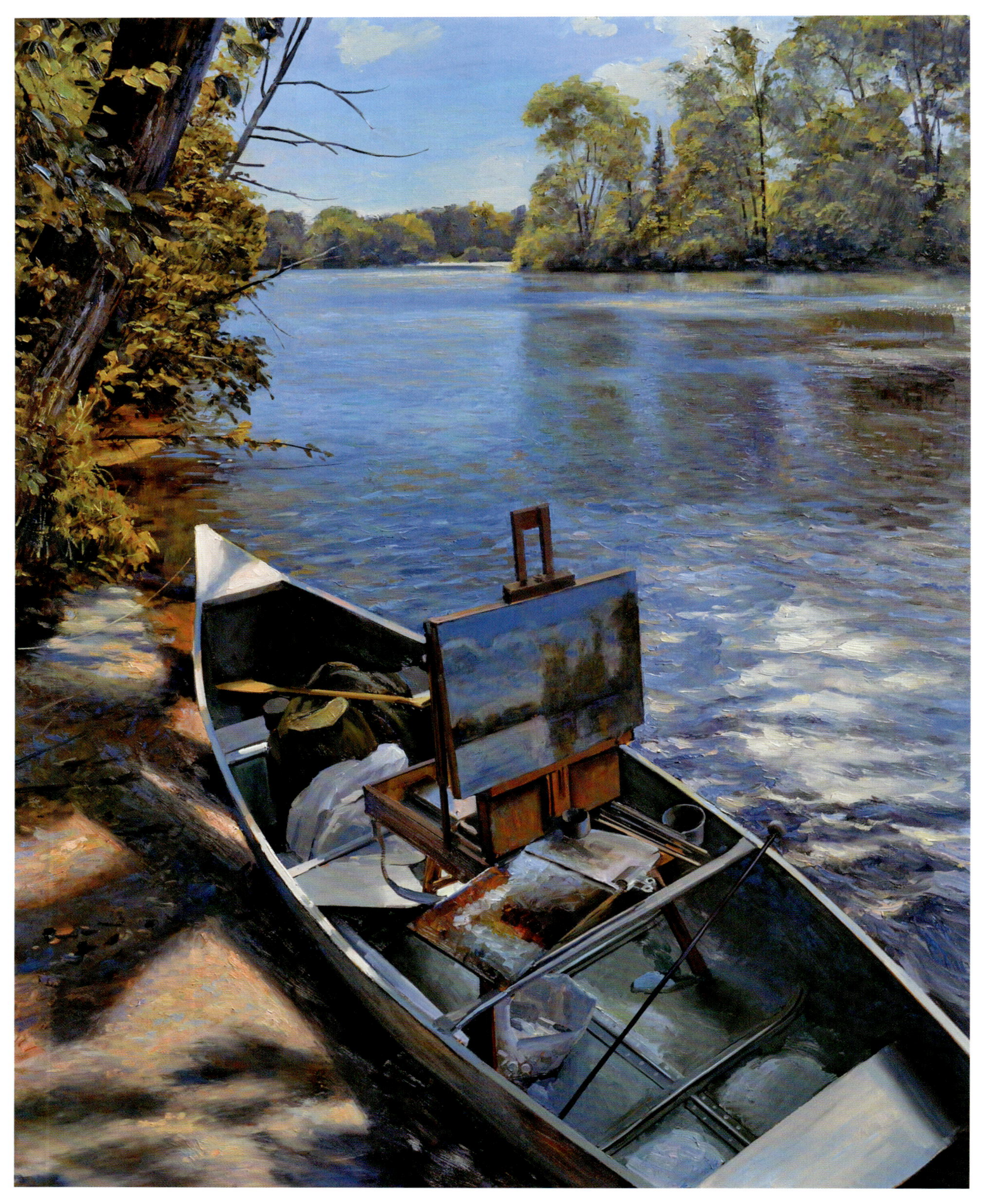

Painting from the Canoe, 2011
Oil on linen, 53 x 42 inches,
Collection of the Artist

Joel Babb: Nature & Culture

Carl Little

A LARGE LANDSCAPE BY JOEL BABB FEATURES A CANOE pulled up on the bank of a river with the accoutrements of a plein air painter set within it. It is a self-portrait of sorts: the artist presented as the materials he employs to capture the world around him. Sunlight falls on the water, distant trees stand against the sky, and the river—the Nezinscot—invites the viewer around the next bend. Displayed in the floating studio is his study of this very bend. Nature sustains Babb; he turns to it as a place of retreat and renewal—and, for his remarkable forest paintings, inspiration. He has achieved a balance in which the excitement of painting outdoors lends new energy to his studio work.[1]

Babb is known equally for his urban views. He divides his time between country and city, continuing to explore both places even as he builds on his repertoire of subjects. He also sketches outdoors (even from helicopters) for these hyperrealistic panoramas and intimate streetscapes of the Boston and Portland, Maine, environs. For Babb, realism represents a philosophy of art. As such, he says, the realist painter is constantly discovering "new understandings, new realizations" of the mysteries of existence. "Realism as a philosophy," he muses "suggests that a small corner of the universe, when rightly observed, may open up universal laws in action." A modern-day Thoreau.

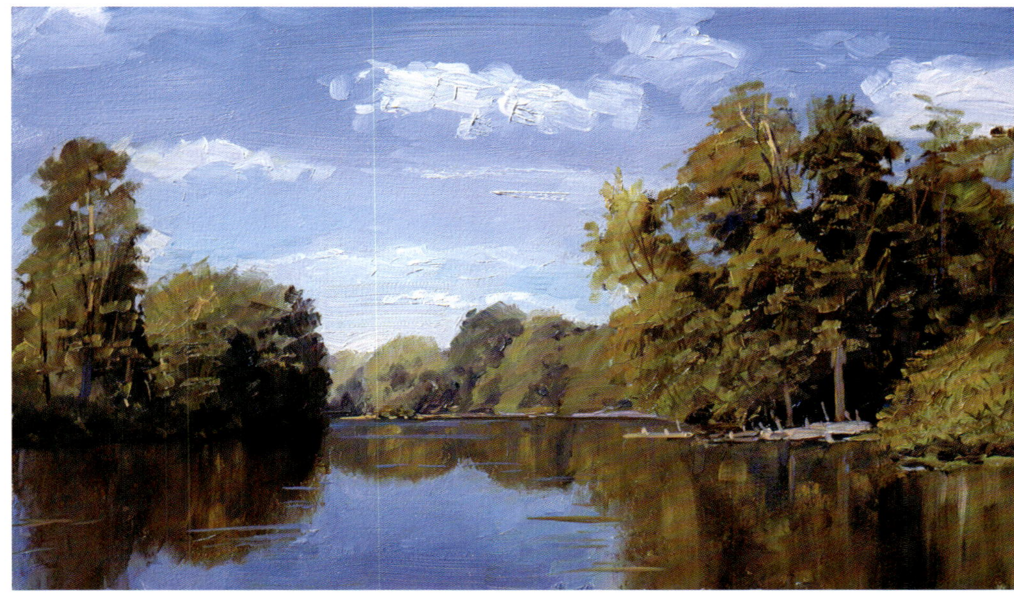

Joel M. Babb was born in Waycross, Georgia, on May 31, 1947. Because his father worked for the U.S. Department of Agriculture, the family (including Babb's two sisters) ended up settling in Lincoln, Nebraska. From an early age, Babb considered art a viable livelihood. "My mother's father painted a bit, I had an uncle who was the art director of TWA, and one of my cousins was an artist who studied at Cranbrook," he stated in a 2002 interview, "so I thought of art as being a potential career."[2]

Art awareness began in high school through chance encounters with the work of contemporary artists. At one point, for example, Babb came across a profile of painter Edwin Dickinson in *Time* magazine.[3] He was struck by one of the paintings reproduced, a moonlit interior titled *The Fossil Hunters*, 1926–1928. The suggestiveness of the subject appealed to him. Dickinson's painting may have inspired the central figure in the largest canvas Babb painted in high school, *Wounded Figure*, 1965. The painting shows a male figure, its face dark and mask-like, with its chest torn open. A sophisticated vision well beyond the budding artist's age is apparent.

In his room in Nebraska, Babb worked at an easel that had belonged to his grandfather. He pinned up sheets of newsprint and, using large brushes, painted in ink wash in a way he has described as "the typical Rorschach approach of Abstract Expressionism." He listened to Bach and to Vivaldi violin concertos as he worked.[4]

Another Dickinson painting, *Ruin at Daphne*, 1943–1953, had a similar impact on the young artist.[5] Influenced by this architectural fantasy and by the eighteenth-century Italian artist Giovanni Battista Piranesi's *Carceri* engravings—the so-called "prison series"—Babb set out to create his own painted compendiums of bits and pieces of places and objects. One of these, *Architectural Fantasy*, 1964–1965, blends Dickinson's cryptic symbolism and Piranesi's evocative settings. This painting received a favorable notice from Babb's uncle, Trans World Airlines art director Rex Werner, who boldly claimed that a New York City art gallery would be glad to show them if his nephew could produce twenty-five more. The praise was inspiring but also rather confounding, coming from "an admired uncle" who otherwise paid little attention to his art.

In 1965 Babb entered Princeton University, where he majored in art history.[6] Among his teachers was George Ortman, a California artist known for his geometric constructions. Ortman was straightforward in his opinions—he called Dickinson a

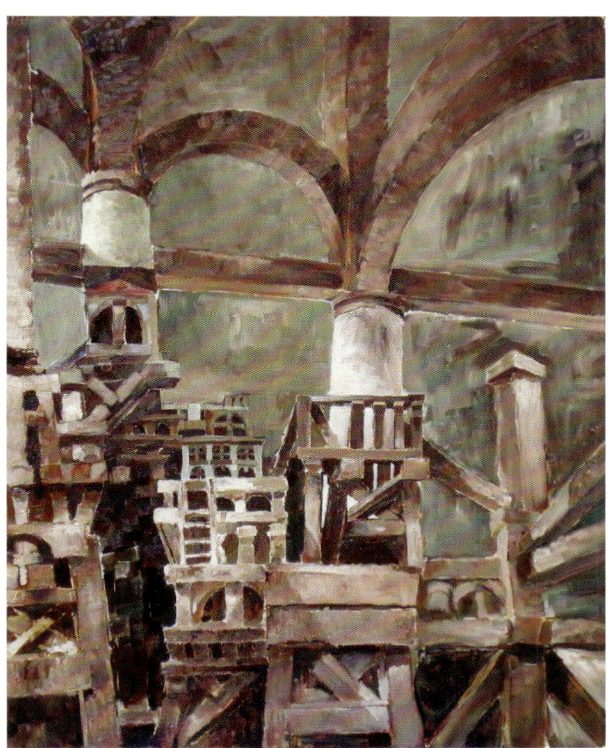

third-rate artist—and taught an abstract-leaning approach to making art that focused on signs and symbols. Ortman's contemporary perspective and philosophy encountered resistance from students and faculty at the university, but Babb admired his independent vision and enjoyed working with him.[7] He also owed his professor a debt of gratitude: he helped arrange a fellowship in the Creative Arts Program at Princeton, which allowed Babb to stay at the university one summer to work in a large studio of his own.[8]

That summer was a productive one. Babb made large brush paintings inspired by the trees outside his studio window "as if they were surreal personages gesticulating, interacting and gesturing to each other." Inspired by a portfolio of Henri Matisse's paintings and drawings in the French art journal *Verve,* he created a book of Chinese ink paintings alternating with oil paintings that included the window and the trees beyond. He spent evenings in the university's Theatre Intime, sketching rehearsals with a reed pen.

While at Princeton, Babb established the discipline that has marked his life as a painter.[9] Whenever he could, day and night, he sketched and painted, discovering motifs during the long walks he took around and beyond campus—excursions that also served to relieve him of some of the stress of academics.[10] He recalls carrying his studio easel, canvas, and paints to distant prospects.

Babb also studied with George Segal, whose tableaux of modern life featuring life-size plaster-cast figures are icons of twentieth-century American sculpture. Though he found Segal to be perceptive and intelligent—and an astute observer of art of all periods—the course itself was "something of a disaster," with students unprepared to respond to their professor's directives in a meaningful way. Like his classmates, Babb sought to emulate his teacher, creating some installation pieces that even Segal judged to be over the top.[11]

At the same time, Babb was fully immersed in art history, relishing many of the classes at Princeton. He particularly enjoyed, and excelled in, Kurt Weitzmann's medieval course and Wen Fong's class in Chinese art. In some cases, only many years later did he appreciate the genius of his teachers.[12]

Fong's course and a graduate seminar that he also taught were among the high points of Babb's education. The brilliant scholar, who later became a special consultant to the Department of Asian Art at the Metropolitan Museum, relied on "intense connoisseurship," as Babb has described his teacher's methods of addressing the problems of style and historical development. Students developed a habit of long and careful study of original works of art and were taught to base attributions on "known and verifiable archaeological landmarks." Babb was also drawn to the idea of the Chinese scholar-painter, "living in seclusion in the mountains, in poetic dialogue with his great ancestors, but dealing with nature and eternal forces in original ways." He embraced this vision and has, to some extent, pursued it in his life as an artist. Indeed, he has noted that in his landscapes of Maine he feels the presence of those studies of Chinese landscape painting at Princeton.[13]

Babb's reading list included such landmark studies as Heinrich Wölfflin's *Renaissance and Baroque* and E. H. Gombrich's *Art and Illusion*. From each, he took insights: the former's admonition that an artist's work must be "of his own time" and the latter's focus on the graphic conventions that artists adopt on the way to developing a personal style. Through reading Bernard Berenson, he discovered Giovanni Morelli, the nineteenth-century Italian art historian, whose scholarly method resembled that of a detective. "I loved the intense observation and the challenge of connoisseurship as opposed to…theoretical abstractions," Babb recalls.

As he delved into the history of aesthetics, Babb came to realize that a responsiveness and interest in art did not necessarily make one capable of formulating art-historical ideas. Although the art history department at Princeton, one of the best in the land, excelled at building the "wide foundations" of art appreciation, Babb felt he and his fellow majors needed "a Brunelleschian genius to roof over the foundations that had just been laid down."

Babb's Princeton years were ones of evolution and discovery. While he experimented with various modern aesthetics under the sway of his teachers, he also came to realize the need for fundamentals. He confronted a philosophical point of view that held concepts of the modern above the lessons of the past. "The narrative of the arising of modernism as a renewal of art over the decadence of academicism…was unquestioned," Babb recalls. This narrative was reinforced by his friend John MacGregor, a graduate student at Princeton whose thesis focused on psychoanalysis and art. Later a historian of outsider and psychotic art,[14] MacGregor focused on the unconscious elements and inner necessity of art, ideas that appealed to Babb's sense of rebellion. Babb made a connection between the processes of automatism of such artists as the Frenchman Jean Dubuffet

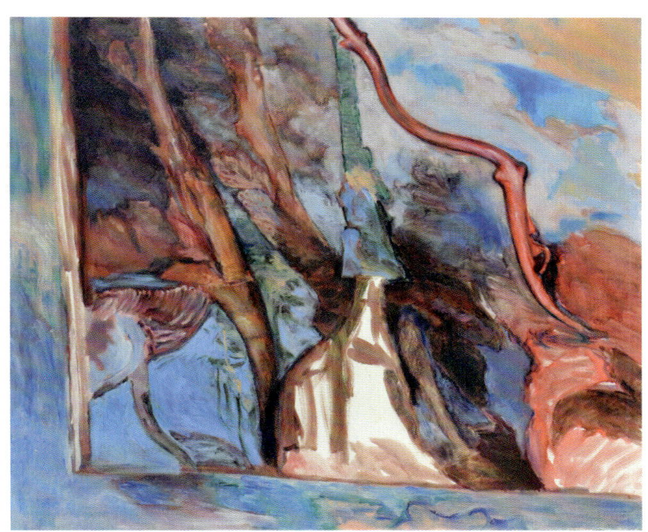

and the concepts of abstract-expressionist painting.

As Babb completed his studies, he continued to be in thrall to modernist concepts, including MacGregor's ideas of the unconscious. He painted in an "unpremeditated" manner that consisted of laying on color in splashes and then shaping images that seemed to emerge in the process. Reading T. S. Eliot's "The Waste Land" added fuel to this surrealist fire, as he sought in visual terms to emulate the poet's use of associations that "hover suggestively around meanings without being reducible to explicit symbolism."

Babb's *Window Abstraction,* 1969, epitomizes his final body of work at Princeton. The painting features an array of random objects—a sitting dog, a gun, a crustacean, a skate swimming away, veins and arteries, a rib cage—suggestive of "anxieties, tensions, pleasures" and existing in "an uneasy arrangement like the elements of a dream." The freedom the artist felt deploying these images was almost therapeutic. William Butler Yeats's poem "The Circus Animals' Desertion" seemed to support his vision:

> Those masterful images because complete
> Grew in pure mind, but out of what began?
> A mound of refuse or the sweepings of a street,
> Old kettles, old bottles, and a broken can.

Babb was drawing on the elements of the "rag and bone shop of the heart" to create a new image. The poet's words, he felt, justified his own "experiments in a new style delving into the contents of the unconscious."

As an art history major at Princeton, Babb discovered that his studies "made a framework" for his thinking about the creative act. Indeed, exposure to art-historical literature had a direct impact on his development as an artist. "Over time the encounter with historical art undermined my youthful confidence in experimentation with abstract expressionism," he has noted, "and probably had a lot to do with my painting taking the turn it did." Babb felt he had arrived at a crossroads: on the one hand, the unconscious aspect of art-making seemed rich in possibilities; on the other, was an existentialist view of culture a reason to abandon all tradition, to avoid the mastery of technique? The young artist found himself pulled between a desire to practice a modern art and a growing passion for the past. He thought a European sojourn might help guide his future direction. Packing his copies of Yeats, John Keats, and Shakespeare's sonnets, he went abroad.

THE SUMMER AFTER GRADUATING FROM PRINCETON, Babb went to Munich, where he had a temporary job at a bank arranged through the university's German Department. Discovering he was an art major, the bank later arranged for him to stay longer and work in the library of the National Museum. In addition to taking in the opera, Babb explored the city's art treasures. The Alte Pinakothek offered an exceptional collection of Rubens and Rembrandt as well as Titian's masterpiece *Christ Crowned with Thorns,* which he drew many times. He found fresh and unfamiliar examples of the work of Cézanne and Picasso and immersed himself in the collection of German painters, from the nineteenth-century master Caspar David Friedrich to such important twentieth-century figures as Lovis Corinth and Max Liebermann. The expressionist and psychological cast of the art offered a welcome contrast to the minimalism and hard-edge abstraction prevalent in America.

On the advice of Munich friends, Babb set out to explore Italy, stopping first in Florence and then traveling to Rome, where his "frugal pilgrimage" ended up lasting seven months. He rented a room from a family near the Vatican and took meals at a hospice run by Bavarian nuns. He vowed to see everything in his Touring Club Italiano guide.

The European tour is often the occasion for epiphany in an American artist's life, and so it was with Babb. "When I went to Rome," he remembers, "I was overwhelmed by the rich matrix of architecture, sculpture, and painting—from Greco-Roman to the Baroque." Standing in front of the monumental ancient marble statue *Laocoön and His Sons* in the Vatican, Babb was aware that British artist Joshua Reynolds had stood in the same spot over two hundred years earlier. Likewise, viewing the Belvedere Torso, he knew that Rubens had made drawings of this powerful sculptural fragment even a century before that.

More or less disconnected from his family and America and not enrolled in any school, Babb set out to draw the city, focusing on its architecture and Roman sculpture. He also furthered his art-historical studies: obtaining a reader's card for the Bibliotheca Hertziana, he discovered published drawings by the seventeenth-century French artist Claude Lorrain. "Here was something similar to Chinese landscape painting," he recalls thinking, "but the conventions were of my own western tradition."[15]

The paintings of Nicolas Poussin also had a profound impact on Babb. He was drawn to the seventeenth-century French painter's classical style, its clarity, order, and logic. "The style is the personal manner and method of painting and drawing," Poussin had written, "and arises from each artist's particular genius in the application and use of the ideas."[16] That Rome had played a significant role in Poussin's artistic development was not lost on Babb, who was casting about for a model.

Babb's immersion in Rome's art and history had a lasting effect. "Once you have seen the Sistine Chapel and the Raphaels of the Stanze," he has noted, "your scale is set to a different starting point." Yet however stunning the treasures in the Vatican and the Uffizi Gallery were, it was not to a career in art history that Babb felt drawn. He would become an artist. Returning to the states, Babb visited the art schools to which he had applied and been accepted (with the help of a recommendation from George Segal). His goal was a master of fine arts degree, which would allow him to teach while he addressed the "deficiencies" in his traditional studio studies. The School of the Museum of Fine Arts, in Boston, seemed like the best fit, a major selling point being access to the museum's formidable collections, which included substantial holdings of Chinese art.

Babb leapt into the studio courses, taking figure drawing and John Burns's renowned class on technique, known as the Renaissance Workshop.[17] In the latter, students learned how to prepare canvases and grind colors and were introduced to silverpoint, egg tempera, and other techniques. The class had a "secret studio" in the attic of the museum, where students could study old master paintings chosen by Burns for their value in teaching various processes.

Another highlight was T. Lux Feininger's course on light and color. The German-born artist's in-depth knowledge of art history and the ingenious nature of his exercises were enhanced by firsthand accounts of the Bauhaus and his illustrious family's role in twentieth-century aesthetics.[18] "He seemed a conduit to great modern movements of Europe," Babb recalls, "and to a world of higher achievement."

As he pursued his studies, Babb became acutely aware of his shortcomings while realizing that many more years would be required to achieve mastery of mediums. At the same time, needing to support himself, he signed on as a night watchman at the museum. If a comedown for a former coddled Princeton student, the job was well suited to someone studying art. Babb would roam the galleries with a small sketchbook;

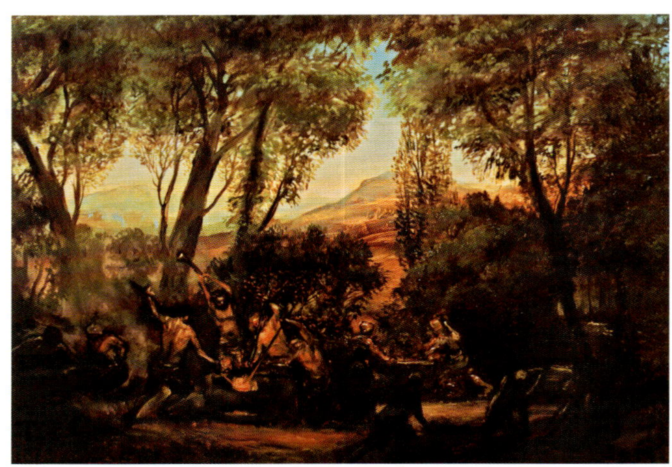

"every night," he said, "was full of discoveries and encounters with new works in the collection." Again, a Yeats poem seemed to Babb to reflect his situation. Reading "Sailing to Byzantium," the painter identified with the poet's desire to be gathered "into the artifice of eternity." For Babb, it meant to somehow absorb the mastery of great art—or at least to be made worthy of making such an attempt. Rome had been Babb's Byzantium, but also a kind of Holy Jerusalem. Now he was in Boston, a new city, where he might begin his voyage of discovery.

In 1974, with his MFA in hand, Babb launched his career by teaching painting and drawing at Tufts University for one semester. More prophetic of his future, that same year he taught basic drawing as well as watercolor, portrait, and oil painting for the education department of the Museum of Fine Arts. He continued offering these courses for the education department for another twelve years. Teaching proved beneficial to his own development as an artist: accompanying his students into the museum to study specific works enhanced his knowledge as well. In addition, in preparation for an "anatomy for artists" course, he monitored dissections at the Boston University School of Medicine and purchased a skeleton.

Beginning in 1982, Babb also taught a painting course in the galleries of the Museum of Fine Arts for the Harvard University Extension School. He contrasted old master techniques that would have been employed by Rubens with impressionist approaches such as pointillism, drawing on French artist Georges Seurat's color theories and Ogden Rood's classic *Modern Chromatics* (1879). While teaching for Harvard for the next sixteen years, Babb continually learned more about the technical aspects and the fundamental concepts of painting. During many of these same years, from 1986 to 2003, he taught classes in realist painting at the School of the Museum of Fine Arts. For both institutions, he aligned the coursework with exhibitions at the Museum of Fine Arts.

Babb was highly inventive in his pedagogy. In an interview in 2006 he described some of the courses he taught, including one that was organized around the idea of Leonardo da Vinci and Seurat meeting in a field in France. Would the two men actually see the same thing? "I was trying to get at questions pertaining to the nature of style," he explained, "and the effects of expectation and knowledge."[19]

Babb's part-time schedule—Fridays and Saturdays were devoted to teaching—allowed him to paint the rest of the time. In these early days, he often made copies of

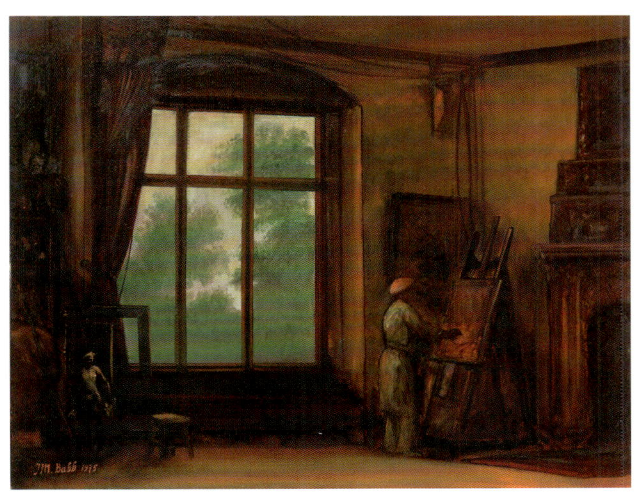

AN ARTIST IN HIS STUDIO, 1975
OIL ON PANEL, 12 x 16 INCHES
COLLECTION OF THE ARTIST

paintings in the Museum of Fine Arts galleries. He copied Rubens's *Head of Cyrus Brought to Queen Tomyris*, ca. 1622–1623, and Eugène Delacroix's *The Entombment of Christ*, 1848, for example. He studied the technique of the old masters in order to learn the ways of paint. He also looked closely at the canvases of Rembrandt and other painters of the Dutch Baroque era, including Jacob van Ruisdael, another favorite. He emulated their dramatic contrasts of light and dark, which they achieved by using very little color but a range of subtle values. From these examples he learned to use a combination of transparent washes of earth colors for an underpainting, a practice he continues today.

At first Babb painted landscapes from his imagination, which is the way he thought Rembrandt and the Chinese painters had worked. Gradually he evolved the goal of painting modern subjects that had the look of an eighteenth-century style, "as if Thomas Gainsborough had come back to life and painted contemporary scenes." Many of Babb's early paintings reference old masters. The setting for *Men at a Forge in the Wilderness,* 1975, owes something to Italian Baroque landscapes in the school of Salvator Rosa even as it conjures certain run-down neighborhoods around Boston. Several figures in the painting were inspired by the men in Francisco Goya's *The Forge*, ca. 1817, which Babb had encountered on a visit to the Frick Collection in New York City.

Another early painting, *An Artist in His Studio,* 1975, drew its inspiration from a small painting by Rembrandt, *Artist in His Studio* (ca. 1628), one of the treasures of the Museum of Fine Arts collection. Babb's aim was to take something of the idea and technique of the Dutch master's canvas and make it his own. Thus, the studio is based on a memory of a room in the Ivy Club at Princeton; the painter wears Babb's smock and tam, and the easel is the one he had built himself. The painting is a self-portrait of the artist finding his way.

Moving into the World

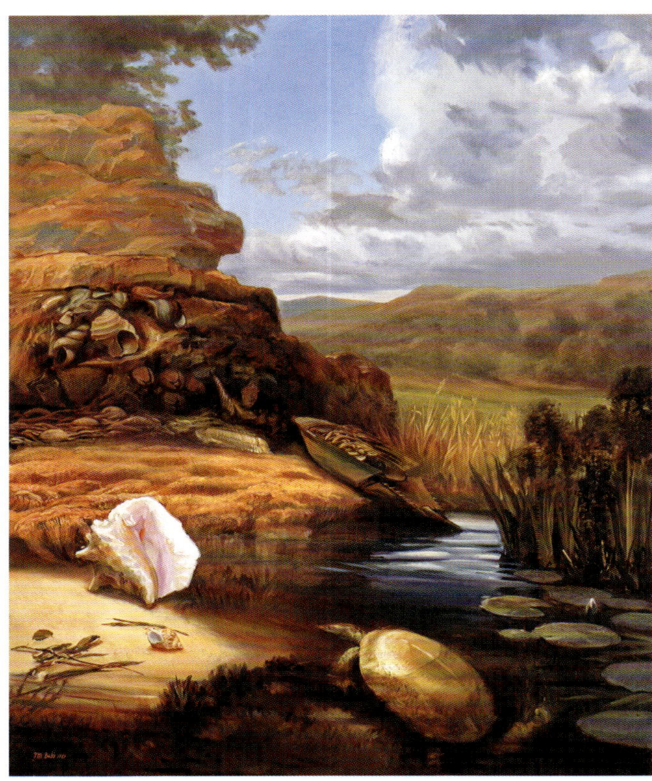

LIVING FOSSILS: EVOLUTION ALLEGORY, 1976
OIL ON PANEL, 48 x 36 INCHES
BEVERLY KING

BABB CONTINUED TO EXPLORE IMAGINARY SUBJECTS, influenced by old-master approaches and subject matter, but also by his ongoing studies. Reading art historian Anthony Blunt's famous study of Poussin, for example, he was drawn to the idea of the landscape as a philosophical statement of a world view. Babb felt that symbolic representations would enhance his landscapes by adding layers of meaning. In *The Creation as a Workshop,* 1974, he scattered various tools in the landscape to imply some master "designer of nature." Time, evolution, and the role of nature are the subjects of several other paintings from this early period, including *Allegory of Fossils,* 1976, and *Circe,* 1980.

As his aesthetic evolved, Babb began relying more on sketches and watercolors made on site, as well as photographs. The animals in *Circe* were based on photographs and studies from a visit to the London Zoo; other elements in the painting derived from photographs taken in the Villa Garzoni gardens in Collodi in Tuscany. Using these studies back in the studio, he blended the imaginary and the real.[20] This composite vision is also present in several paintings of imaginary factories. The machines and the landscape in *Titans and Olympians,* 1979, derive from a watercolor he painted of a quarry in Quincy. At the same time, this painting reflected personal issues: the artist included himself in the group of laborers in the foreground as a vision of the painter "fallen from a state of grace while at Princeton" to a "much lower standing in the world."

In many respects, *The Iron Works* and *Carrara,* 1979, which were conceived as pendant paintings, represent the transition from the imagined to the real. For the former, Babb spent several days around the Bath Iron Works in Maine, making drawings and watercolors of the warship-building complex. The latter canvas, of the marble quarry in Tuscany, is almost entirely invented from memory, with photographs from a visit serving as initial memory aids.

In painting the view of the Bath Iron Works, Babb discovered that making watercolors on site led to observing, and absorbing, more natural effects of light, the form and color of clouds, and other elements of the scene. He was moving away from fantasy and allegory, outward into the world, even as his confidence and skills advanced exponentially. An argument Babb had had with his friend John MacGregor illustrates the artist's shift in perspective. Immersed in what he calls "archaism," Babb stated that an automobile should never appear in a painting. MacGregor replied that in his opinion the car should be mandatory in order that the image be "of our time."

Now working more on location, Babb found himself drawing those formerly forbidden automobiles. He also painted on-site watercolors, in Boston and elsewhere, working with layered washes. He enjoyed the quick and direct manner the medium demanded. Studying the watercolors of Americans Winslow Homer, John Singer Sargent, and Edward Hopper, as well as those of the British painter Joseph M. W. Turner and other earlier masters, helped him move beyond the idea of creating paintings from imagination alone and employing a limited palette. Watercolor proved liberating.

Babb also began to take more photographs, both for their own sake and as sources for paintings. He eventually gave up developing his own prints and began using slide film. Almost immediately, the photograph became a significant resource in conceiving compositions, superseding the careful pencil-and-wash drawings he had been making for that purpose.[21] The camera could capture a wealth of information in an instant. Babb discovered that the extent of that visual data did not become apparent until he started working up the painting from the photographs. He came to realize that this sort of "detached rediscovery of places visited" had a charm and a power all its own. Over the years, Babb has used photography in different ways, from a prompting source of visual information to a tool for more photorealistic purposes. He has consistently both painted on site and worked from photographs, comfortable with each approach and aware that they require different ways of considering subject matter.

Around this time, Babb also found himself turning more to architectural subjects. His 1982 show *Providence: American City* consisted of oils and watercolors of various views of Rhode Island's capital. The watercolors were painted on location and also with the aid of photographs, the first of his cityscapes to be executed with the help of the latter. He was drawn to the city's mix of old and new world architecture and the contrasts of classical and modern building types.

Some of the paintings, such as *The Agora,* 1981, a view of downtown Providence, were highly complex and required that Babb devise new technical means. Adding a rail along the bottom and top of the canvas and using two T squares, he was able to control the brush so as to create the impression of the relief and regularity of the multi-windowed facades. He was becoming a topographic artist, skilled at depicting tall buildings with stunning verisimilitude.

AUTOMOTIVE US, 1982
OIL ON PANEL, 30 x 45 INCHES
BOB AND JACKIE LASKOFF

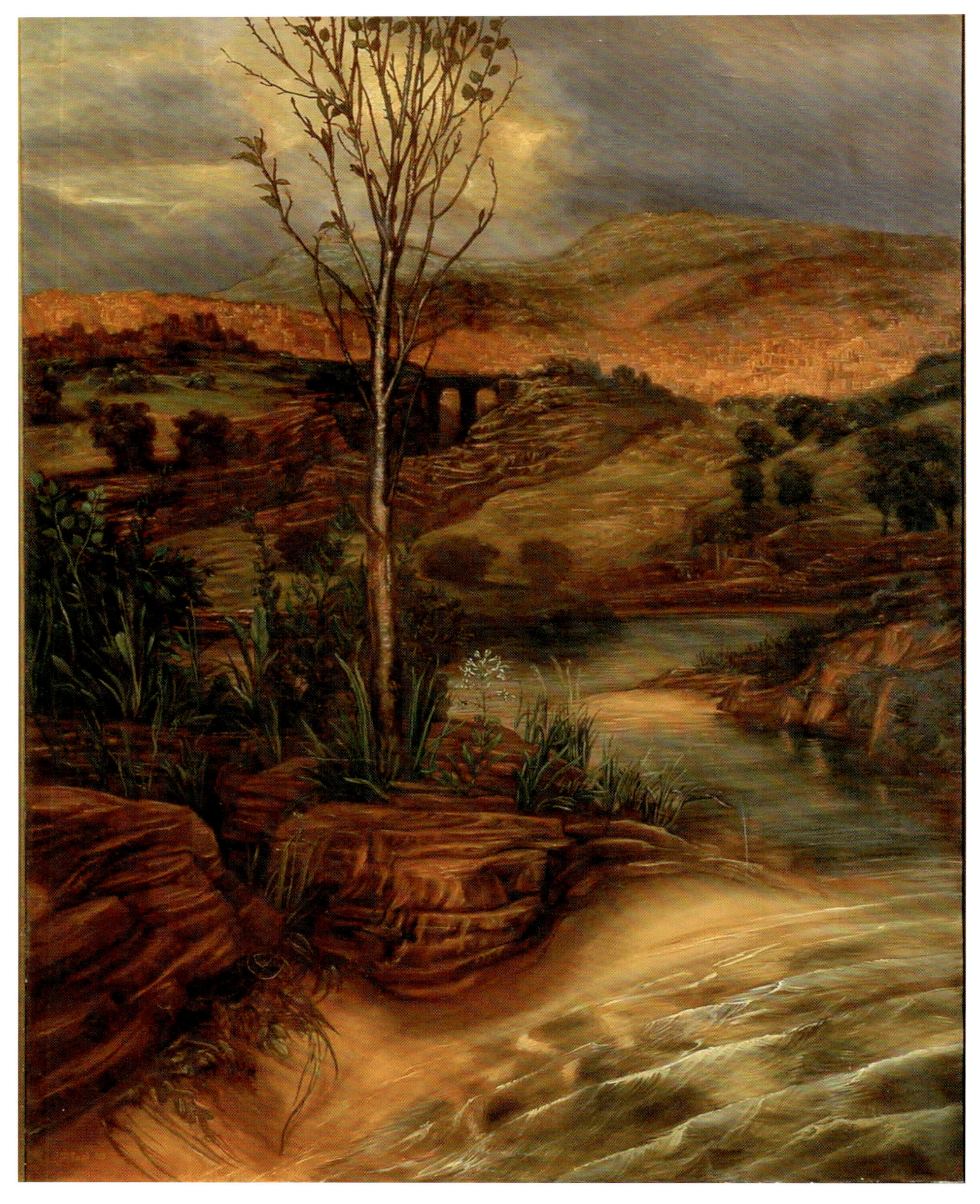

Early History, Imaginary Rome, 1975
Oil on linen, 54 x 42 inches
Collection of the Artist

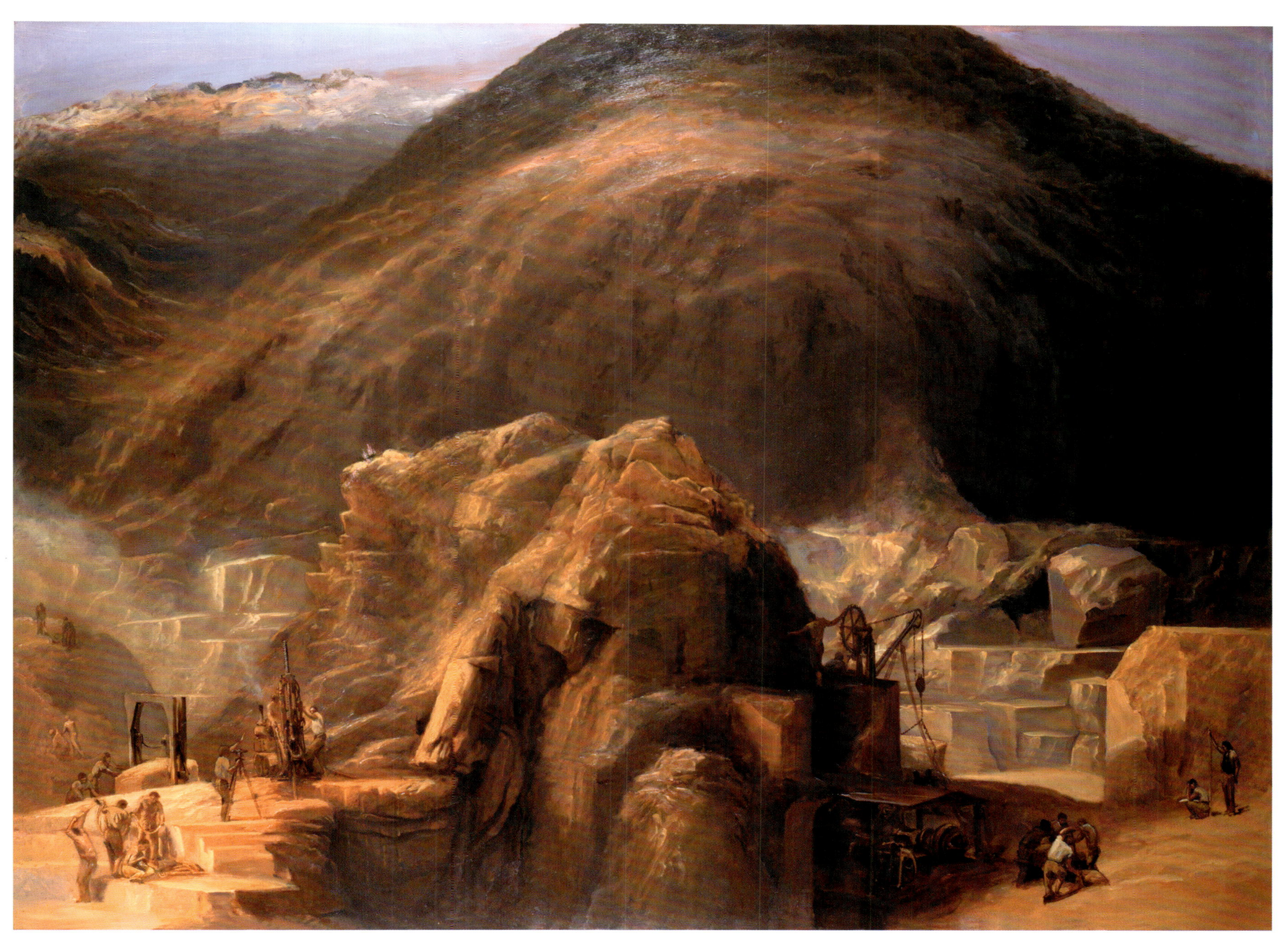

CARRARA, 1976
OIL ON PANEL, 36 X 44 INCHES
COLLECTION OF THE ARTIST

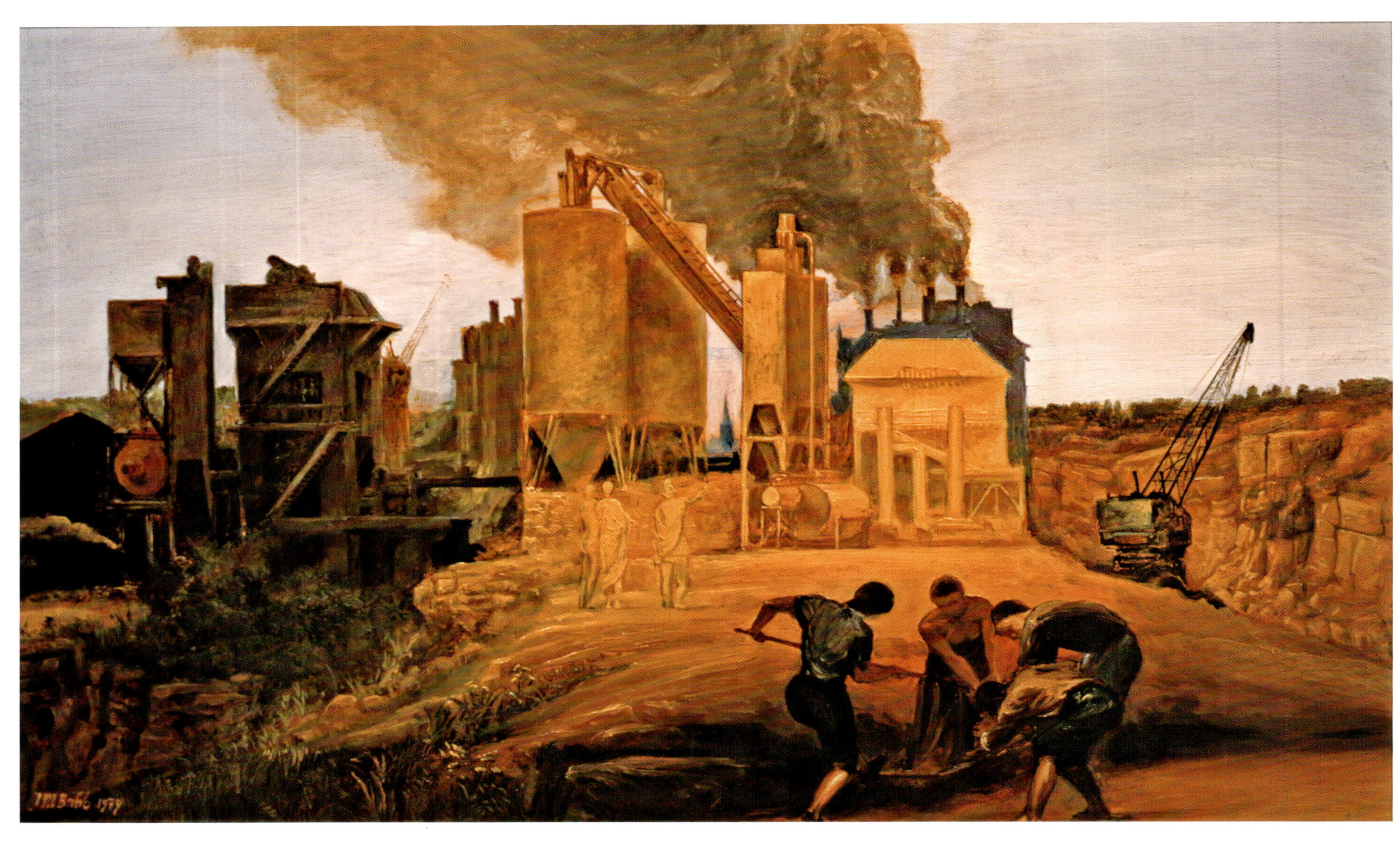

Titans and Olympians, 1979

Oil on panel, 12 x 19 inches

Janet Starr

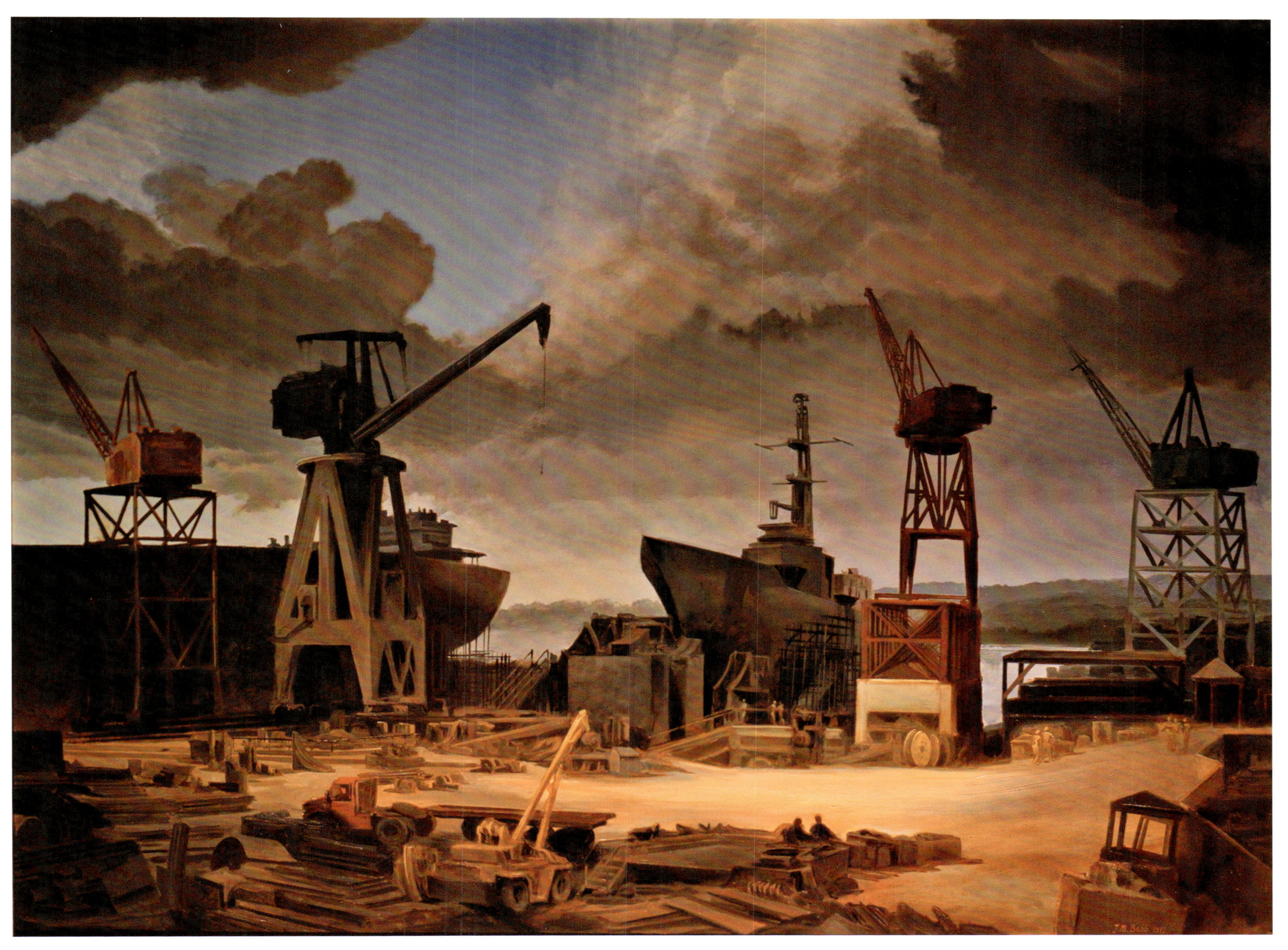

THE IRON WORKS, 1979
OIL ON PANEL, 36 x 48 INCHES
ZACHARY AND CAROL BAKER

A painting of a landscape consisting almost entirely of cars in a parking lot, *Automotive US,* 1982, proved something of a turning point in Babb's progress as a painter. Working from photographs, he became mesmerized and obsessed by "reflection phenomena" to the point where he began to drive by watching the reflections on the hood of his car.

Babb had moved to "the extreme opposite pole" from where he had started as a painter, trading in allegories and a restrained color scheme for near-photorealistic images of the contemporary environment executed with a full-spectrum palette. Though his image of the parking lot might be read as a commentary on modern life, the meaning of the subject was secondary to his amazement at the world that appeared before his eyes.

BOSTON: ABOVE, BELOW, AROUND

IN 1983, BABB WAS INVITED TO TAKE PART in a competition to design a large-scale work for the Broadway South Boston subway station as part of the Massachusetts Bay Transit Authority's Arts on the Line program. Studying the space, he came up with an ingenious idea: to present aerial views of the neighborhoods of South Boston on the ceiling above the train platform as a kind of inverted "through the looking glass." The concept owed something to the trompe l'oeil illusionism Babb had marveled at in Roman palazzos and was further inspired by reading Douglas Hofstadter's brilliant 1979 book, *Gödel, Escher, Bach: An Eternal Golden Braid,* which focused on an awareness of the logic of math, art, and music.

In order to get the aerial perspective he desired, Babb found a pilot and a small helicopter to fly him over Boston. Removing the door from the passenger side allowed near perfect visibility as he took photographs of rooftops and intersecting rail lines and streets. From these photographs he developed a series of large Escher-like drawings and watercolors from which to work up the idea for his presentation to the jury. In these speculative pieces Babb navigated another reality.

Although he did not receive the commission, Babb found the idea of aerial cityscapes exciting; he was soon working on a series of oil paintings and watercolors based on photographs taken during his flyovers. At the same time, developing the ceiling piece led him into new areas of inquiry around visual representation. He found

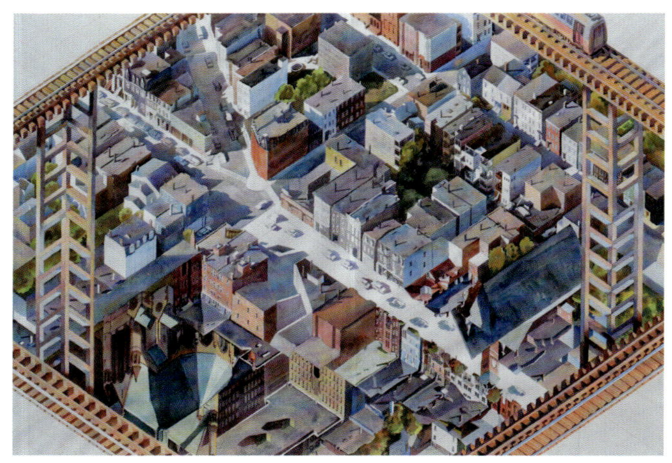

SUBWAY PLATFORM CEILING DESIGN, 1983
WATERCOLOR, 53 x 77 INCHES
COLLECTION OF THE ARTIST

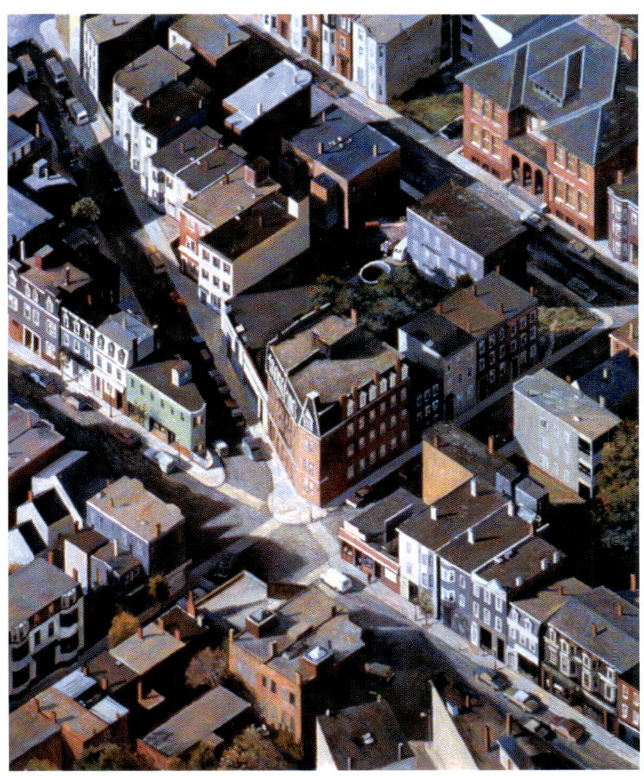

EMERSON STREET AERIAL, SOUTH BOSTON, 1984
OIL ON LINEN, 72 X 60 INCHES
PRIVATE COLLECTION

himself experimenting with different perspectives and alternative ways of projecting ideas of space. The from-the-air perspective offered an out-of-the-ordinary frame of reference for the landscapes and byways navigated by people every day. In a number of paintings, Babb heightened this unusual sense of space by way of an isometric projection. For example, in *Emerson Street Aerial,* 1984, which was based on photographic material from the South Boston helicopter flight, the system of grids contradicts the expectation of the eye, even though, as the artist notes, it "satisfies the requirements of the mind."

Babb has played variations on this aerial perspective, adding his own take to the rich array of representations of space found in different artistic traditions. He acknowledges the historical context for perspective, from Italian Renaissance architects' innovations through Italian Baroque ceiling paintings that integrate the real space of the viewer into the pictorial space. This tradition of illusionism has made him constantly aware of the viewer's location and its relation to the perspective within the painting itself. He is continually fascinated by the quirks and paradoxes that arise in the representation of a city view.

Two major commissions in 1984 underscore Babb's sense of invention. The first was a painting for the lobby of the Charles Hotel in Cambridge. At the time art consultant Portia Harcus approached the artist, the building was still under construction. They settled on a panoramic Cambridge street scene that would measure five feet high by twenty feet long. Babb photographed street corners near Harvard Square and worked up large drawings (one of them was later framed and hung behind the receptionist's desk). Once the view was selected, the artist set up his four-by-five-inch camera on top of a wooden stepladder, in order to raise himself above the level of the rooftops of cars, and took a series of chromes panning down Massachusetts Avenue to the Holyoke Center. Once approved, Babb had seven weeks to complete the picture. The first week was spent building the outsized stretcher and gessoing the twenty-foot-long canvas. The painting was made in Maine, in an uninsulated space with a woodstove and kerosene heater. Babb worked through his Christmas vacation from teaching to complete the painting.

Mass Ave Cambridge has remained in place since its installation nearly thirty years ago. Part of the painting's appeal lies in its visual dynamics: as one approaches it from either side, the changes in foreshortening create the illusion that the painting is moving—

adjusting, as it were, to the passerby.[22]

The second work commissioned in 1984, also twenty feet long, was painted for the lobby of the Cambridge Savings Bank at Harvard Square. Knowing that the painting did not need to be completely naturalistic and might include elements of relief, Babb decided to create an architectural fantasy that would weave together various buildings in Cambridge in a kind of urban frieze. He developed an unusual process for designing the painting. The buildings would be rendered as if based on architects' drawings and projected in axonometric and isometric fashion to show what they would look like prior to being built. At the same time, the facades would be portrayed in both bird's- and worm's-eye views arranged on the same diagonal grid. Finally, some of the planes would recede in a sculptural fashion, and the painting itself would feature a picture plane existing on three levels.

The design offered special challenges. The painting was on Masonite, while the receding planes were cut out of poplar, with hundreds of passes on a table saw necessary to get the correct contours. The relief elements had to be consistent with the angles of the grid, which were followed by the painted portions of the image. Unable to find architectural drawings for any of the well-known older buildings in Cambridge, Babb photographed the structures and made his own drawings from them. The color scheme was challenging, too: if the colors for the finished painting contrasted with one another too much or were too naturalistic, the light on the painting would not appear to model the planes of the relief section.

The painting brought to the fore many of the issues of perspective Babb had been exploring.[23] Though the piece initially made use of photographs for collecting information, the visual data was recast by a process of the artist's intellect, modeling the real into a kind of new visual order. In his later work, Babb would experiment less with invented points of view, but these earlier explorations remained a foundation for the way he viewed the world. Studying perception made the process of representation "far more elusive and fascinating than a mere mechanical transcription."

One of Babb's most fascinating perspectives is one found in *Copley Plunge*, 1990—a kind of suicide's view, looking straight down from the John Hancock tower in the Back Bay.[24] A classic one-point perspective, the verticals of the buildings lead to a vanishing point straight down—beneath, as it were, the viewer's feet.

Over time, Babb did more aerial views of Boston based on helicopter flights. *Park Street Aerial* and *Federal Reserve Aerial,* both 1987 and commissioned by the investment firm Fidelity, incorporate discoveries Babb had made about color while working in watercolor. He found himself mixing colors with the brush on the canvas, but allowing them to work on their own so that they did not become completely gray. He painted more in progressions and reflections, connecting colors into the overall picture scheme.

Watercolor aerials of the city made around this time are stunning in their complexity and control. For a medium that was known to misbehave, in Babb's hands the paint remained fluid even as it achieved the range of values and finish found in his oils. The watercolor *The Construction of Rowe's Wharf,* 1987, harks back to those imaginary views of factories—and even to the "cult of ruins" of Piranesi, Hubert Robert, and other artists of Rome he admired. Babb stopped working from helicopters and small planes after September 11, 2001.

Babb was also working on the street level in Boston, painting views of intersections in the Back Bay and elsewhere. He places the viewer in situ; in a manner of speaking, we join the pedestrians as they move from place to place in the bustling metropolis. Part of the appeal of these canvases lies in Babb's precise eye. In depicting the corner turret of a Back Bay brownstone, he captures the handsome lines of the windows and roof. His is an aesthetic of sight lines and detail. Compared to the loosely rendered paintings of Boston buildings by his contemporary George Nick, Babb is a constructivist.

Though he shares Hopper's passion for New England architecture, Babb is not so much interested in its psychological aspects. His *Blue Victorian,* 2007, painted on Nantucket, engages the viewer by its unusual framing of the subject—the facade recedes upward into the sky—not by any sense of human drama. Yet Babb is as fascinated by the play of light and shadow as Hopper was.

Other cities, including Cincinnati; Providence; New York; and Portland, Maine, have attracted the artist, but Boston has been his steady and principal passion. His panoramas of the city are brilliant in their detail but also in their composition: the painter encompasses great swaths of the metropolis with an eye for what one might call the greater picture. Babb's panoramas, many of them based on views from tall buildings, stand among his supreme achievements as a painter. Many of them have been painted on commission and now hang in conference rooms and offices high above the city. The captains of industry who meet in these rooms can view the city from their aeries at any given time, but they will never perceive it as Babb has: the particular slant of light, the cloud-shadowed areas in the distance, the cars in the streets.

Over the years, Babb has drawn inspiration and enlightenment from museum exhibitions. As with his commitment to the literature of art history, he has spent time with old and modern masters of various aesthetic bearings. Whether Canaletto at the Metropolitan Museum of Art; Ruisdael at the Fogg Art Museum; Lucian Freud at the Hirshhorn Museum; or Richard Estes, Alfred Leslie, and Antonio López García at the Boston Museum of Fine Arts, he has learned from close appraisals of the kind Wen Fong encouraged, gleaning impressions and ideas that have enhanced his appreciation of the artistic process.[25]

In the case of the Metropolitan's exhibition of works by Canaletto, mounted in 1989–1990, Babb was inspired to "crank up a notch" the realism in his painting.[26] The level of detail in his *Copley Square from 500 Boylston,* 1991, was greater than the artist had ever achieved. The rendering of reflections distorted in the glass of the John Hancock building is astounding in its resolution. At the same time, inspired by a Canaletto painting of London, Babb presents distant sections of the city as abstract geometric patterns.

As he created these panoramas, Babb further fine-tuned his use of photography. Rather than try to take one perfect photograph that would capture everything in a particular view, he would integrate several different shots into a single composition.[27] He had also made the transition from four-by-five-inch to digital camera and began using a computer as an aid in producing his paintings, all the while recognizing that photography was "something of a compromise" when compared to how the eye actually sees. Some of Babb's paintings took on the finish of photorealism, yet when studied up close, the brushwork remains visible and the treatment of color inventive. His broken colors are partly mixed on the canvas.

"No matter how familiar a city is," Babb has written, "there is something fascinating about a broad view from a high place, in which familiar landmarks are seen in new relations." More than spectacle, this elevated viewpoint helps solve the puzzle of the maze of streets below, heightens our awareness of the way a river shapes a city, and even underscores the importance of green spaces in the urban environment. A broad view of the city may elicit a sense of detachment, as Babb has noted, but as he states in the next breath, "one sees the city as an organism with a life of its own."

Babb's panorama of the John W. Weeks Bridge, the footbridge that connects Cambridge with the Allston section of Boston, ranks among his most poetic views. The painting offers a broad turn in the Charles River, from the Weeks Bridge to the Weld Boathouse and the Anderson Memorial Bridge. Casting an eye over its breadth, various cultural references come to mind, from Thomas Eakins's *Max Schmitt in a Single Scull,* 1871, to the park in Michelangelo Antonioni's 1966 movie *Blow-Up.* Yet finally it is Babb's vision alone: a handsome pedestrian bridge holding together a sweeping landscape of river, highway, and trees, with the tower of Harvard's Eliot House lit by strong late summer light leading the eye into the landscape.

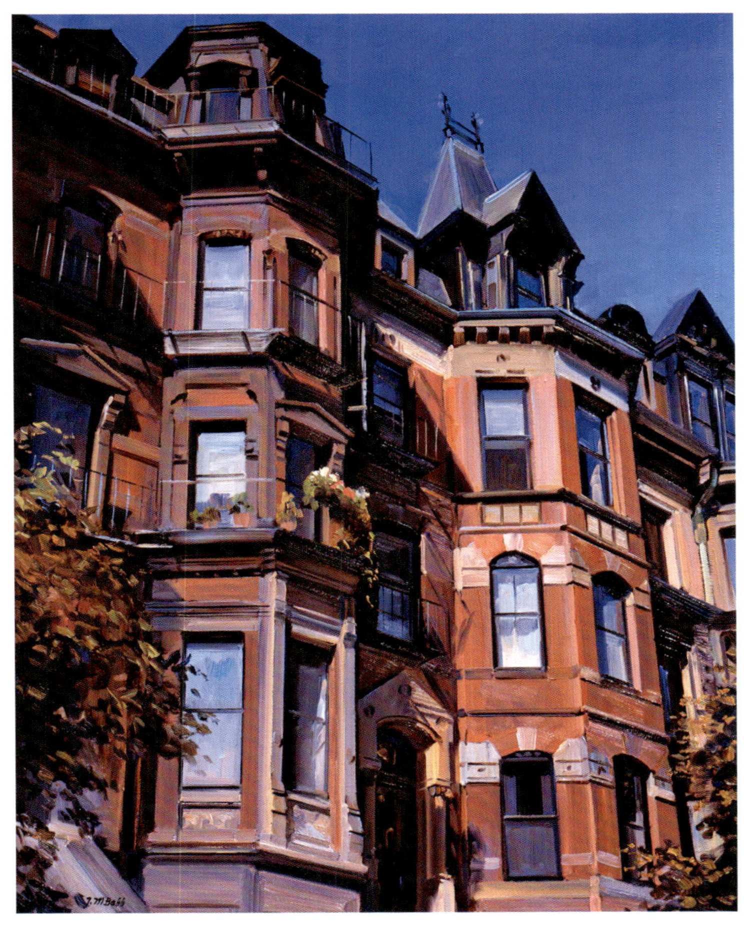

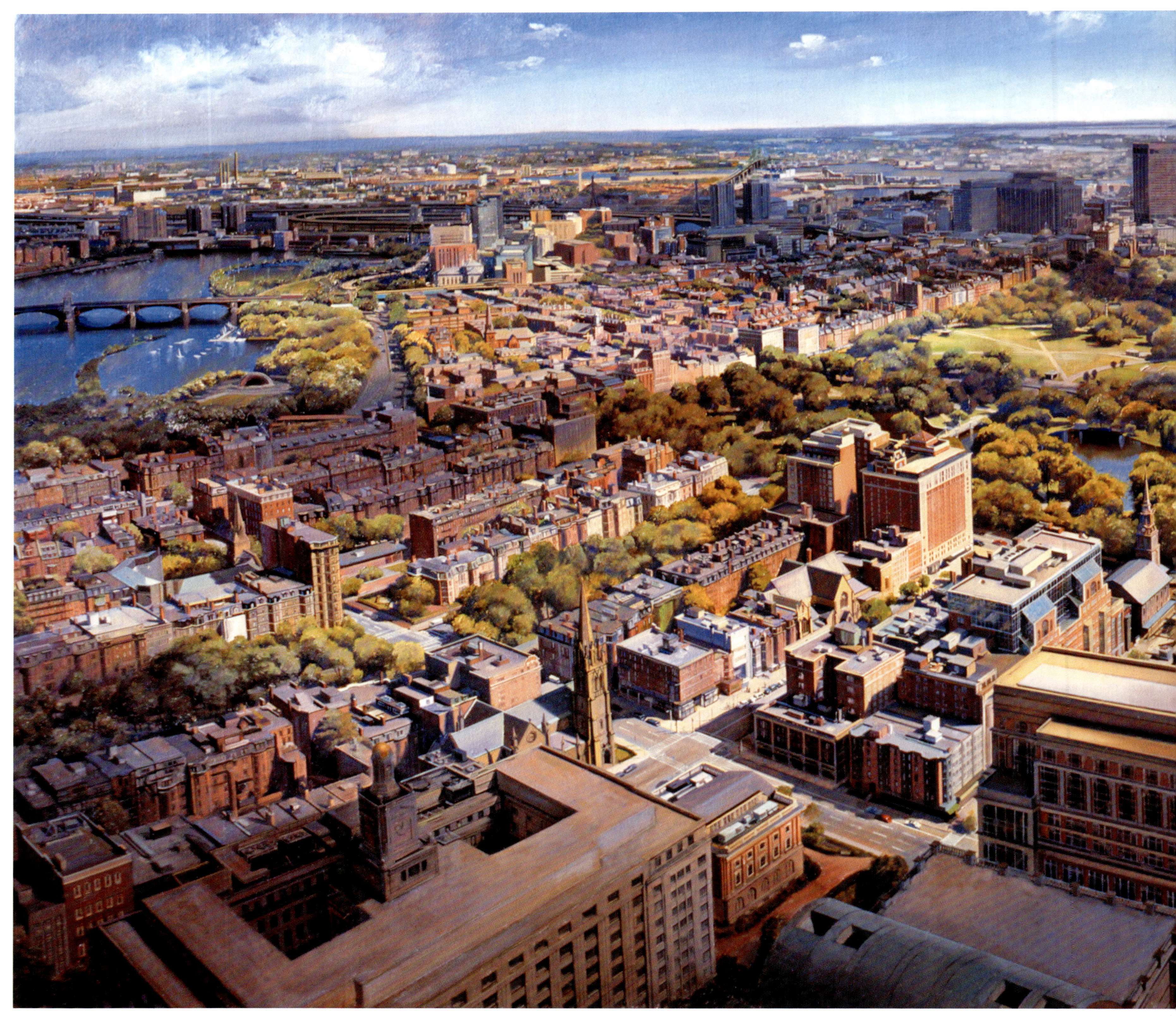

36   Boston from the Hancock Tower, 2008, Oil on linen, 36 x 84 inches, The Tia Collection, on loan to New Britain Museum of Amer can Art

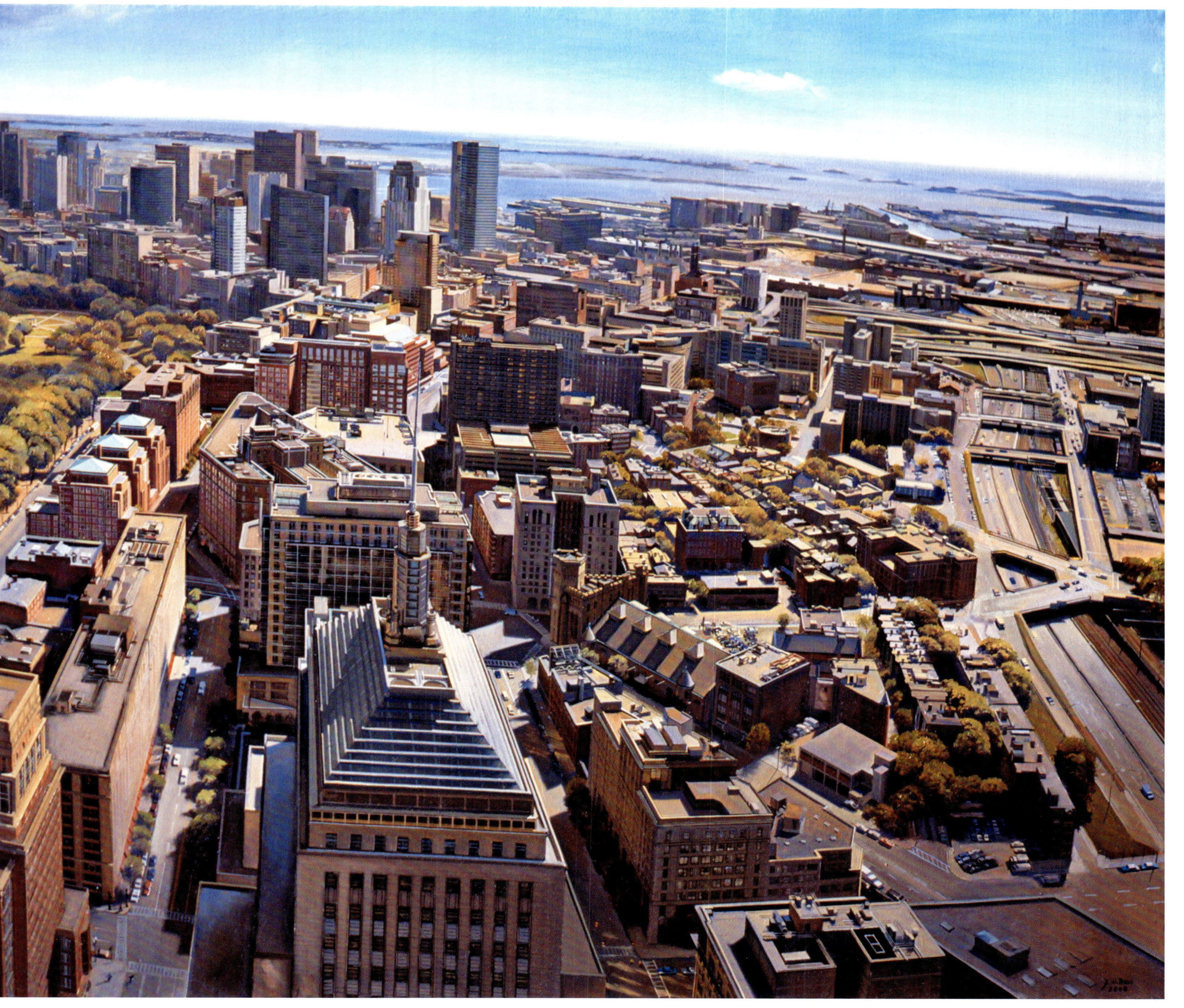

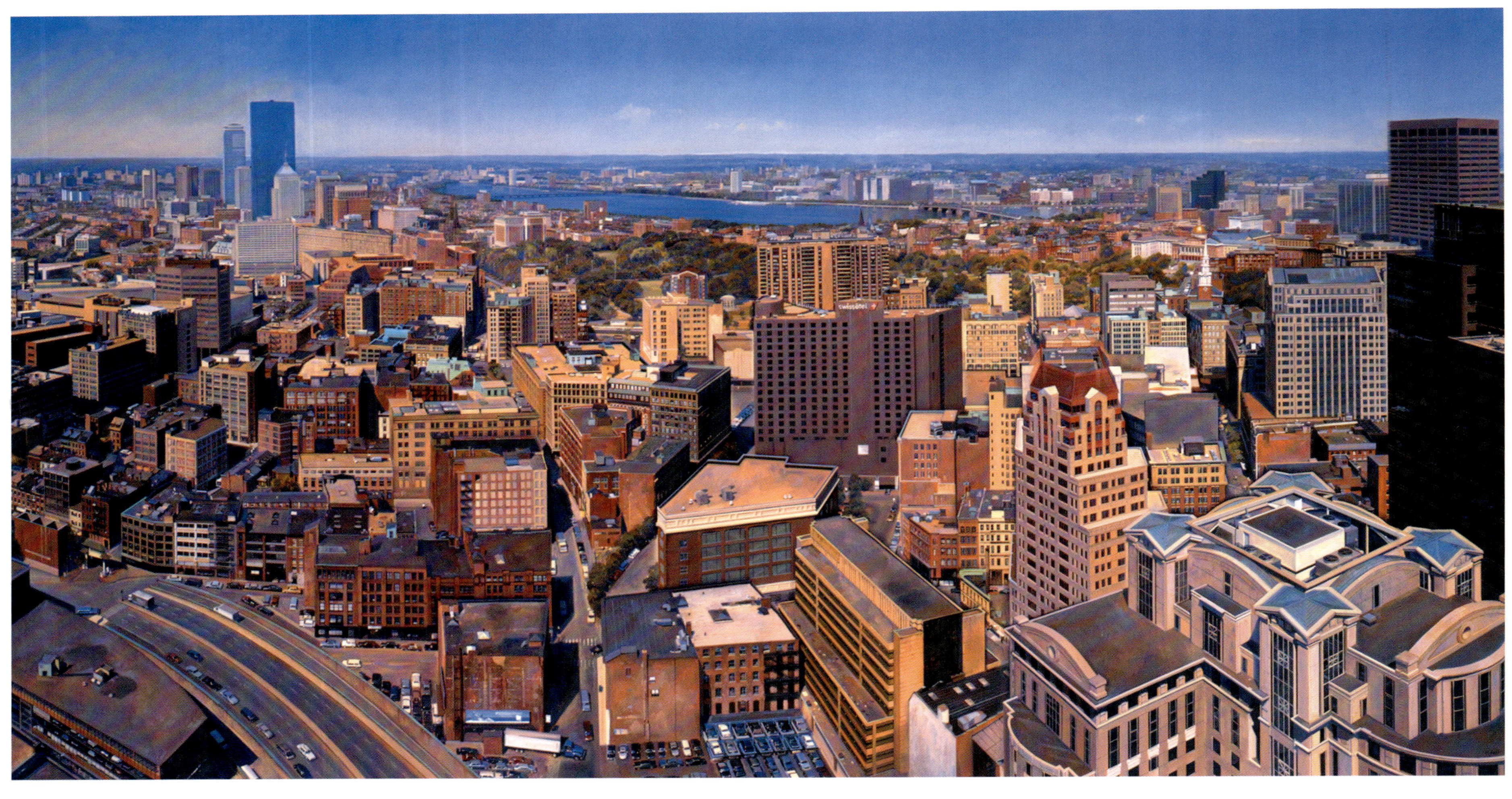

PANORAMA FROM ONE FINANCIAL, BOSTON, 1996
OIL ON LINEN, 58 x 110 INCHES
STANDISH MELLON ASSET MANAGEMENT

In the panoramic view of Boston from the financial district, I wanted to see how far I could go to capture the stupefying complexity of a real panoramic cityscape. There is something fascinating about a broad view from a high place, in which familiar landmarks are seen in new relations. In a sense one travels out and around the city by a process of imaginary flight instead of wandering the customary maze of streets. Something is overwhelming about the complexity of a city, the sheer number of private spaces and interiors, the suggested stories of individuals and institutions—as if my perspective as an individual, from where I am standing, contains tens of thousands of other perspectives and points of view. There are many ways to paint a city, but this one maintains topographical accuracy, so that anyone who looks at the painting can travel through familiar spaces, and so that in time the painting may come to have a certain historical value because of its accuracy.

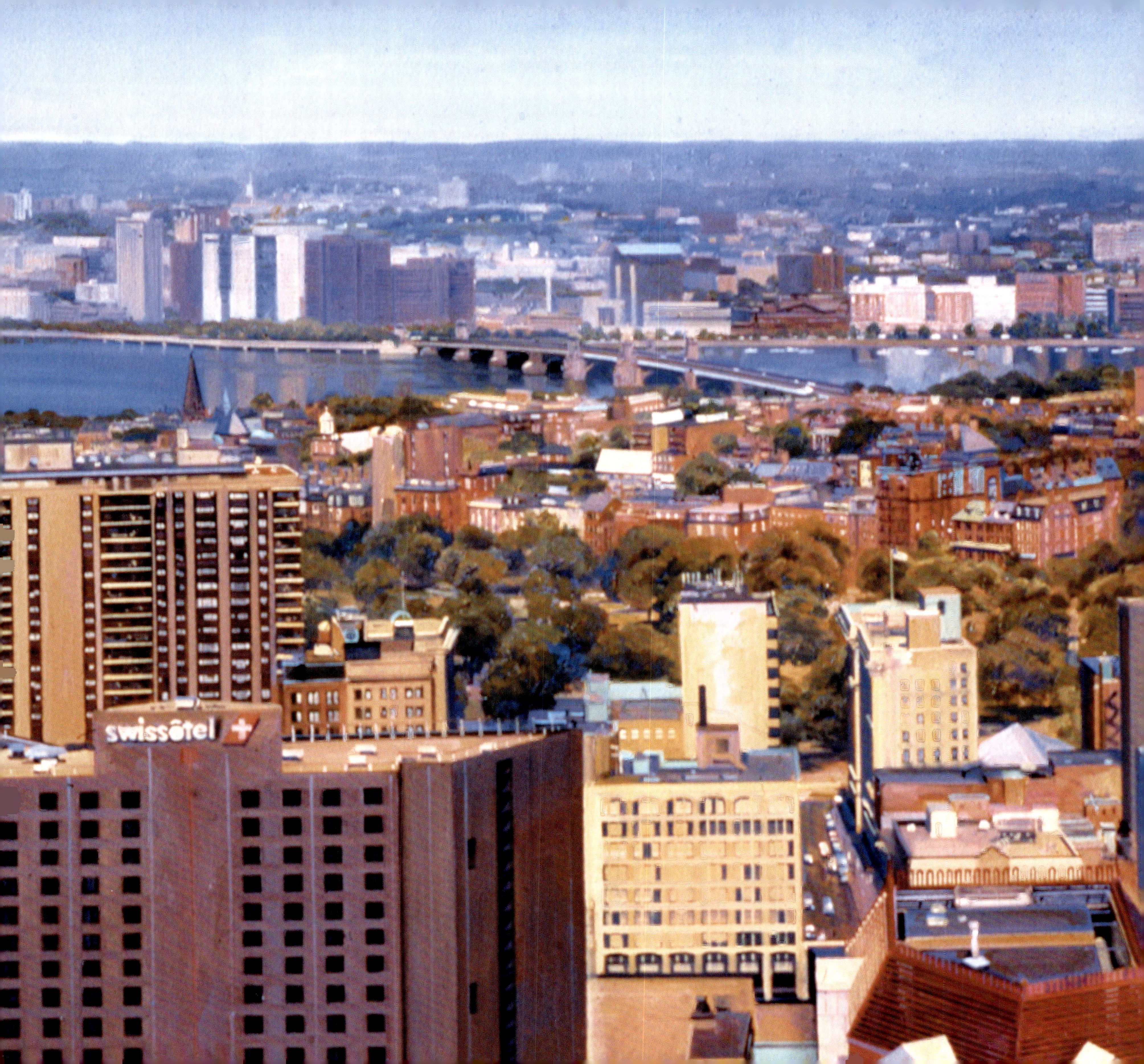
swissôtel

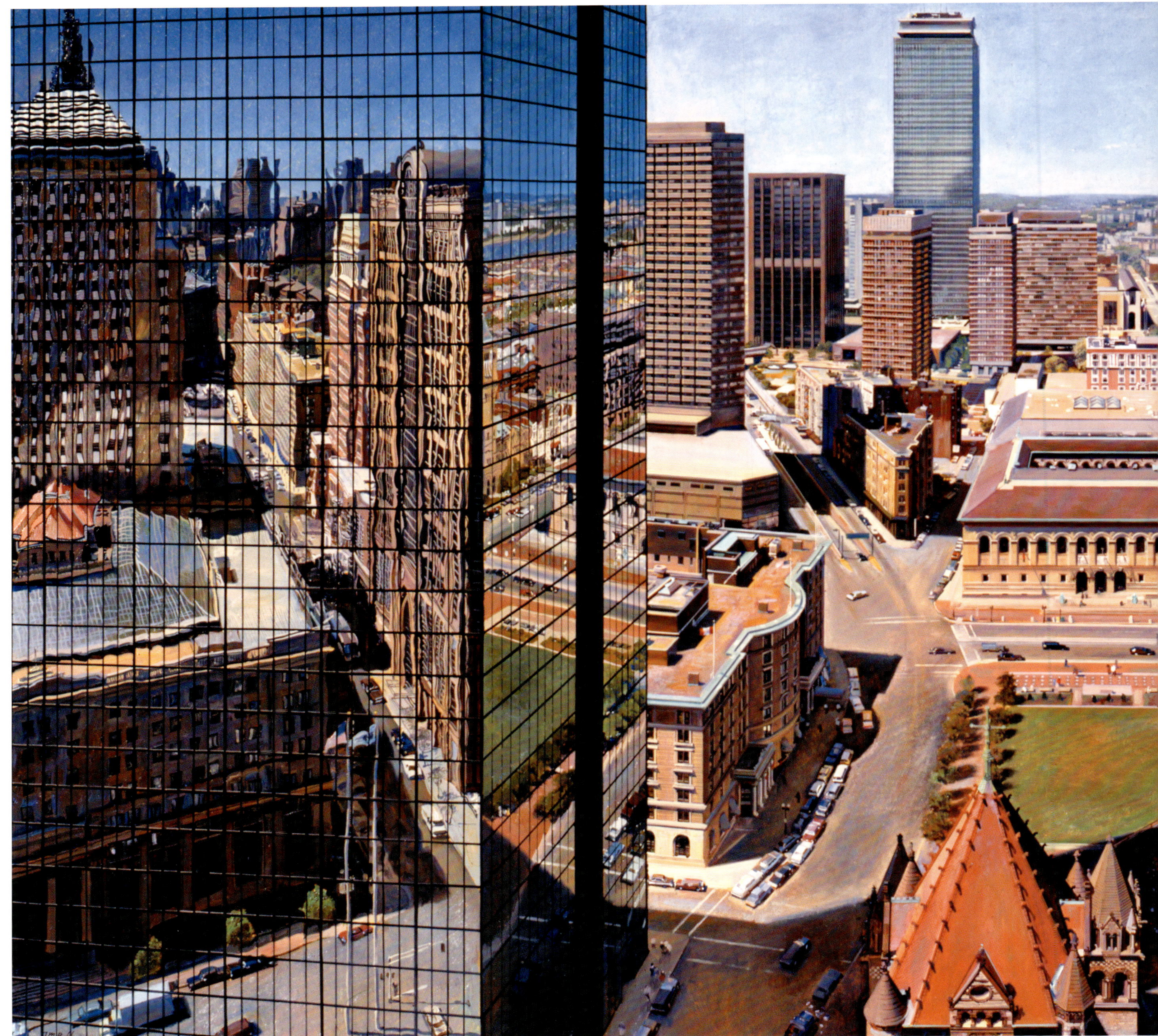

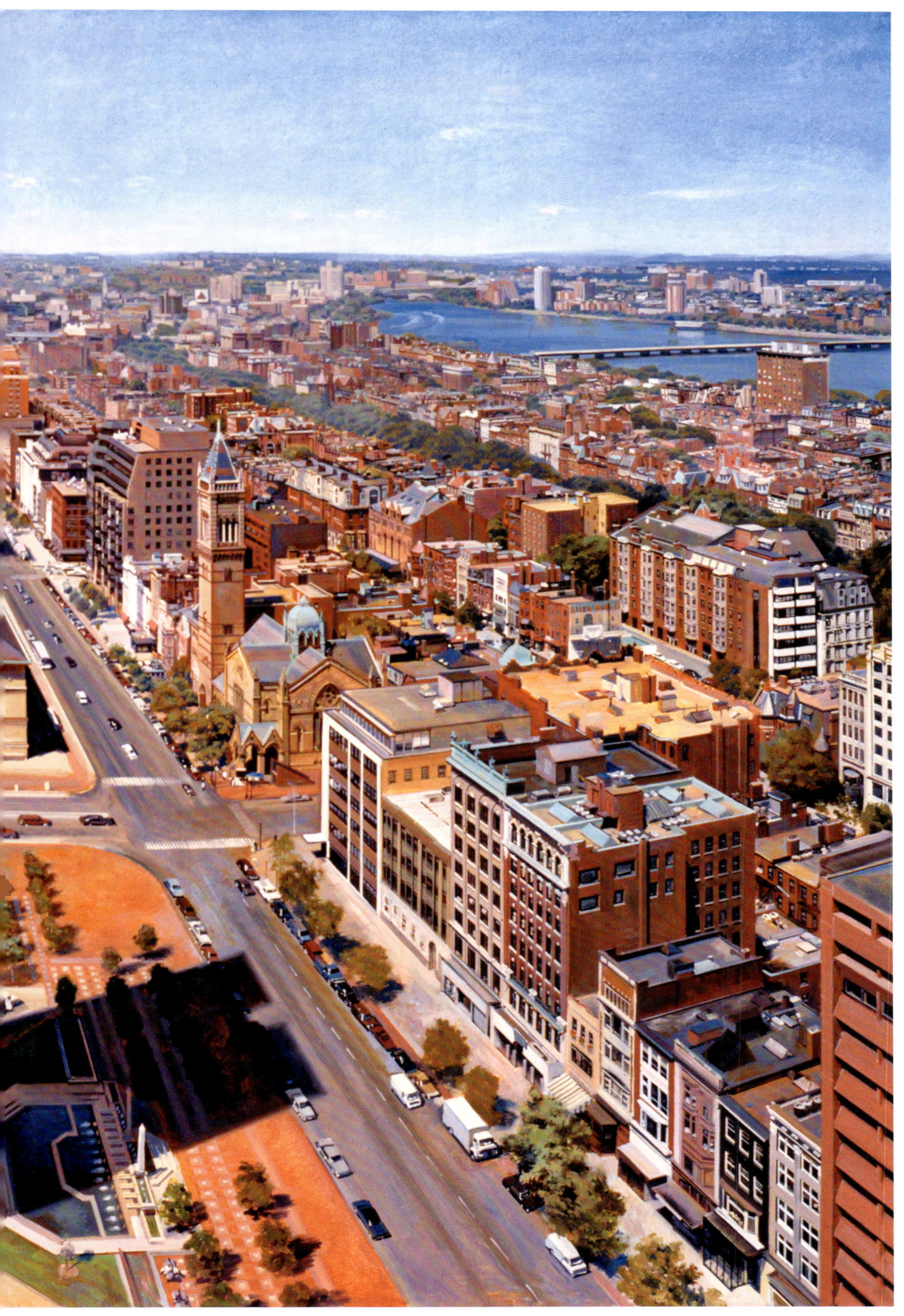

Of course, having photographs is a tremendous advantage
in studying the almost mystifying complexity of reality at a
fine scale. In the distance things begin to break down into
abstract patterns of squares and dots and smears. The lines
of panes of glass in the Hancock building, drawn first, become
a grid in which each area can be graphed and studied
separately, expressing the distortions of the reflections in
each rectangle. Areas in the far distance would be nearly
impossible to reduce to canvas because of the complexity if
it were not for having the photograph. Turn your eye away
and you could never find your place again. Canaletto had
a camera obscura, which greatly enhanced his ability to
reduce complex patterns to paper, and there are drawings
by him tha suggest having been done with the device. But
neither the modern camera nor the camera obscura solves the
problems of doing a panoramic perspective on a flat canvas.

The vertical lines have to be straightened from the conver-
gence of looking downward, and the horizontal lines near
the sides have to be fudged to retain the continuation of a
consistent space. In the end the painting is a combination
of using photographs (or a camera obscura), applying a well
understood perspective system, and keeping in mind a color
system of relative values and intensities to create the painting
you imagined when you were on the spot.

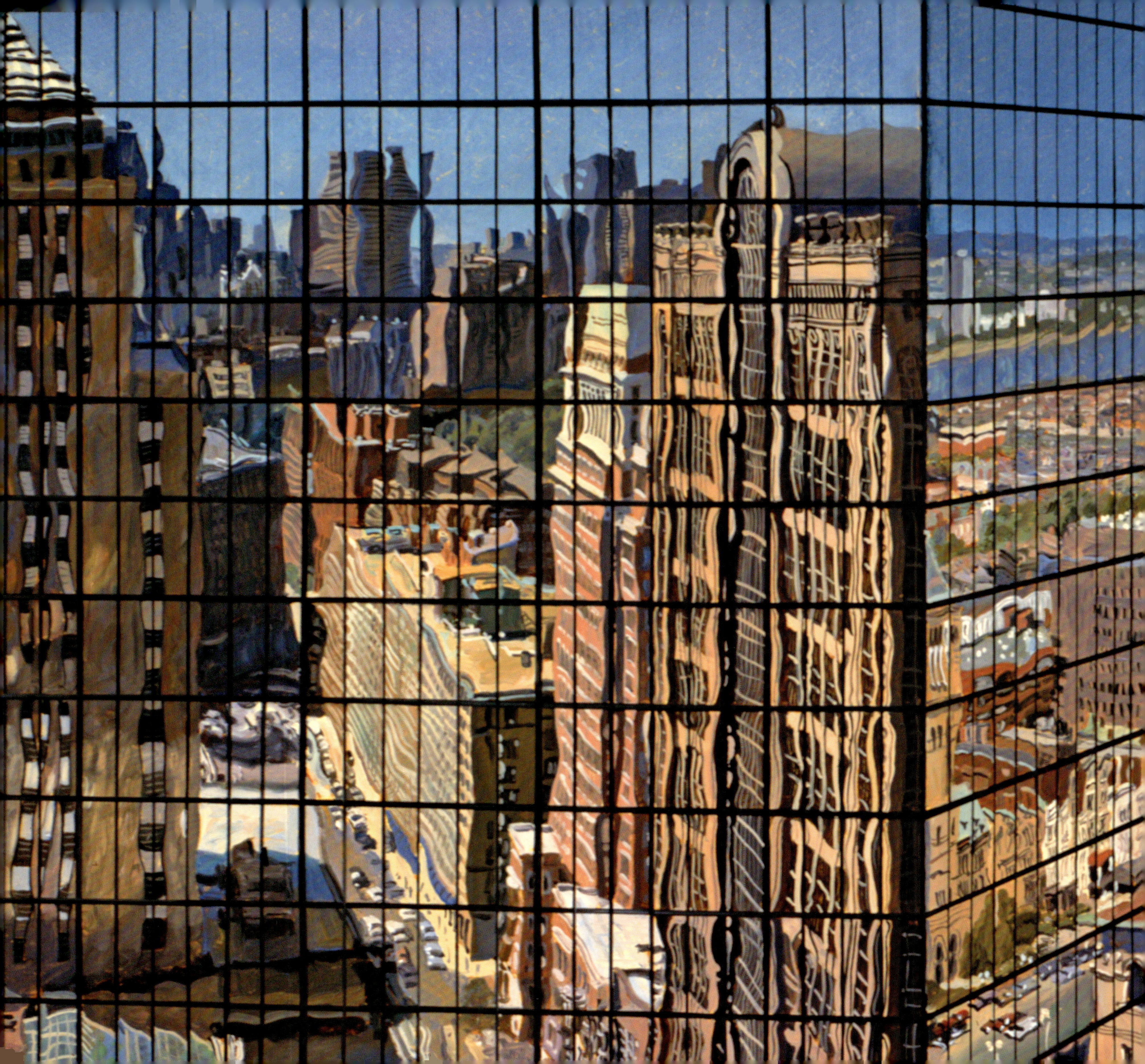

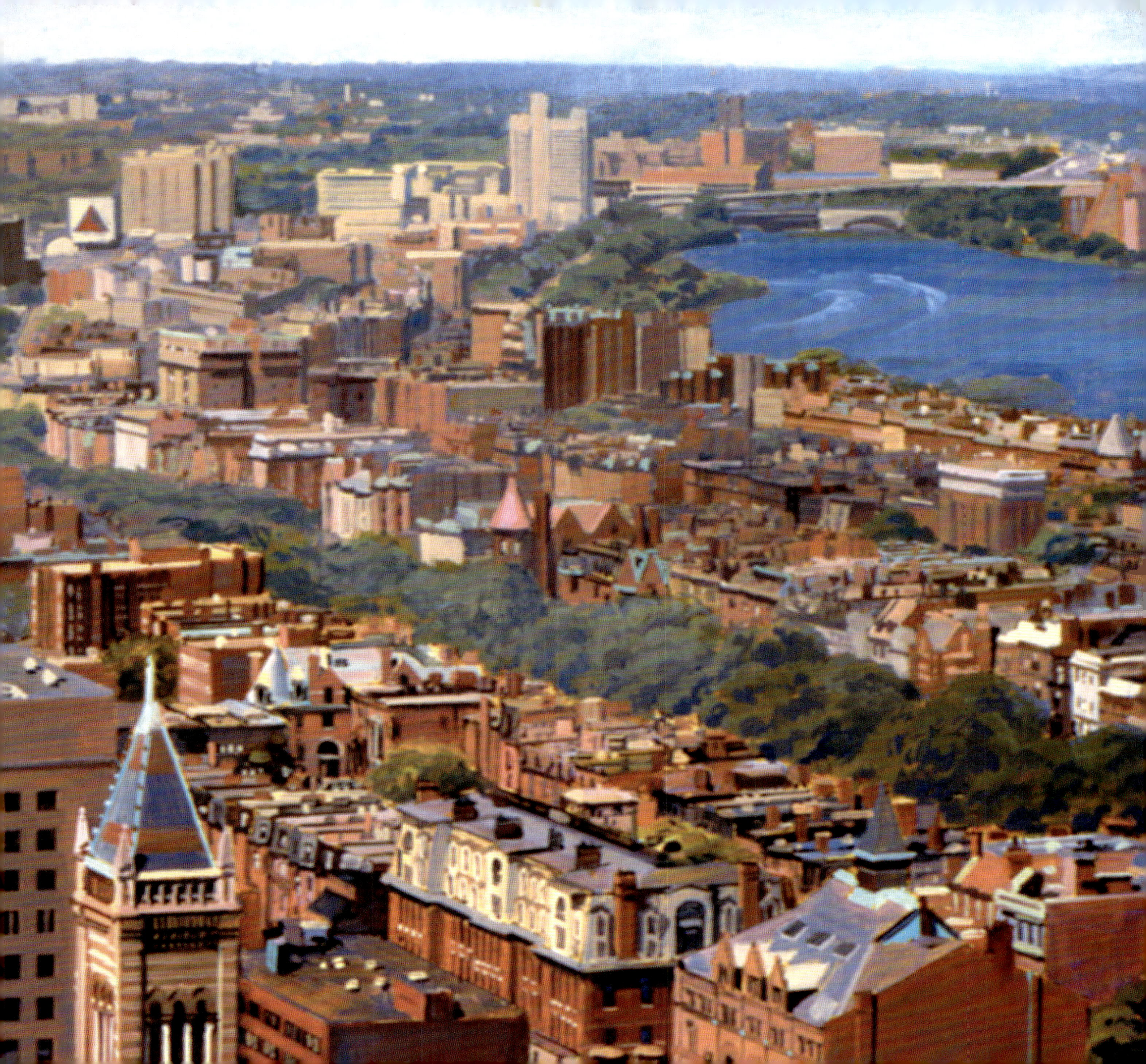

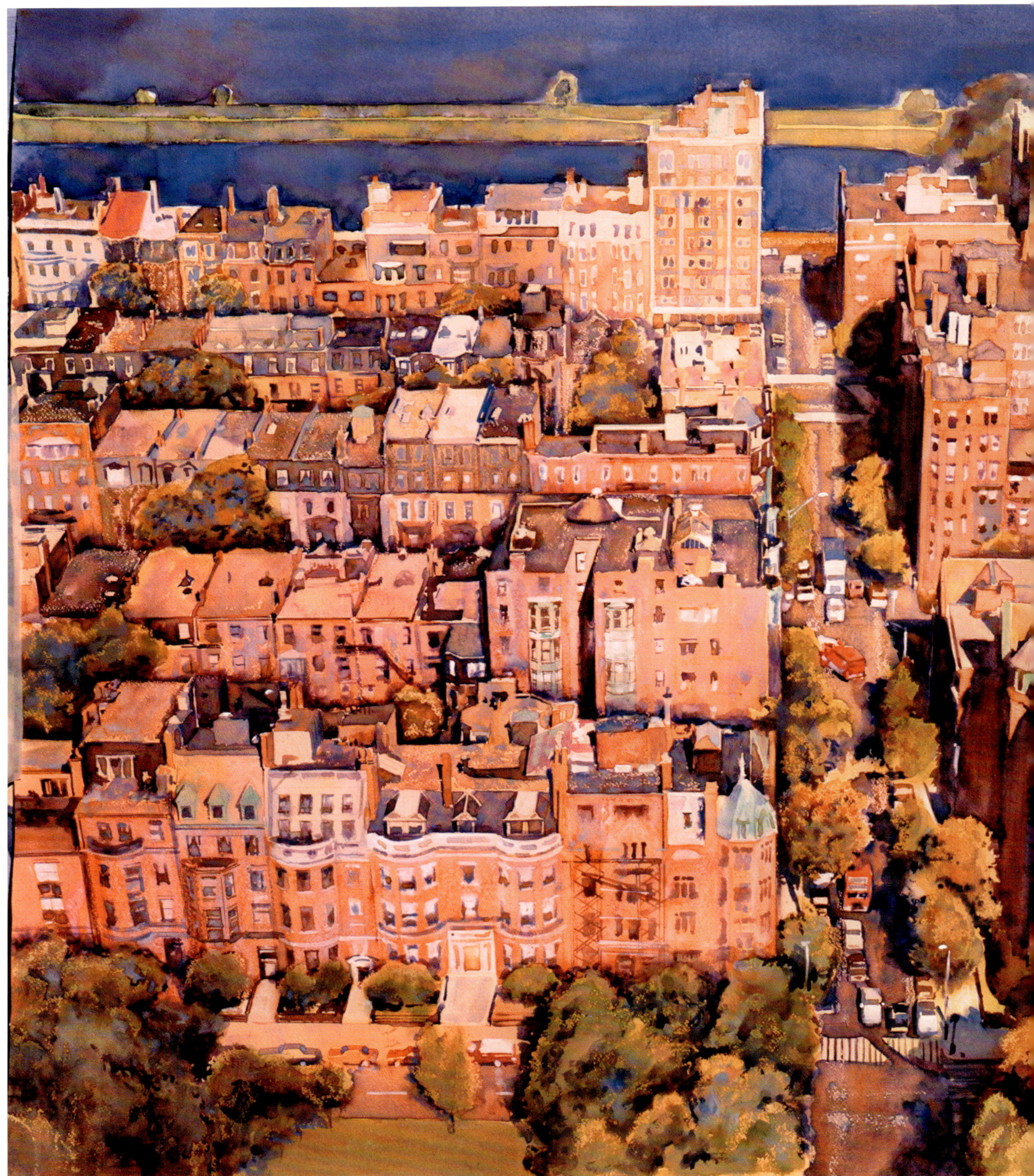

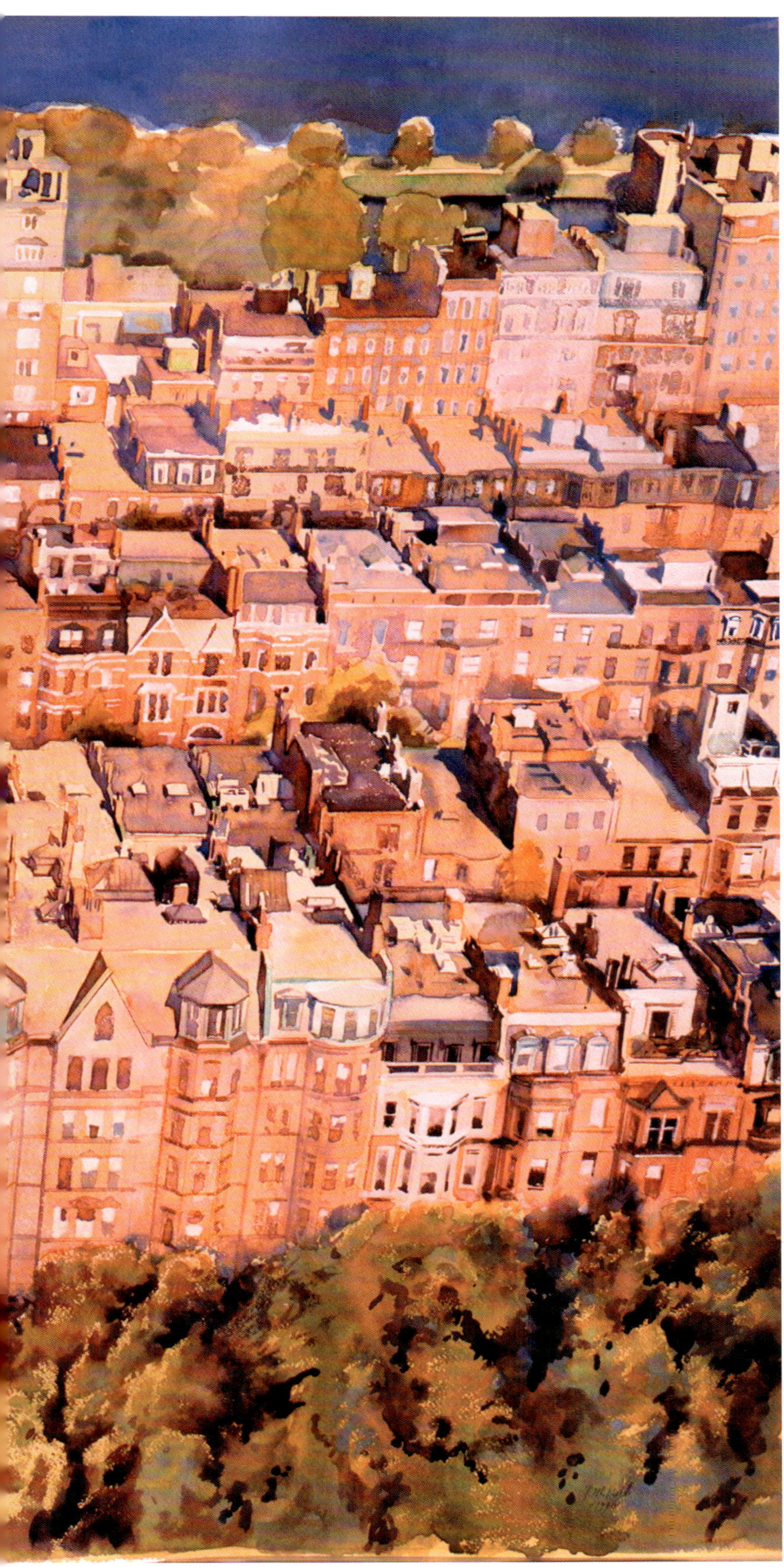

BACK BAY AERIAL WITH LAGOON, 1987
WATERCOLOR, 30 x 42 INCHES
PRIVATE COLLECTION

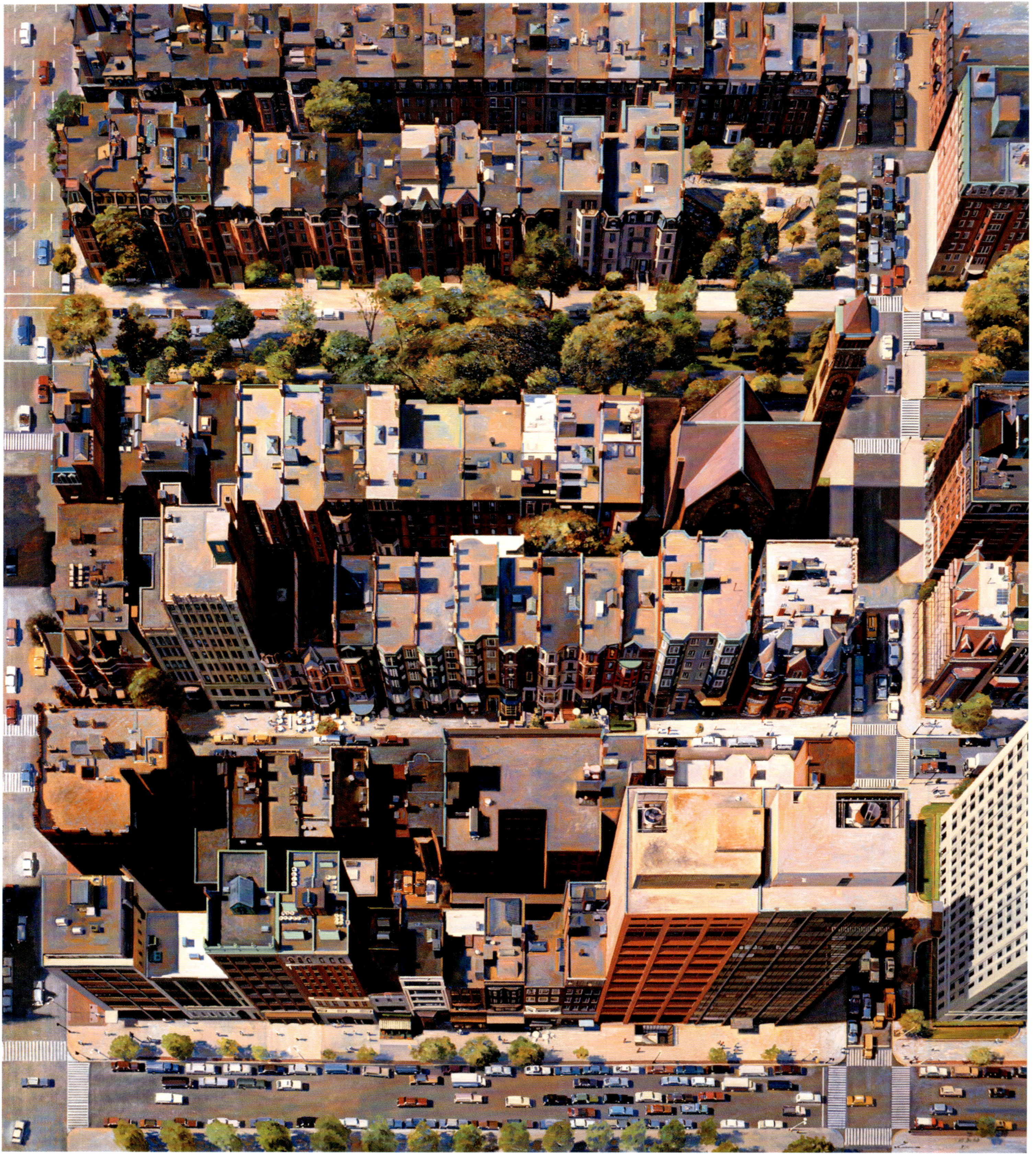

COPLEY PLUNGE *is a simple one-point perspective, like a view looking down a street toward a vanishing point but in this case looking straight down. The vanishing point is at infinity directly below the viewer's feet, and the verticals of the buildings go straight down to that point. The streets parallel the edges of the painting so that cars seem to travel up and down the edges of the picture or across the bottom. The painting shows a view which is not like the view usually seen or photographed—the streets would then be converging to a vanishing point on the horizon. Even though it is a classic one-point perspective, its downward orientation gives it a vertiginous feeling. When hung at the end of a hallway, the effect is that one is plummeting down a shaft to the streets below.* COPLEY PLUNGE *could be exhibited on the floor: it appears interestingly distorted viewed on the wall, but it appears natural when it is placed on the floor and the viewer has the original angle of looking down on the buildings. They appear to pop upright from the canvas, instead of converging.*

COPLEY PLUNGE, 1990

OIL ON LINEN, 82 X 60 INCHES

PRIVATE COLLECTION

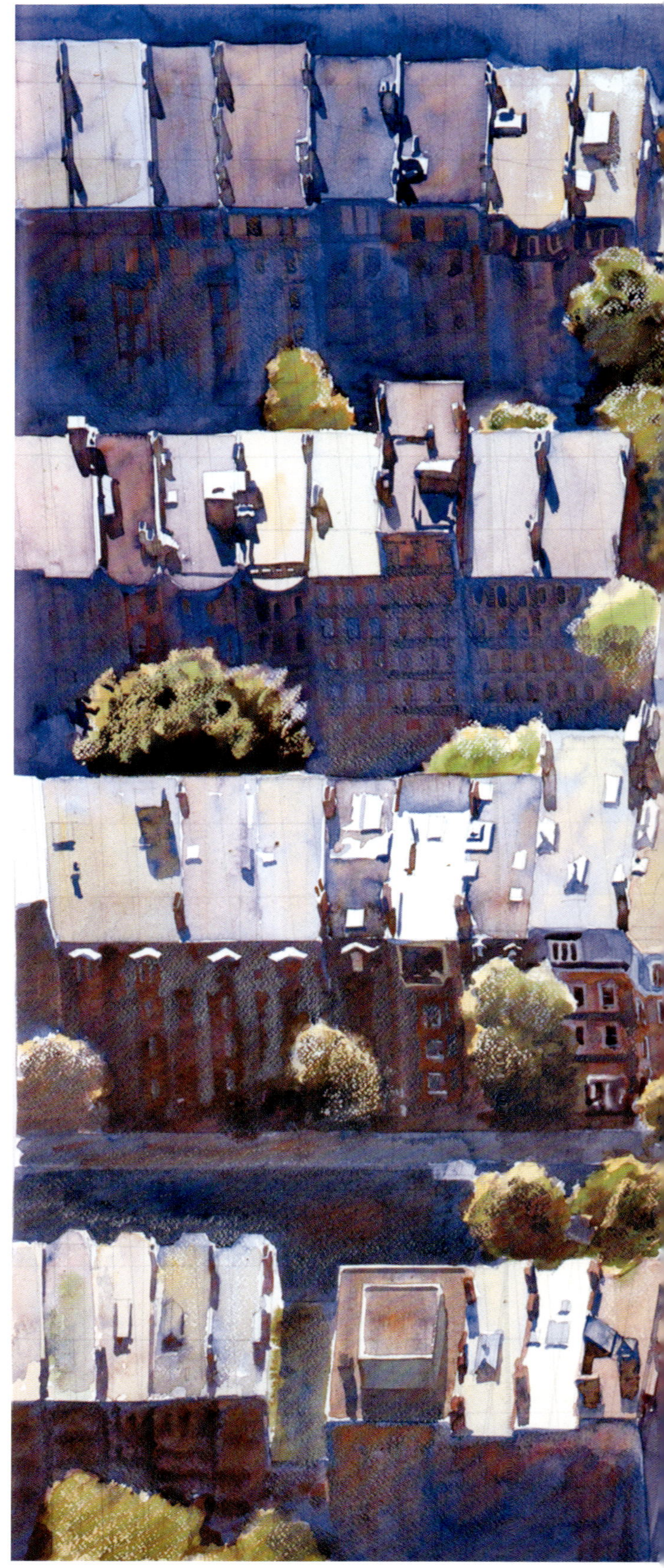

Back Bay Perspective, 1987
Watercolor, 30 x 42 inches
Private collection

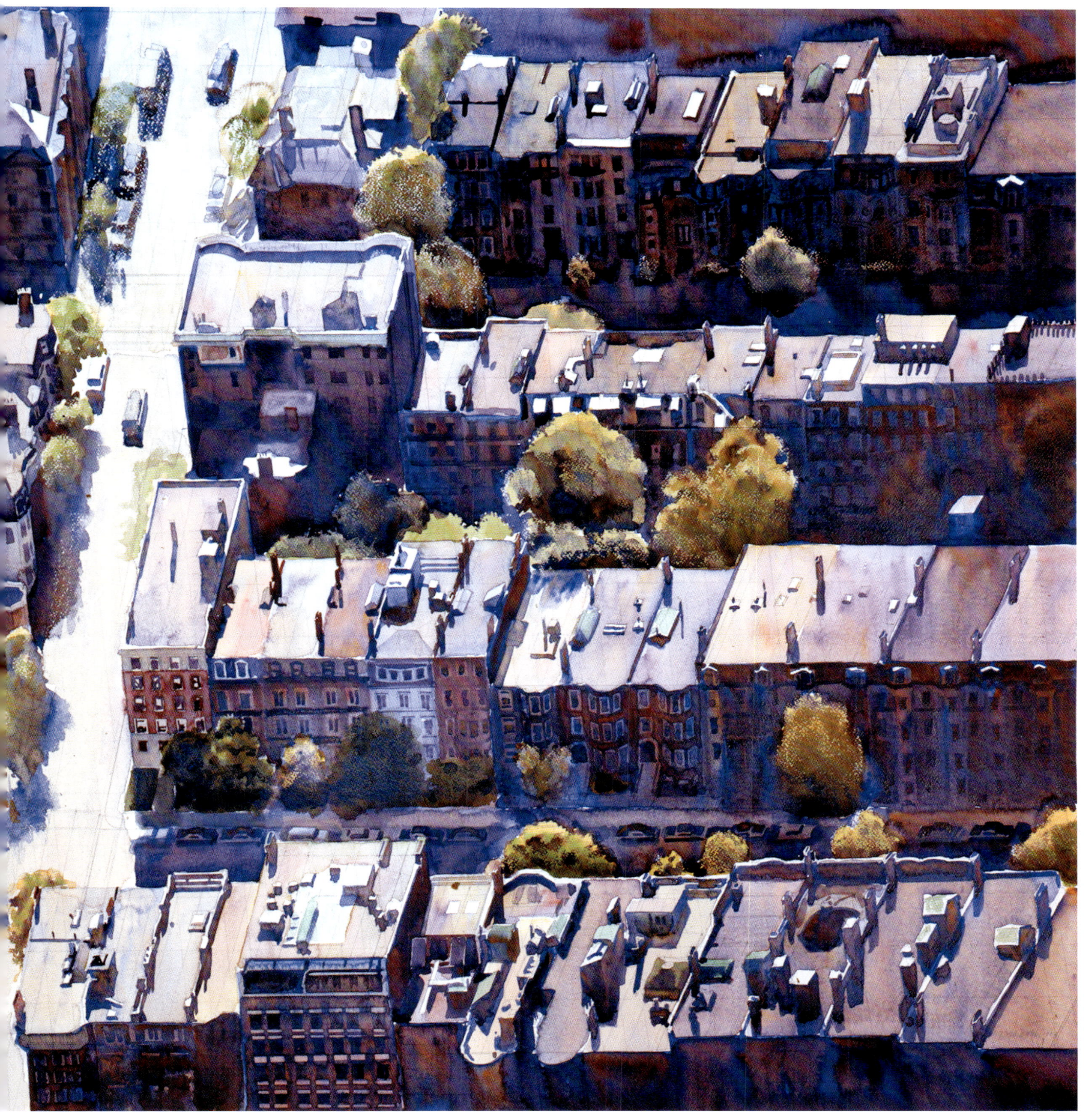

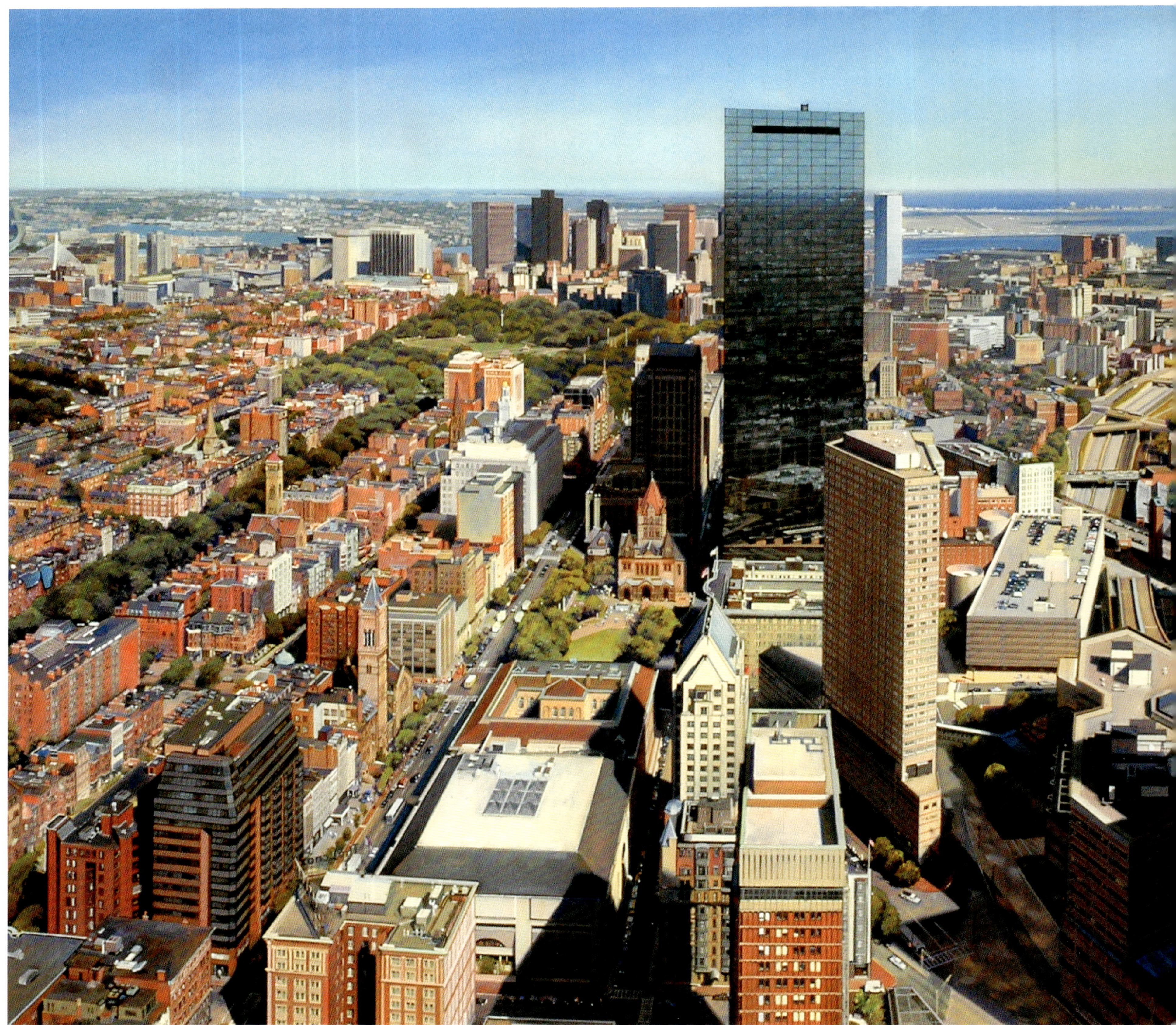

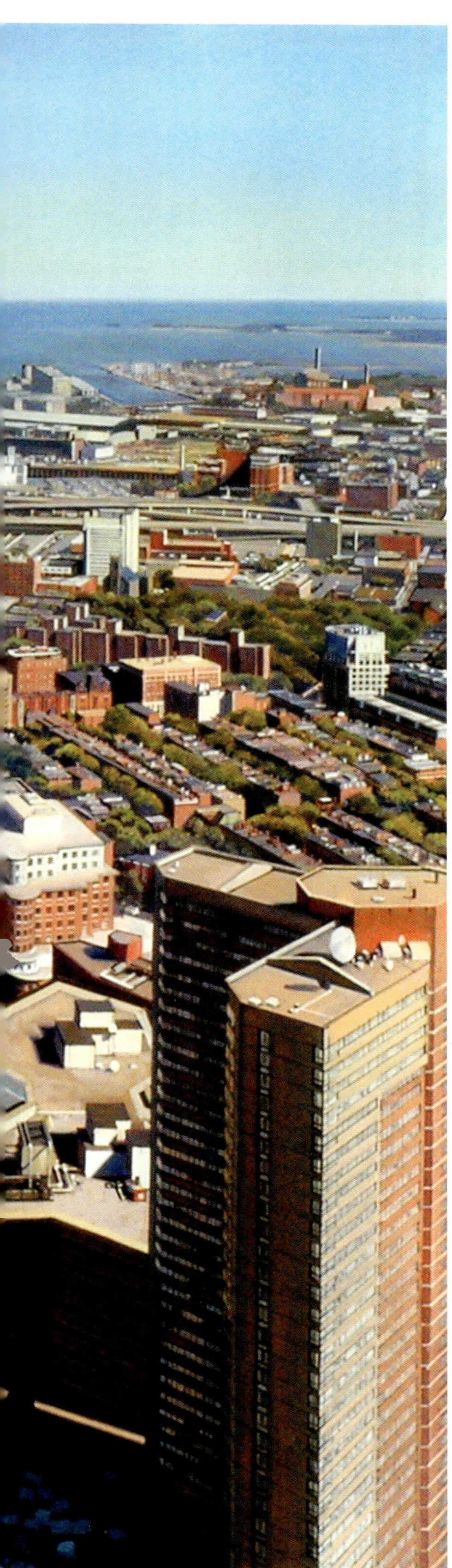

The view from the Prudential building is extraordinary. My painting shows the view looking downtown, toward the harbor. I like the way the John Hancock tower, with its dark glass, anchors the painting. The lines of buildings on the left and right sweep up to the center, with the green tower being the only one breaking the horizon line. The horizon seems to sweep through the Hancock as if it were transparent. But that is because the reflection of the horizon behind us is coinciding with the horizon in the distance over Boston harbor. The level of the horizon is always equal to the viewer's own elevation, so we can pinpoint our height relative to the Hancock with great accuracy—it's right where the horizon line crosses the building. No other building quite crosses the horizon; therefore no other building is quite as high as we are. In a way this painting complements my painting from 500 Boylston Street because it reverses the view of that painting. 500 Boylston is the building seen in the shadow of the Hancock. It was from there that the view looking down on Trinity Church and Copley Square was taken.

BOSTON FROM THE PRUDENTIAL, 2005
OIL ON LINEN, 36 x 52 INCHES
JOHN AND MARGARET STARR

The Green Building at Massachusetts Institute of Technology has a spectacular view of Boston across the Charles where the river is wide and parallel to the streets in Back Bay. When the camera sweeps panoramically to the left or right, the movement does strange things to the geometry of parallel lines, and shapes change. The eye perceives no such change. Wide views are distorted when they are reduced to a flat plane in a painting or photograph. In my painting the river is swept up into a smiling shape.

Likewise, in BACK BAY ROOFTOP PANORAMA WITH THE RITZ, the buildings that are all along the straight stretch of Commonwealth Avenue are swept up into a curve. This is a view gained from climbing out onto the roof of Haddon Hall on Commonwealth Avenue late in the afternoon. Because of the wide sweep of the view, buildings on the left seem to reflect the afternoon sunlight, and buildings on the right seem to be seen against the light.

Interestingly, if both of these paintings could be curved into cylinders and wrapped around the viewer, then all those curved lines would appear straight, just as they would in reality. When the paintings are flattened, all the curves appear.

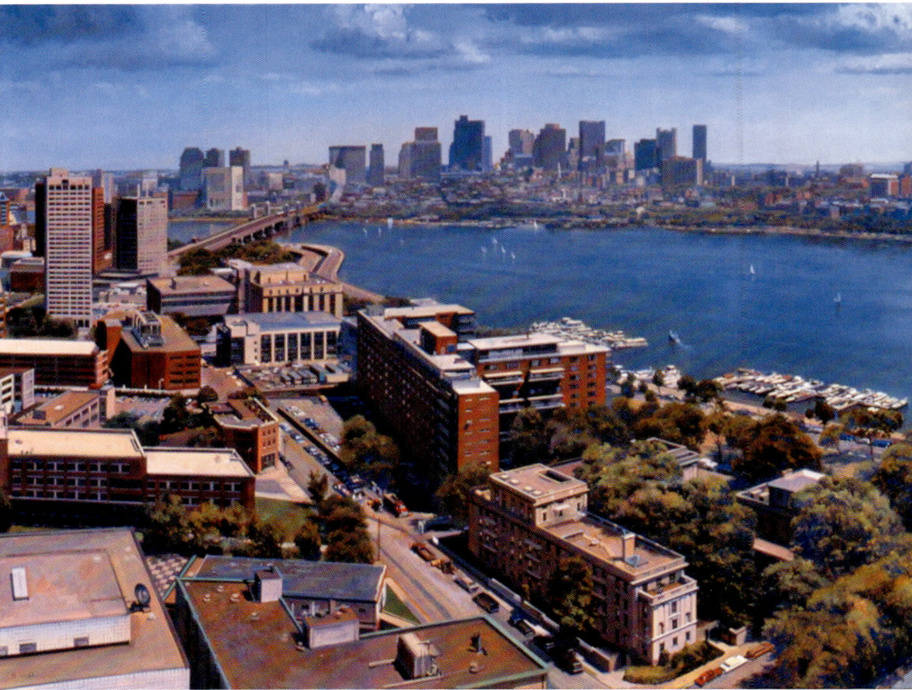

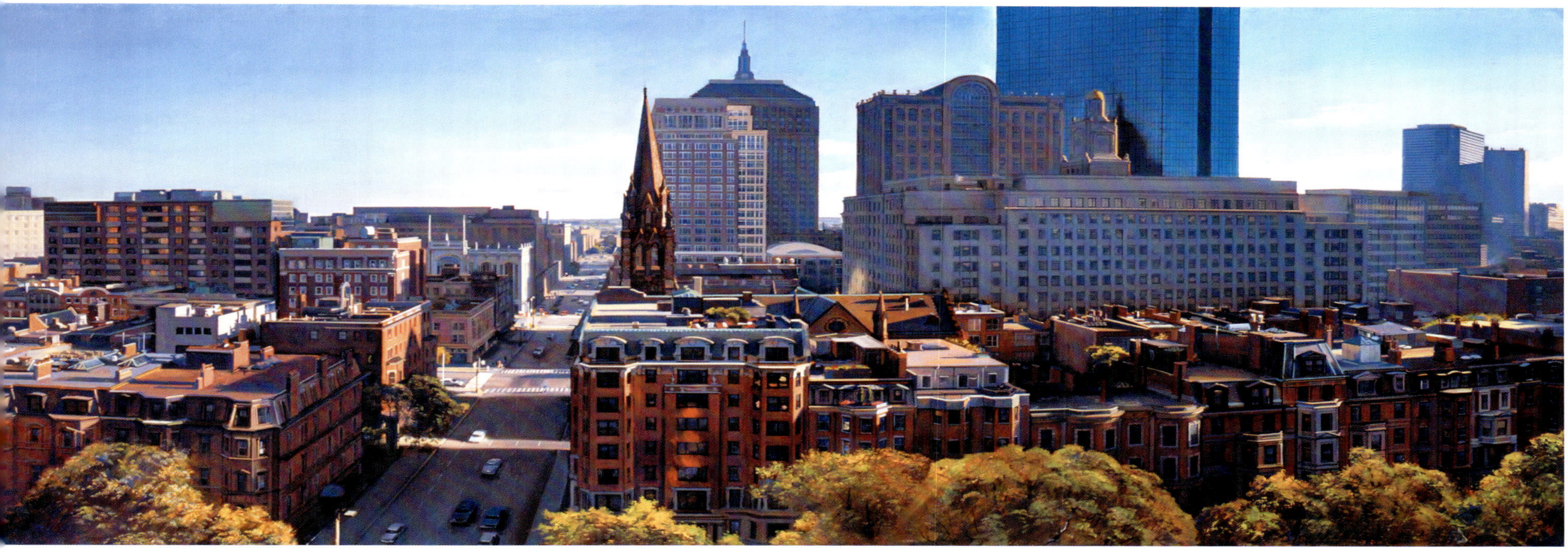

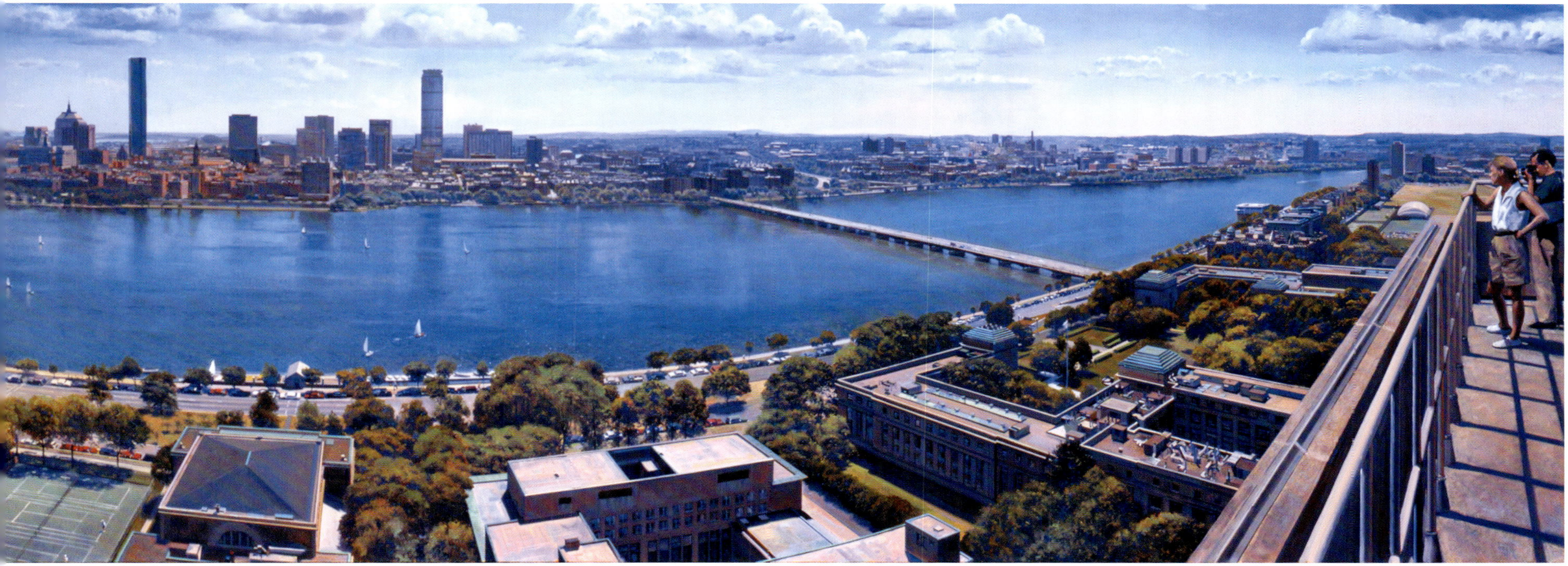

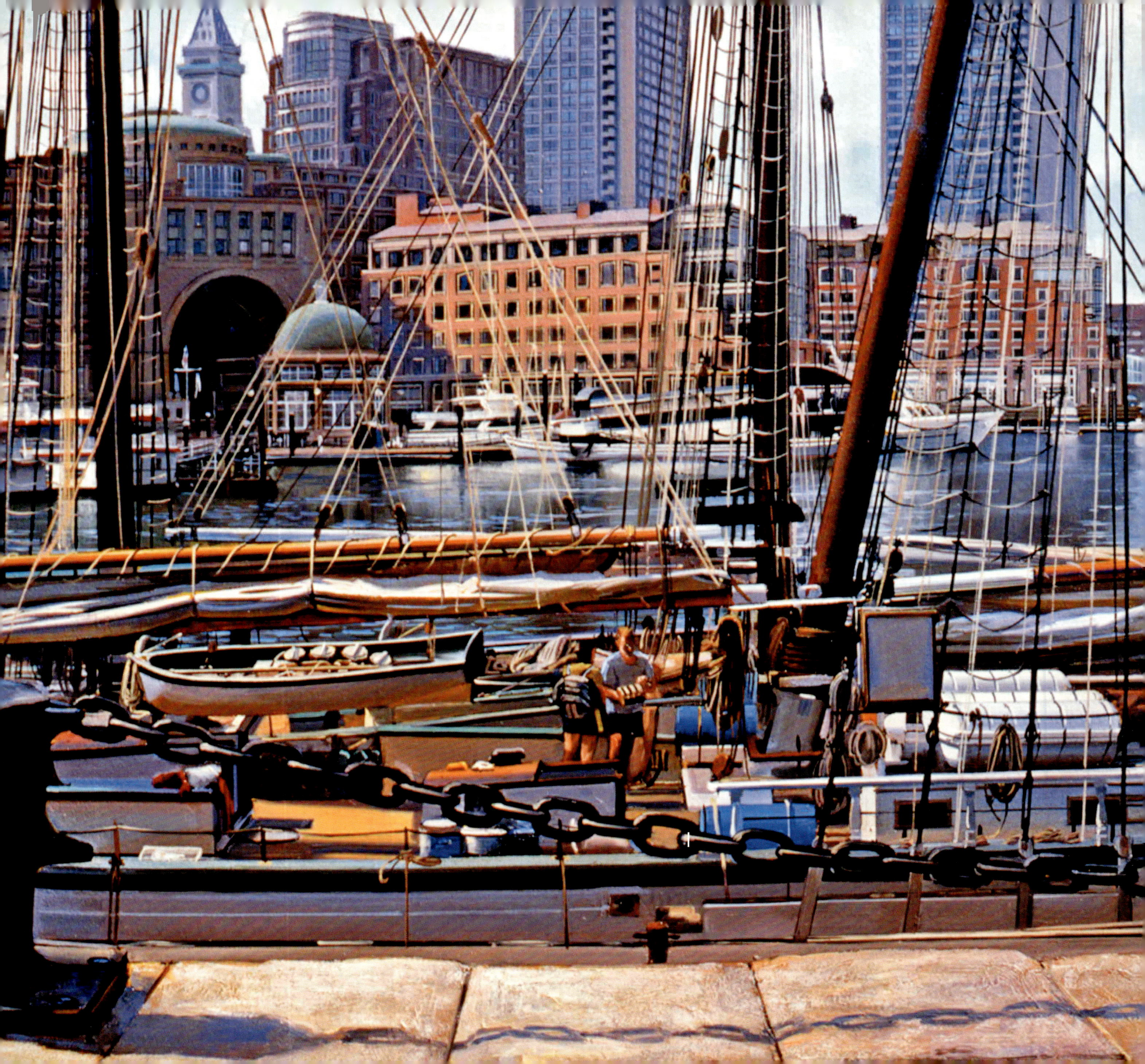

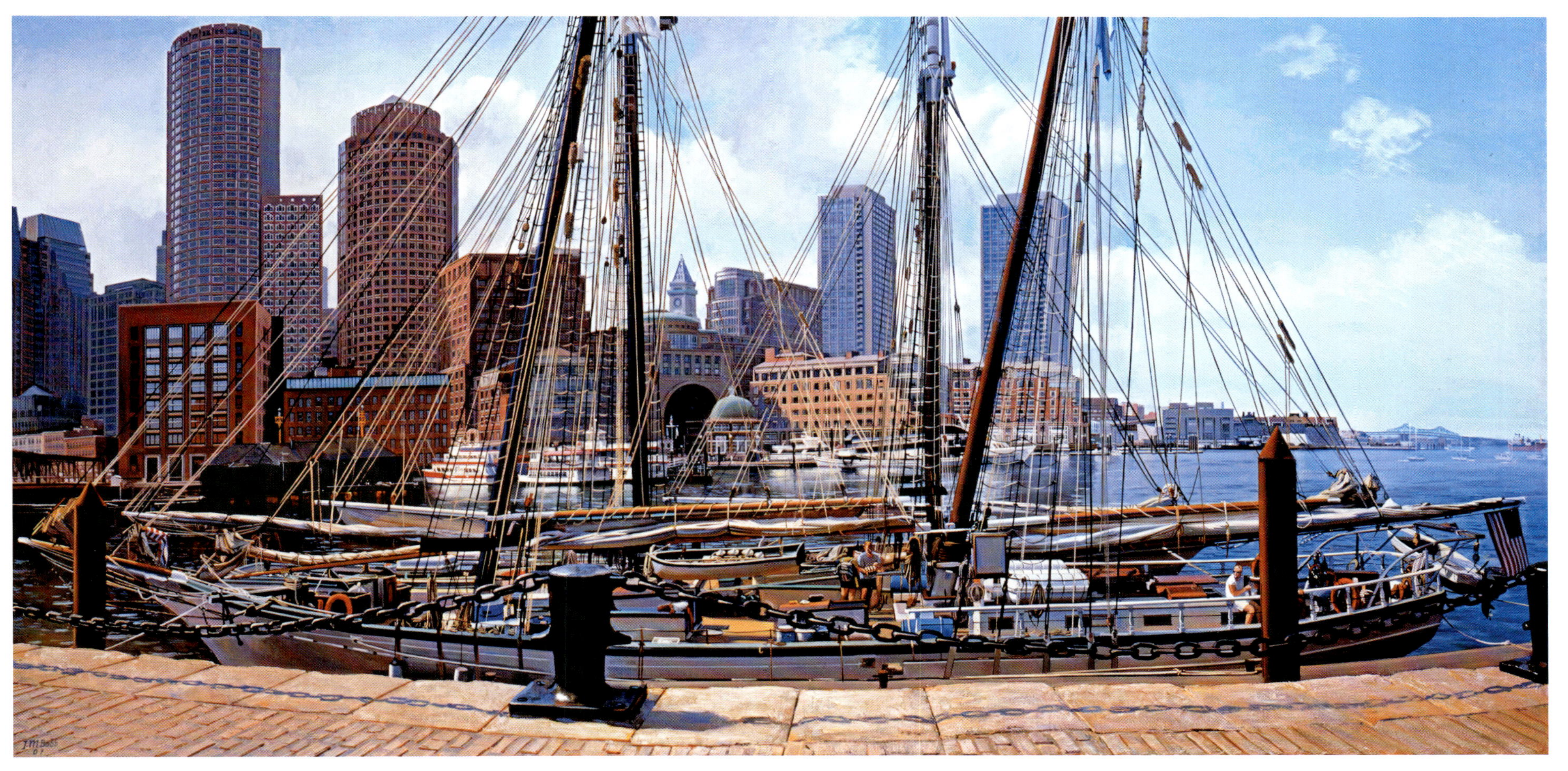

The waterfront has undergone a transformation, and the view from the Fan Pier looking across to Rowe's Wharf is one of the most dramatic. By looking through the rigging of two schooners which are tied up there, we seem to be seeing the new Boston filtered through the image of the past. Canaletto's Venetian views are made so interesting by the traffic of boats and shipping and figures working. My image of the city seen through the old boats suggests a contrast between the vitality of the old city and the new—and a reflection on time and change.

THE FAN PIER, BOSTON, 2007
OIL ON LINEN, 24 x 48 INCHES
ABBOT W. AND MARCIA L. VOSE

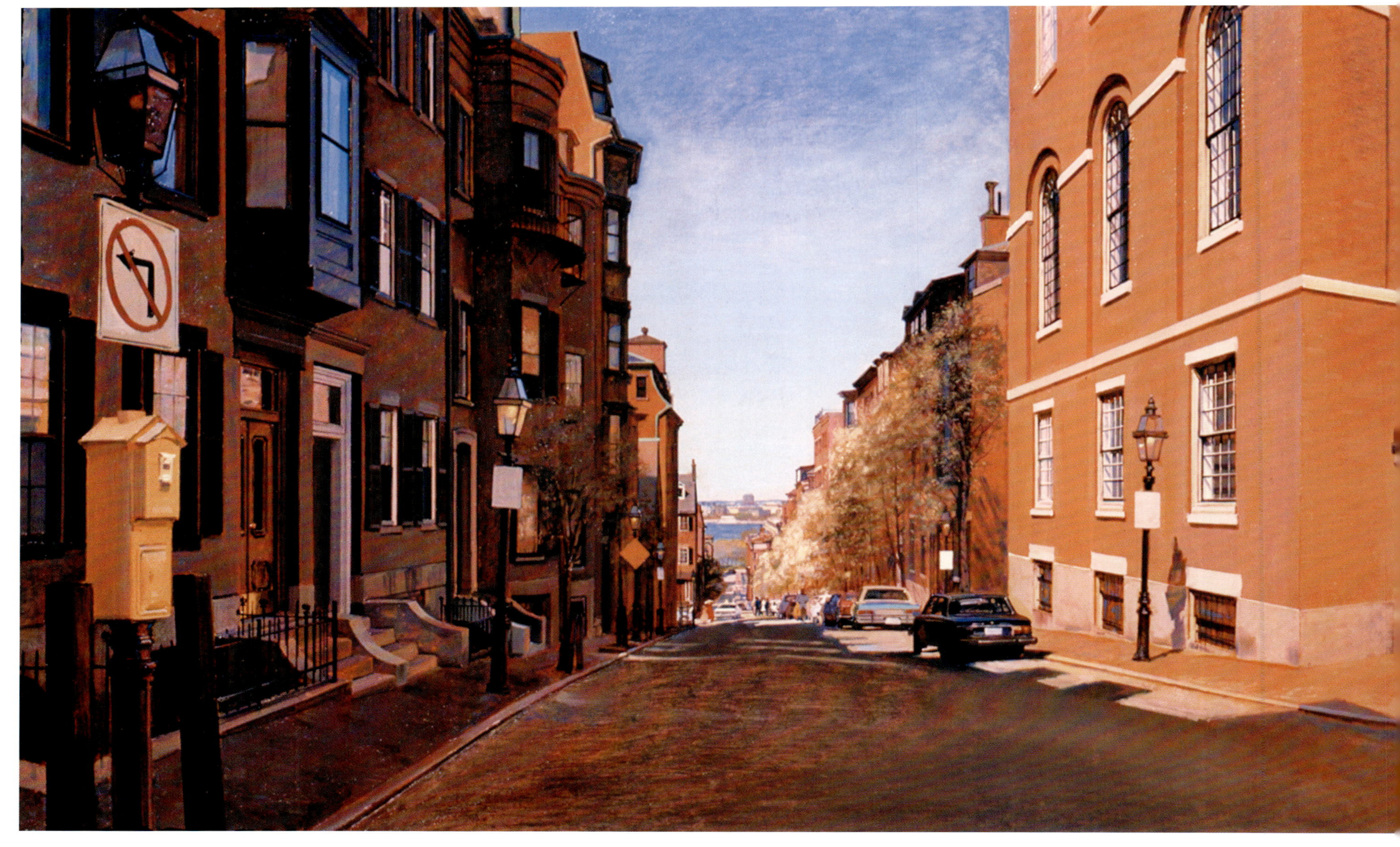

This is an early panoramic painting of an intersection on Beacon Hill just above Louisburg Square. Street corners seem absolutely banal and familiar until you begin to draw them, and then nothing seems to match up or be consistent. The view down each street is a one-point perspective with a vanishing point at the end of the street on the horizon. The view of the corner, in which the central building is seen with its edge toward us, is a two-point perspective. You would think the lines of the building would go to the vanishing points of the streets, but they don't. If you take a series of photos panning across the scene, you will see different geometry for each building as you move the camera. The only way to blend them together is to smooth all the straight lines into curves. But when you are standing on the street corner looking around, your eye never perceives the buildings as being curved! You begin to realize there is something deeply paradoxical and not well understood about the eye and perception of space.

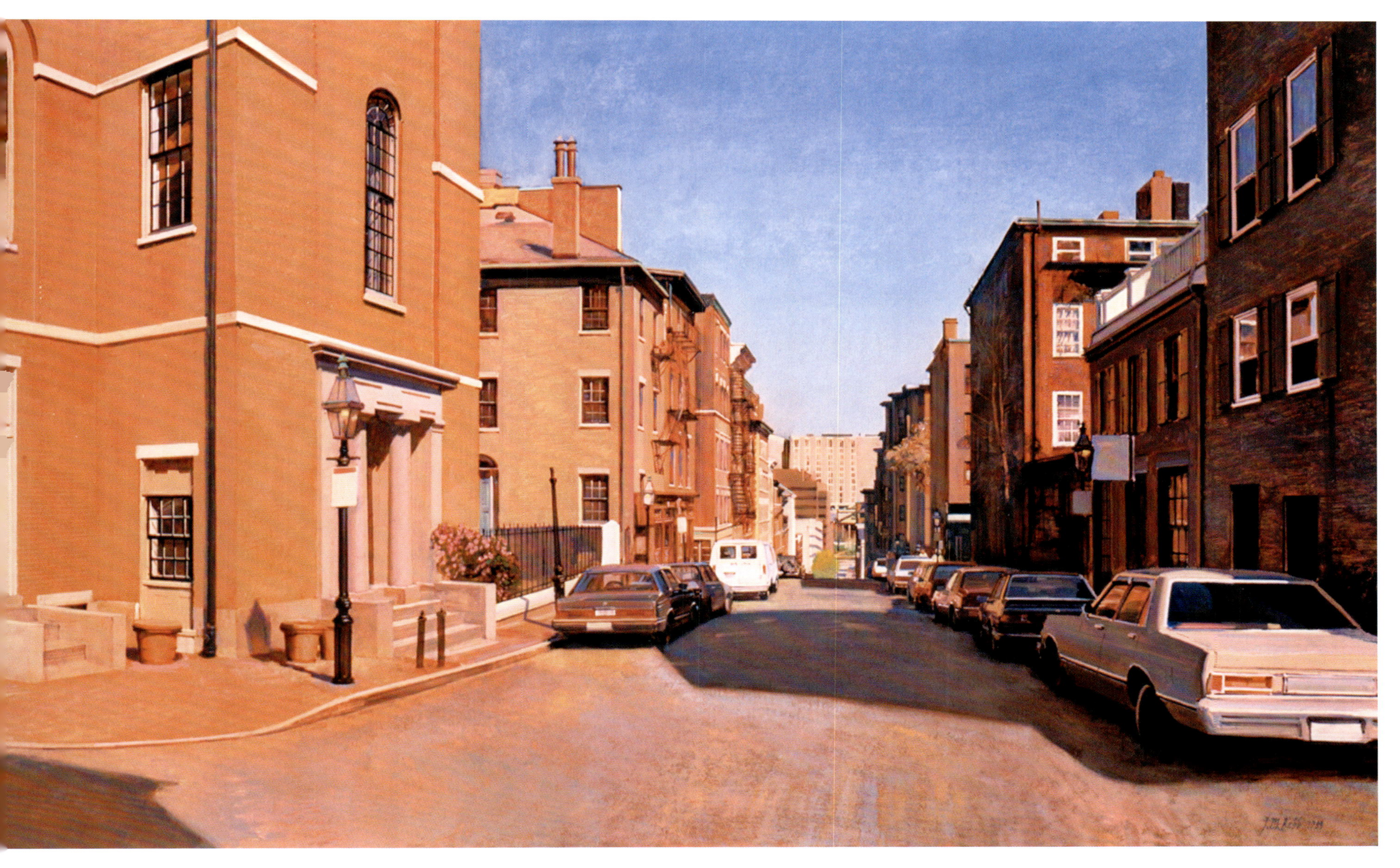

BEACON HILL, 1987

OIL ON LINEN, 22 X 72 INCHES

PRIVATE COLLECTION

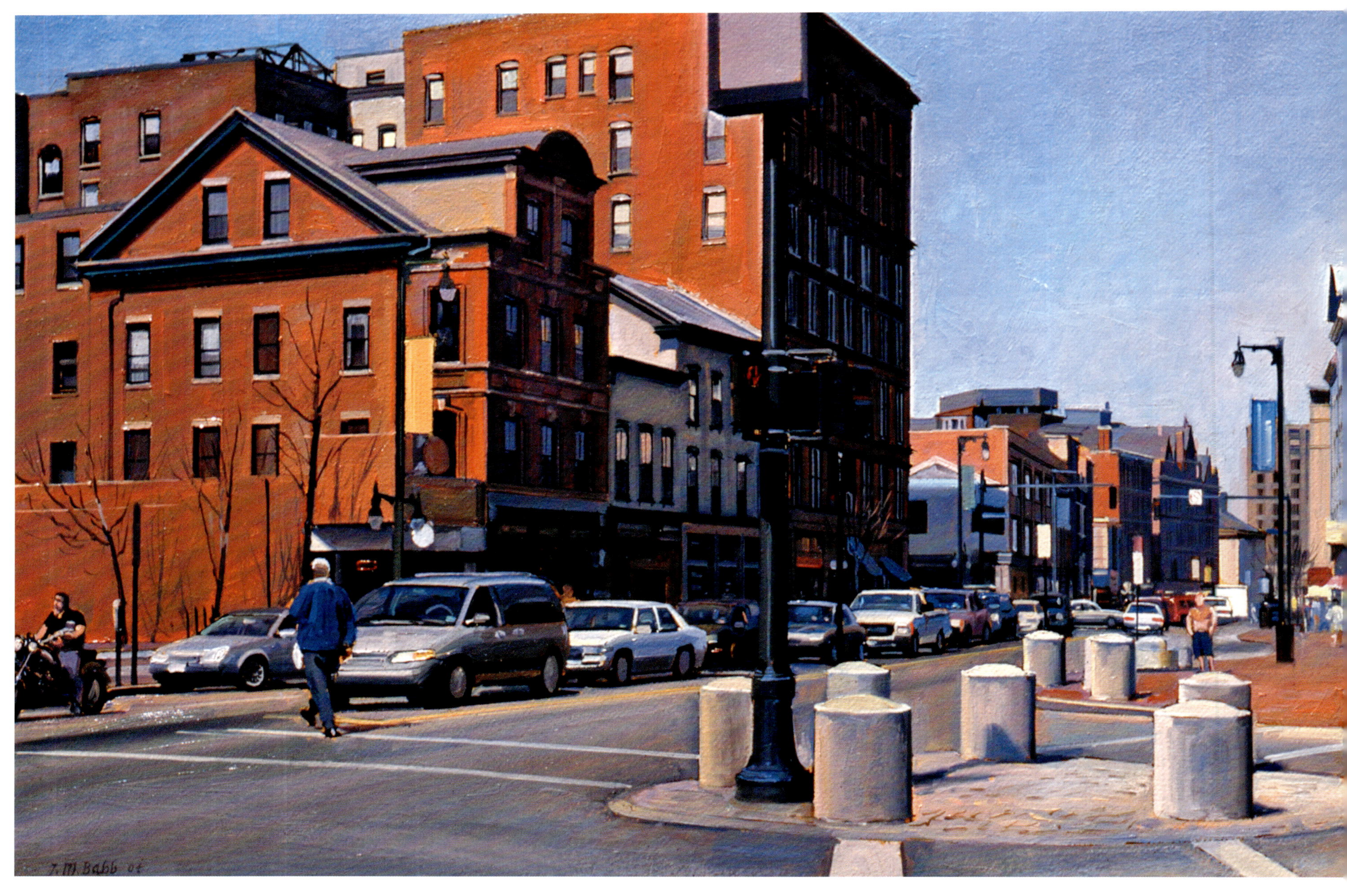

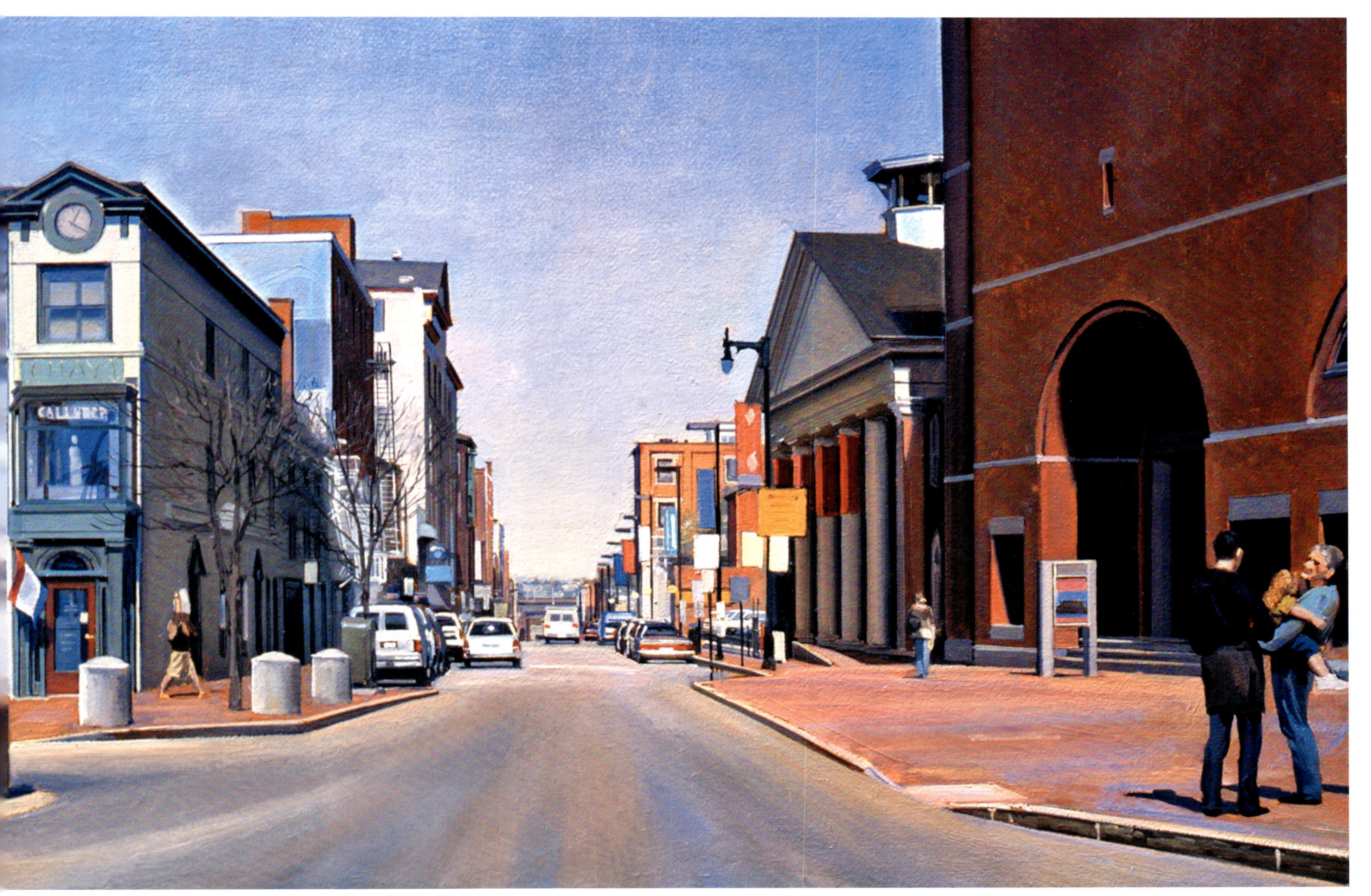

The Hay Building, Portland, Maine, 2004
Oil on linen, 10 x 31 inches
Ralph and Mary Lou Lancaster

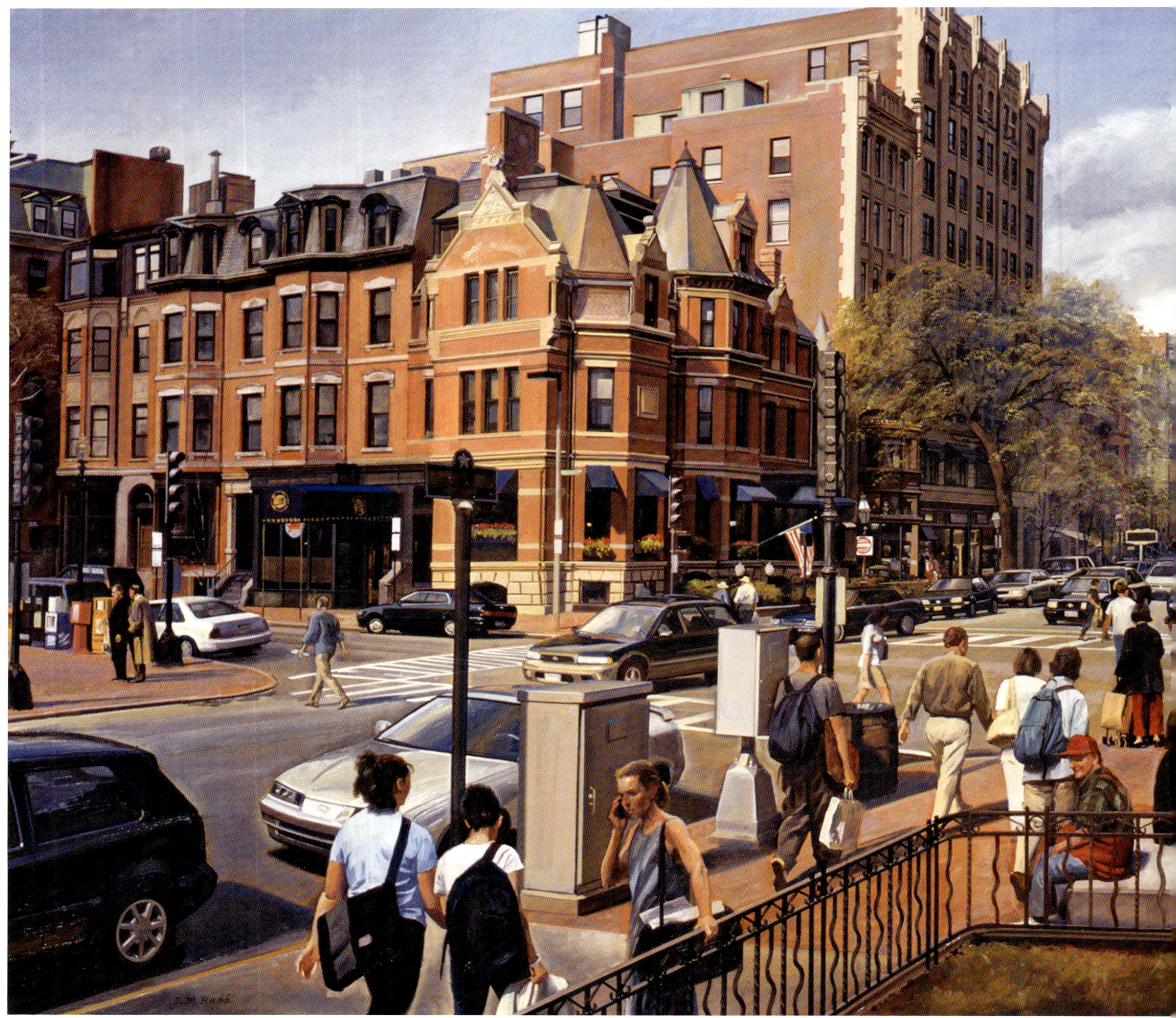

J. M. Babb

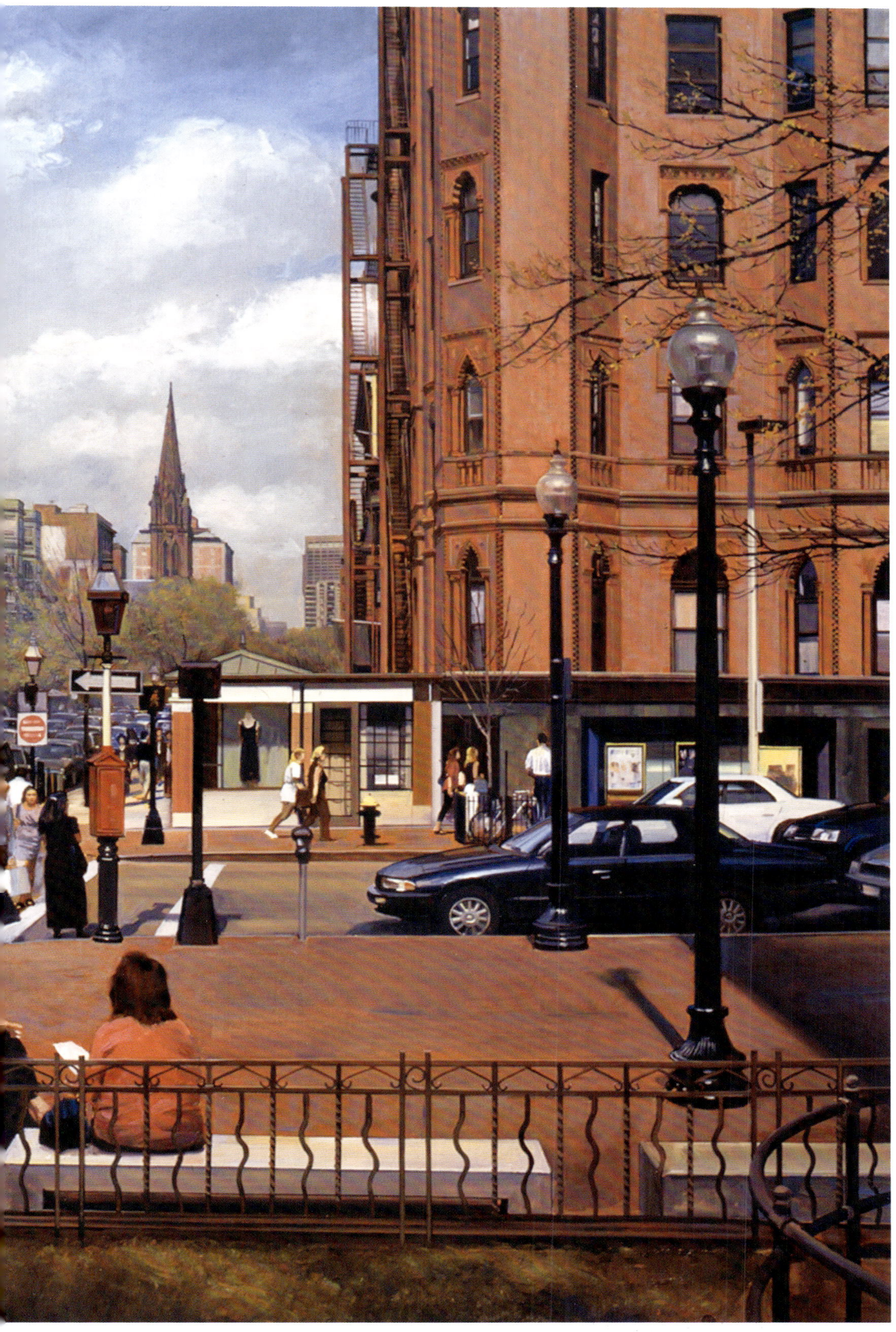

The figures of people going about their business add immense vitality to Canaletto's cityscapes. The life of a city consists of the numbers and varieties of people observed moving in the streets, and the passing of cars which may be familiar today but will appear antique in a hundred years. You imagine possible interactions with the figures, what they might be thinking or feeling, and there is a pleasure in observing the spectrum of humanity. One photograph cannot capture everything. But standing in one place, you may take many photographs to capture people and actions which add to the final conception. Then you must use your knowledge of perspective and scale to integrate the individual figures into the scene. And then everything has to be seen under the same lighting conditions and have a consistent plan of color harmony for the finished painting.

For instance, the Newbury Street painting is organized around the play between blue and orange—but in the foreground, how some of the oranges slide into intense reds is important. I love the color of the reddish shirt of the woman sitting on the bench—how that shirt plays against the color of the bricks behind her.

NEWBURY STREET, BOSTON, 2000
OIL ON LINEN, 30 x 55 INCHES
PRIVATE COLLECTION

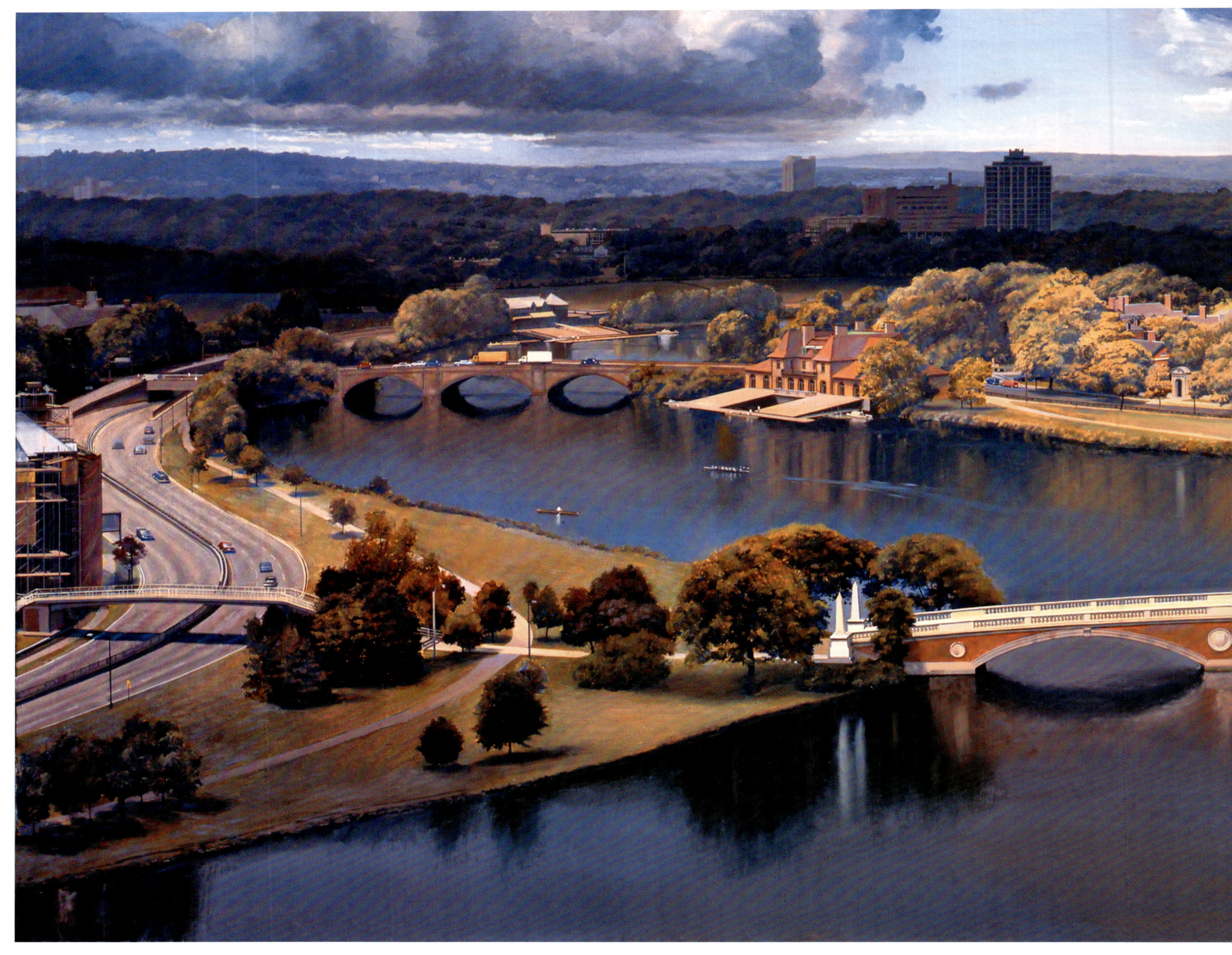

The Charles River adds so much beauty and interest to the city, with Boston and Cambridge viewing each other across the water. There is an immediate release from the congestion of urban neighborhoods to prospects of natural elements and distance. The Weeks Bridge reminds me of Ammanati's bridge in Florence and is even more graceful, being a bridge for pedestrians only. I found this view from the roof of a tall building near the river. It shows the natural beauty so near the intense development of Harvard Square.

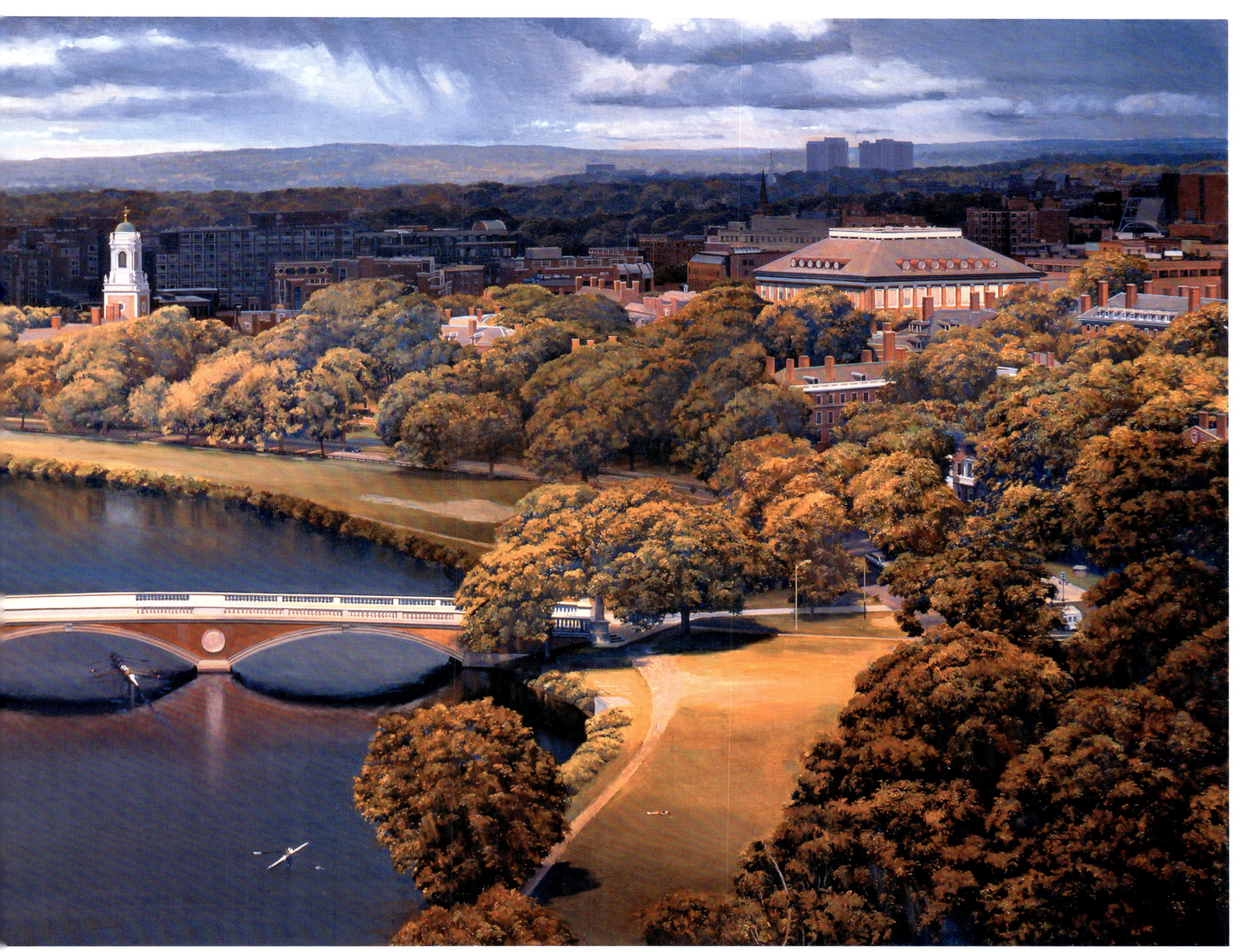

THE WEEKS BRIDGE, 1998

OIL ON LINEN, 37 x 97 INCHES

CAMBRIDGE SAVINGS BANK

Babb began coming to Maine in 1971. Fellow museum employee George Wilkinson and his wife, Mary, had purchased an old farmstead in East Sumner and invited him to visit. In Oxford County, in the western part of the state, the hamlet lies north of the city of Lewiston. Originally called West Butterfield Plantation, East Sumner consists of farms and woodland bisected by two branches of the Nezinscot River, which runs into the mighty Androscoggin in Turner. In 1975, entranced by this remote corner of Maine, Babb was given an acre of land by his friend, who felt that with a roof over his head and no major debt, the painter would have much more freedom to develop as an artist. Not long after, Babb began to cobble together a residence, beginning with a one-room cabin, which he constructed with the help of a local carpenter. The following year he built on a studio, with the windows and much of the interior walls made out of scavenged materials.[28]

The next part of this home in the woods came from an unusual source. In 1988, the Museum of Fine Arts, Boston, invited master metalsmith Gassan Sadaichi to create a sword as part of the exhibition *Japanese Master Swordsmiths: The Gassan Tradition*. The museum built a workshop in its courtyard to accommodate the visiting craftsman. At the end of the show, the structure was put up for sale by sealed bid; Babb and his wife won it. The painter disassembled the wooden structure and moved it to Maine. The present studio was added in 2009.[29]

On his first visit to the land where his house now stands, Babb spent a week camping and sketching, making pen-and-ink studies of wildflowers in the field, inspired by Leonardo's drawings of plants. Looking back from the perspective of having painted such remarkable woodland interiors as *The Hounds of Spring*, *Sonnets to Orpheus*, and *Forest Murmurs*, Babb considers those drawings and the instinct to make them the beginning of "a long artistic discovery."

The Maine home became a place for painting. Indeed, Babb spent more and more time in East Sumner; without a mortgage and economically stable, he had the opportunity to become an artist. As he stated in the catalogue for the exhibition *On the Edge: Forty Years of Maine, 1952–1992,* "Rural Maine has made all the difference in my being able to be an artist."

Somewhat paradoxically, Babb found himself painting mostly cityscapes in his

East Sumner retreat. Over time, however, he began to have success working outside with oil paints, which he had previously found more difficult than plein air watercolor painting. His first on-site pieces were small oils done in Sumner and on the Maine coast.

The inspiration for *The Hounds of Spring*, 1988, came from a walk Babb made in the woods near his home one summer afternoon. While traversing a washed-out logging trace up a hillside across the brook from his house, he suddenly had the feeling that he was walking in a painting, "moving in a work of art," as he put it. The painter felt he should try to capture the moment and place, "the whole environment of stones and plants at my feet, and trees in the distance, and farther hills and the sky and the distant storm." By the time Babb got around to tackling the subject, it was the following spring, and the original spot had lost its magic with the changing of the season. In an attempt to reconstitute the idea, he went to a spot at the base of Tumbledown Dick Mountain in nearby Peru, where he had previously done small plein air oil paintings. He found a spot where the trail was washed out and beech leaves had collected among the stones. New green growth was springing up, and the uphill prospect held the promise of mountaintop cliffs far above.

Deep in the woods, armed with his four-by-five camera and a tripod, and fending off black flies, Babb took a series of color transparencies of what would be the basis of his eight-foot-tall painting. His thought was to render everything in the foreground life-size, an "ant's-eye" view that would convey the illusion of being able to walk into the painting. Indeed, viewing the canvas in the reading room of the Baker Library at the Harvard Business School, one can imagine a student being distracted from his or her work by this beckoning path leading upward to the sky. After working on the painting for several months, Babb moved away from the transparencies he had been using as guides. "The textures and the color harmonies and ideas develop as one works from the photograph," the artist explains, "until the painting takes on a life distinct from the photos."

The subject, too, evolved: regeneration of life in the woods in spring became the presiding theme, which the painter came to associate with Algernon Swinburne's poem "Atalanta in Calydon," from whence comes the title of the work. The painting pays homage to natural forces and the "chaotic, sylvan reality" that arises when they are left to their own devices.[30] Far from the classicized landscapes of Claude Lorrain, *The Hounds of Spring* captures a "sterner" order and harmony. The painting also reflects

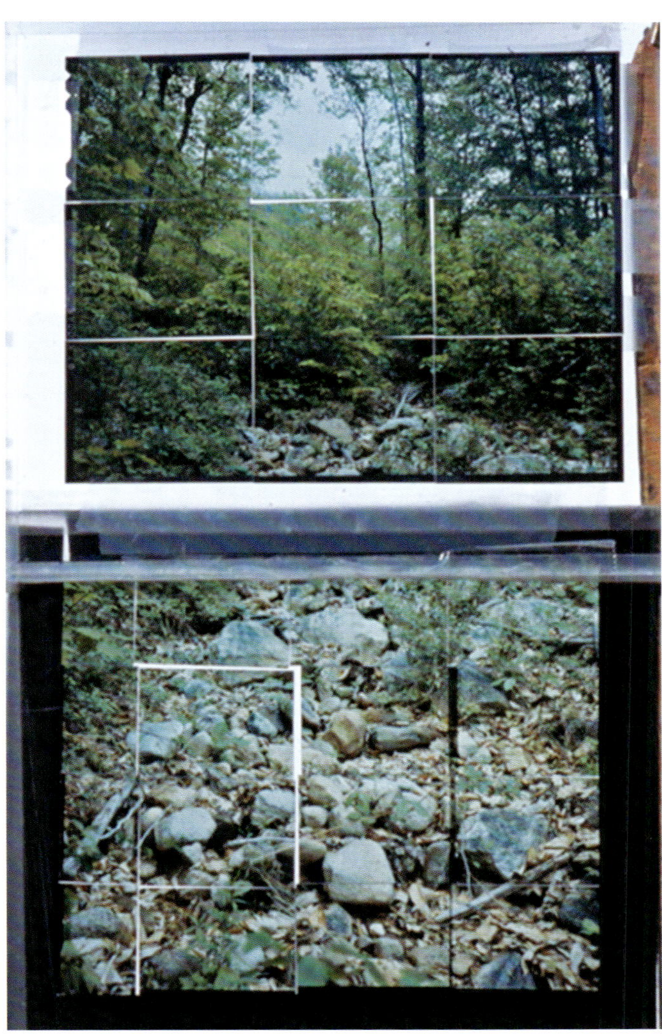

Babb's sense of humility before nature, a stance he had come to through his study of John Ruskin and J. M. W. Turner. He was drawn to the idea of "trying to learn from what is there rather than imposing what you think should be there as the primary impulse in painting."

Building on the success of this canvas, Babb further pursued Maine woodland scenes, deciding to render a view for each season. *Sonnets to Orpheus*, 1990, which takes its title from Rainer Maria Rilke's famous sequence written in 1922, presents the fullness of autumn and the final transition to winter. Leaves are falling down onto dark damp earth—"nature's 'muffled and dumb' storehouse," as Babb puts it, citing the Bohemian-Austrian poet.

Summer came next with the painting *Forest Murmurs*, 1993, a view of a brook near the artist's home in East Sumner. The title refers to a leitmotif in the second act of Richard Wagner's opera *Siegfried*, in which the hero lies down to rest in the forest and yearns for his mother. More than before, Babb sought to represent the absolute chaos of the forest interior; the viewer is situated among and within the trees. "There aren't fields to give distant views the way there are in a Constable painting," the artist notes; "One is completely enmeshed in the forest interior."

Though he has yet to paint a winter view to complete the cycle, Babb has painted a number of other forest interiors, including *The Green Fuse*, 1995, which offers an almost ecological vision of the woods. The painting captures the cycle of energy, growth, and decay—as soon as trees topple, they are colonized by other plant forms, and as Babb states, "nothing is wasted." The title connects the image to Dylan Thomas's poem "The Force That Through the Green Fuse Drives the Flower," in which the Welsh poet considers the power of nature to create and destroy.

Two other woodland paintings, *Gooseye Brook*, 1998, and *The Unnamed Brook*, 2002, were based on locales in the Sunday River region of Maine. In both cases, Babb explored a growing fascination with the dynamics of moving water. He also sought to render the complex patterns of sunlight on brook, rocks, and trees. A combination of on-site oil sketches and photographs helped him develop these canvases into paeans to woodland beauty—to a kind of unspoiled romantic world far from civilization.

Babb has painted further afield, including several canvases in the greater Mount Katahdin area. Such paintings as *Gulf Hagas Brook, Maine*, 2012, and *The Toll Dam, Baxter*

Park, 2004, place the painter in a distinguished lineage of artists of the north woods. Another woodland painting, *Carl's Path,* is a tribute to Babb's friend Carl Straub, former dean of the faculty and professor of environmental studies at Bates College.

Babb displays a similar feel for the natural world in several paintings of Corkscrew Swamp Sanctuary in Naples, Florida, an Audubon preserve established in 1954 that features the largest stand of old-growth cypress trees in the world. Painted in 1998–2005, these views are stunning studies of verdant swampland: ferns, orchids, and other plant life run riot around the base of twisting trees. The painting *Crystalline* is especially notable for its remarkable rendering of reflections. For the artist, forest interiors, north and south, represent the "miracle of being alive and conscious in nature, and standing in the orders of magnitude in nature between microcosm and macrocosm."

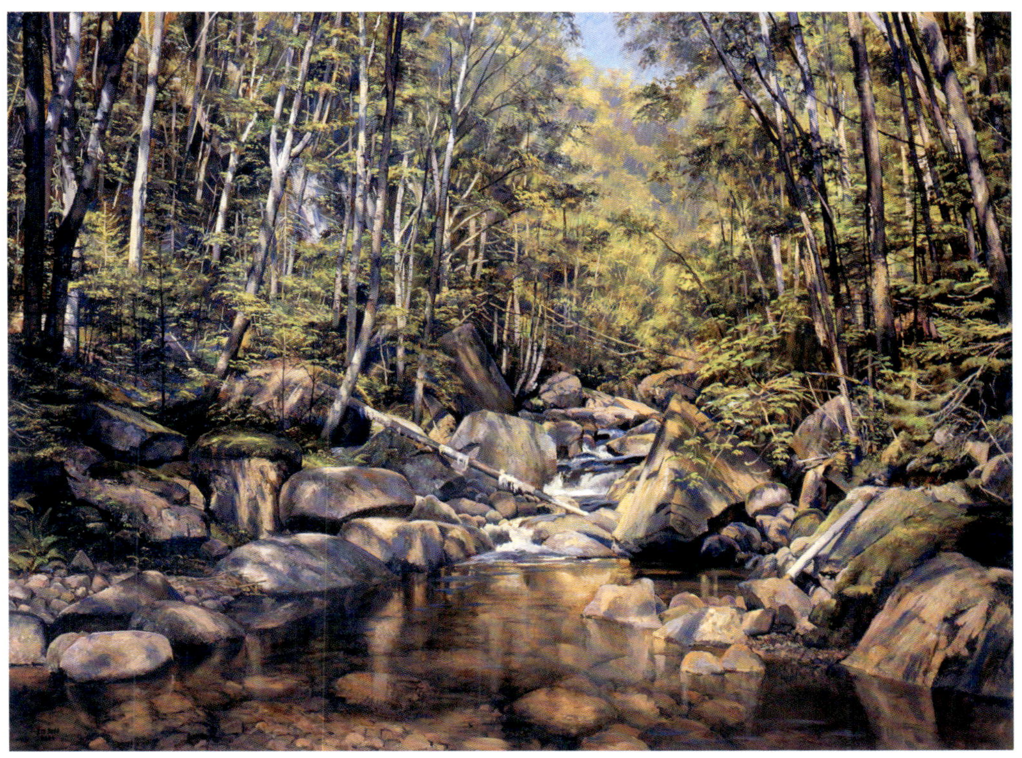

On my first visit to Maine I camped in the field where my studio stands today. I became captivated by the wild-flowers growing there and spent the week drawing them in pen and ink, imitating Leonardo's drawings of plants. I fell in love with the small mountains in our area and occasionally would attempt views in oil or watercolor. But for many years most of my work consisted of complex cityscapes, which I painted in my studio here in Maine. Only later did I use the large camera and the techniques I had evolved for doing the large cityscapes to do large paintings of the woods.

Nature is relatively untended in the Maine woods, and one soon becomes entangled in anarchic competition of self-organizing processes of growth and succession in the forest. Linear perspective, which orders the recession of city streets, seems nowhere in evidence in the woods. And there is hardly any atmospheric perspective to express distance and recession as in a Claude Lorrain painting—in fact there are so many trees there is hardly even a view.

So it becomes much harder to master a way of representing the spaces of the forest—to capture the feeling of looking through lattices of foliage and branches at still more distant patterns and to represent the broken pattern of light that filters down through the trees, making it difficult to read the forms of things but endowing every-thing with the atmospherics of poetic mystification.

OTTER CLIFFS, MT. DESERT, 2008

OIL ON LINEN, 72 x 52 INCHES

JOHN AND MARGARET STARR

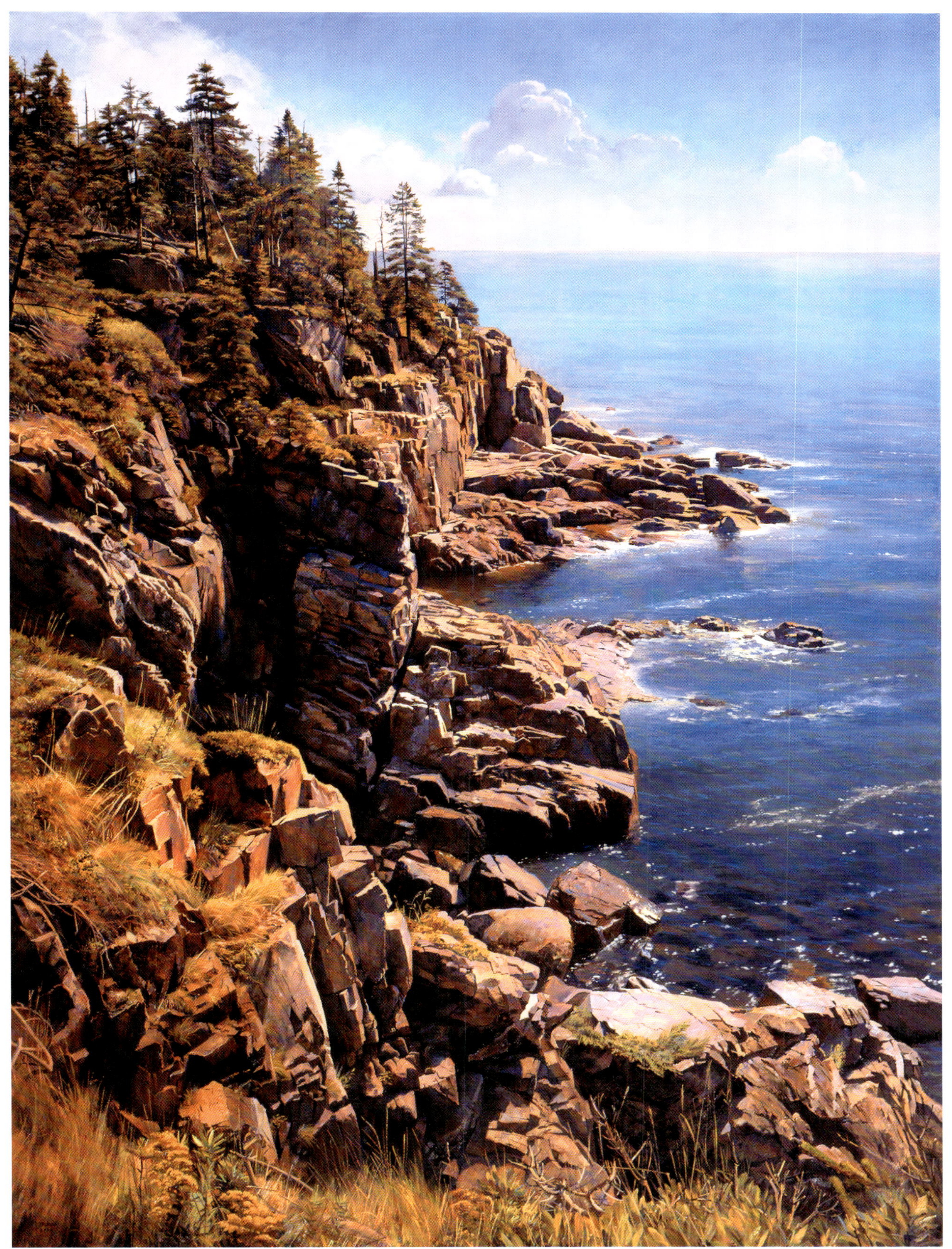

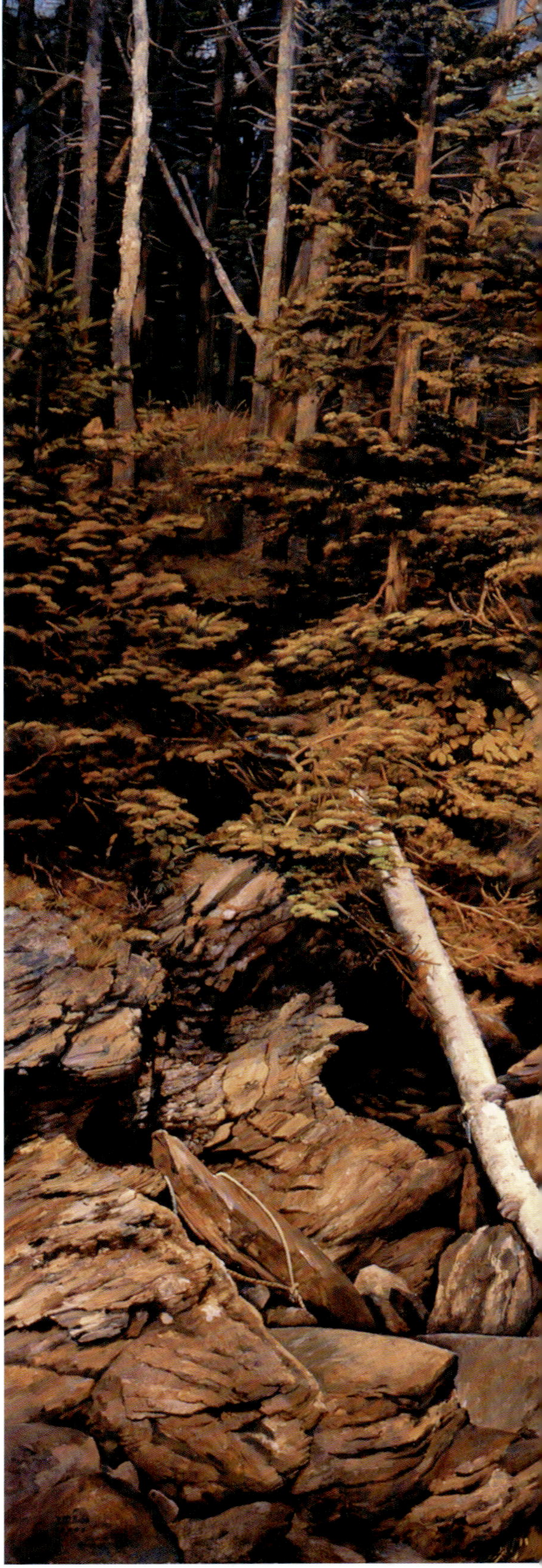

For many years I stopped painting the coast of Maine because it has been painted so much that it is impossible to see it for what it is. We spent a week at a spot on Eggemoggin Reach on Little Deer Isle, in an old farm where the woods came right down to the water. Fishing, and photographing, sketching, and painting, it sinks in how wonderful things are, how much they change with tides and weather. EGGEMOGGIN REACH *is the painting which came of that week. The mares' tail cirrus clouds were there for only fifteen minutes in the whole week, the tide just so at another time. A painting becomes the amalgamation of many observations over time fused in the logic of the art of painting.*

EGGEMOGGIN REACH, 2002
OIL ON LINEN, 60 x 84 INCHES
PRIVATE COLLECTION

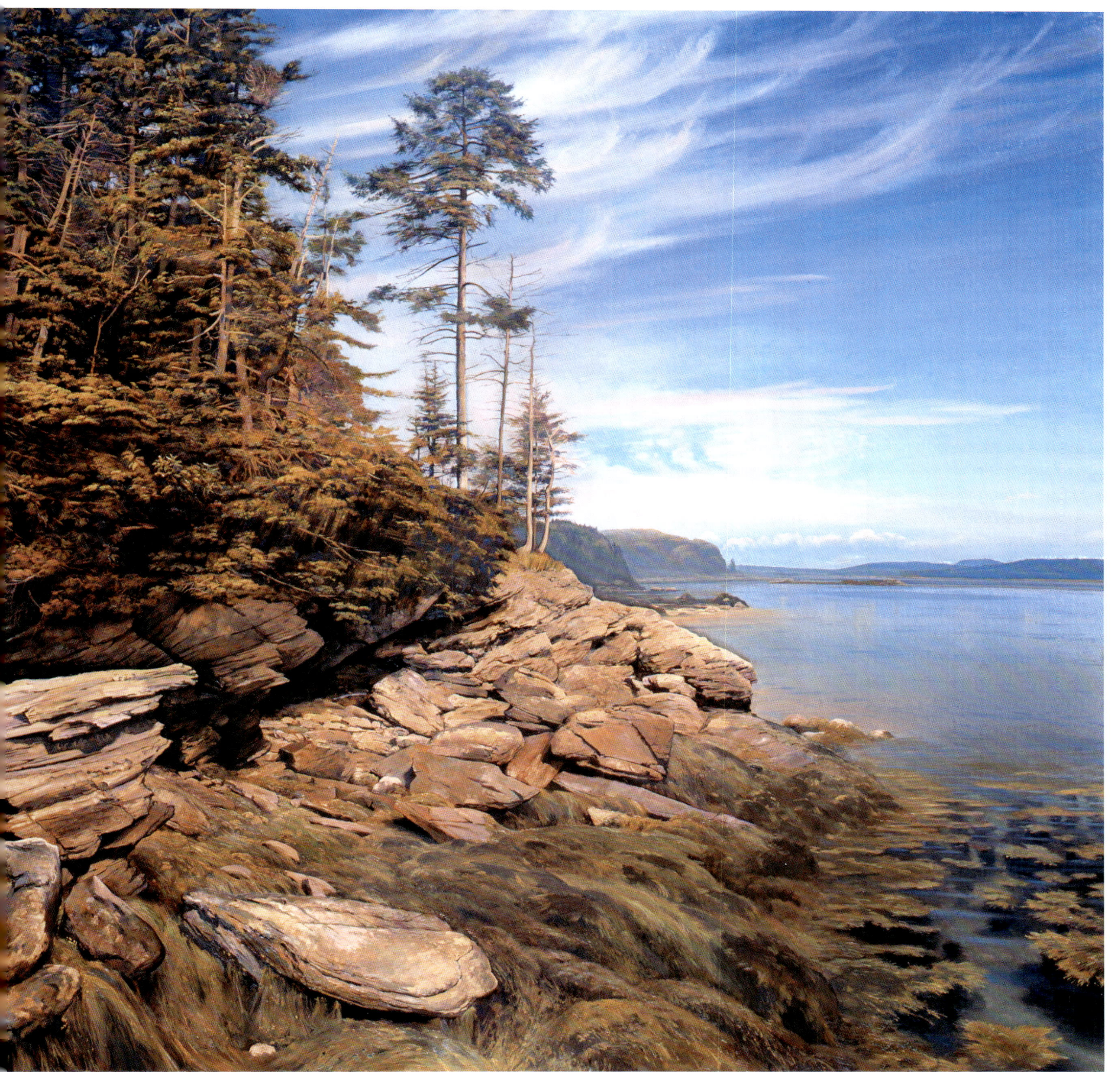

Recently I have been going back to Acadia and really enjoying painting the epic confrontation of sea, granite, pine, clouds. It is as if the Maine woods were being ground away to the foundations by this meeting with the sea. When the water is calm, the shoreline is still evocative of storms of unimaginable scale. I love the architectonic structure of the rocks, and the opposing movement of the water as if resentful of the rigidity, the sway of light and atmosphere over everything.

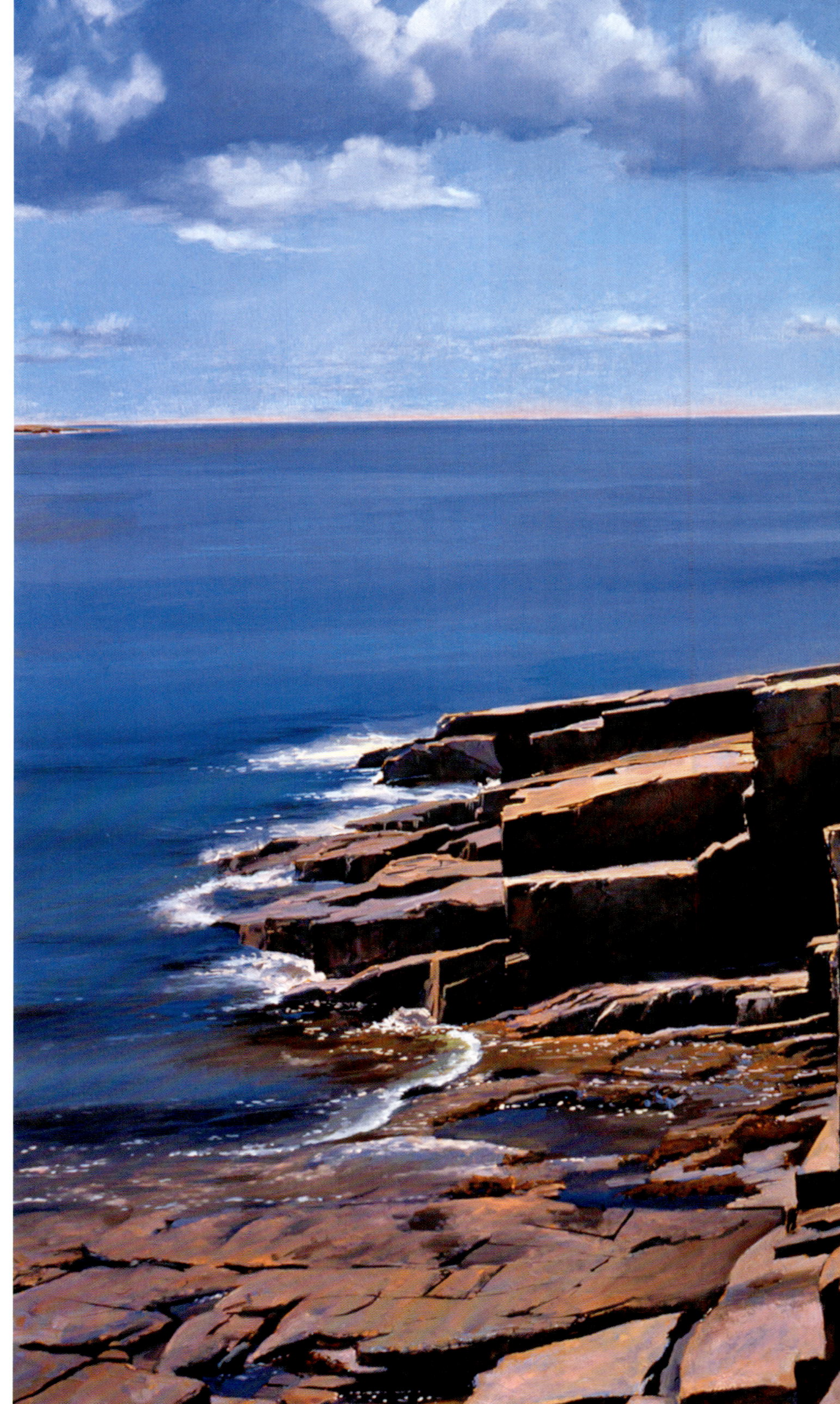

SCHOODIC PENINSULA, MAINE, 2008

OIL ON LINEN, 27 x 45 INCHES

PRIVATE COLLECTION

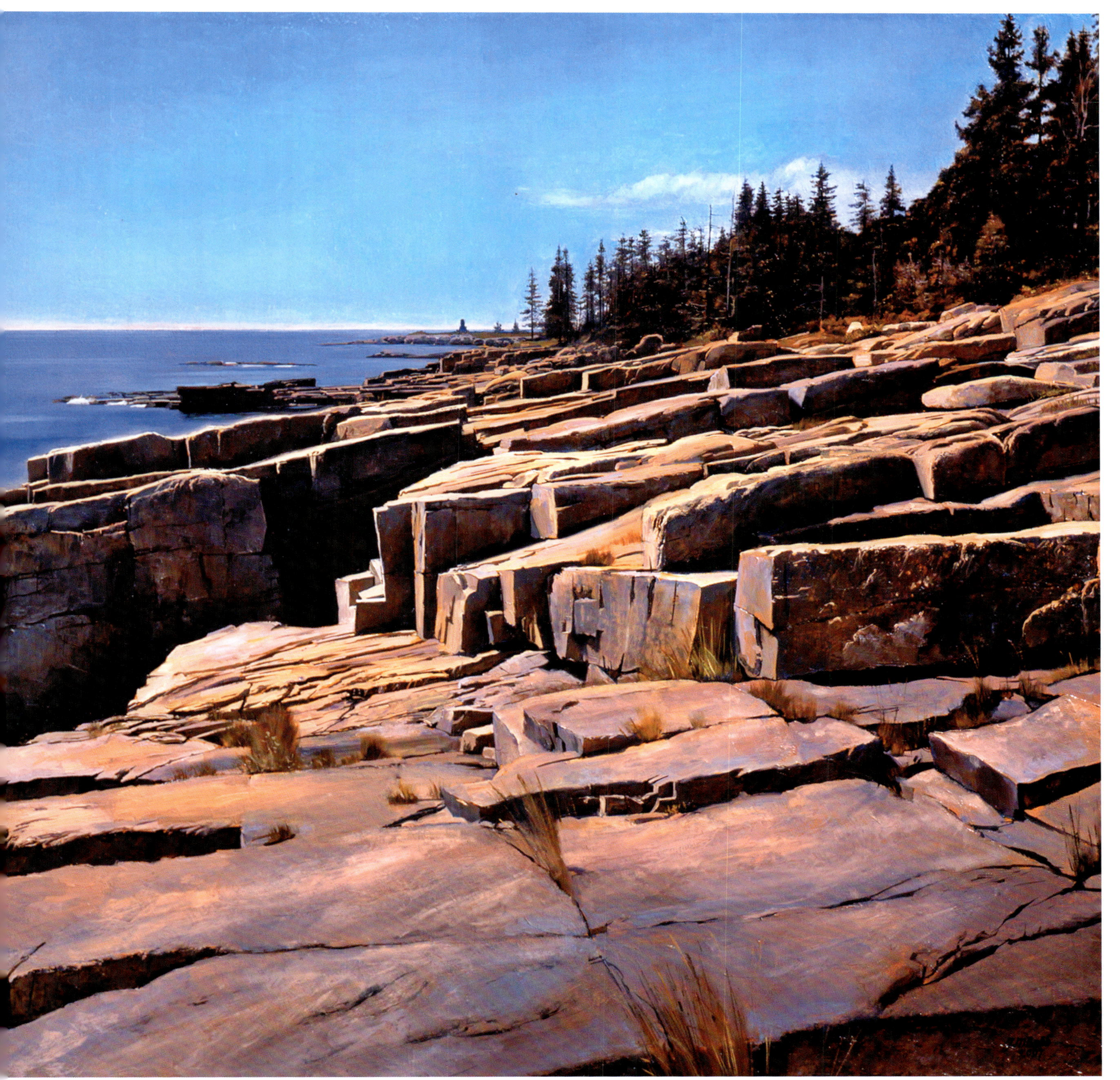

First old logging roads, then gradually streams became my favorite inroads to the secret places in the woods. In a place where a brook is coming down out of the mountains it seems there is always so much going on, nature going about its business in a cheerful way. The sound of the rushing water seeps into you with a message of peace and satisfaction when you spend a day painting by a brook. A phrase in a Shakespeare sonnet describes the morning sun as "gilding pale streams with heavenly alchemy." It's true that the water seems to have no color of its own, but it shows fragments of the rocks on the bottom, shadows, scatterings of the blue of the sky, and shards of sunlight all in motion together, and it is magical.

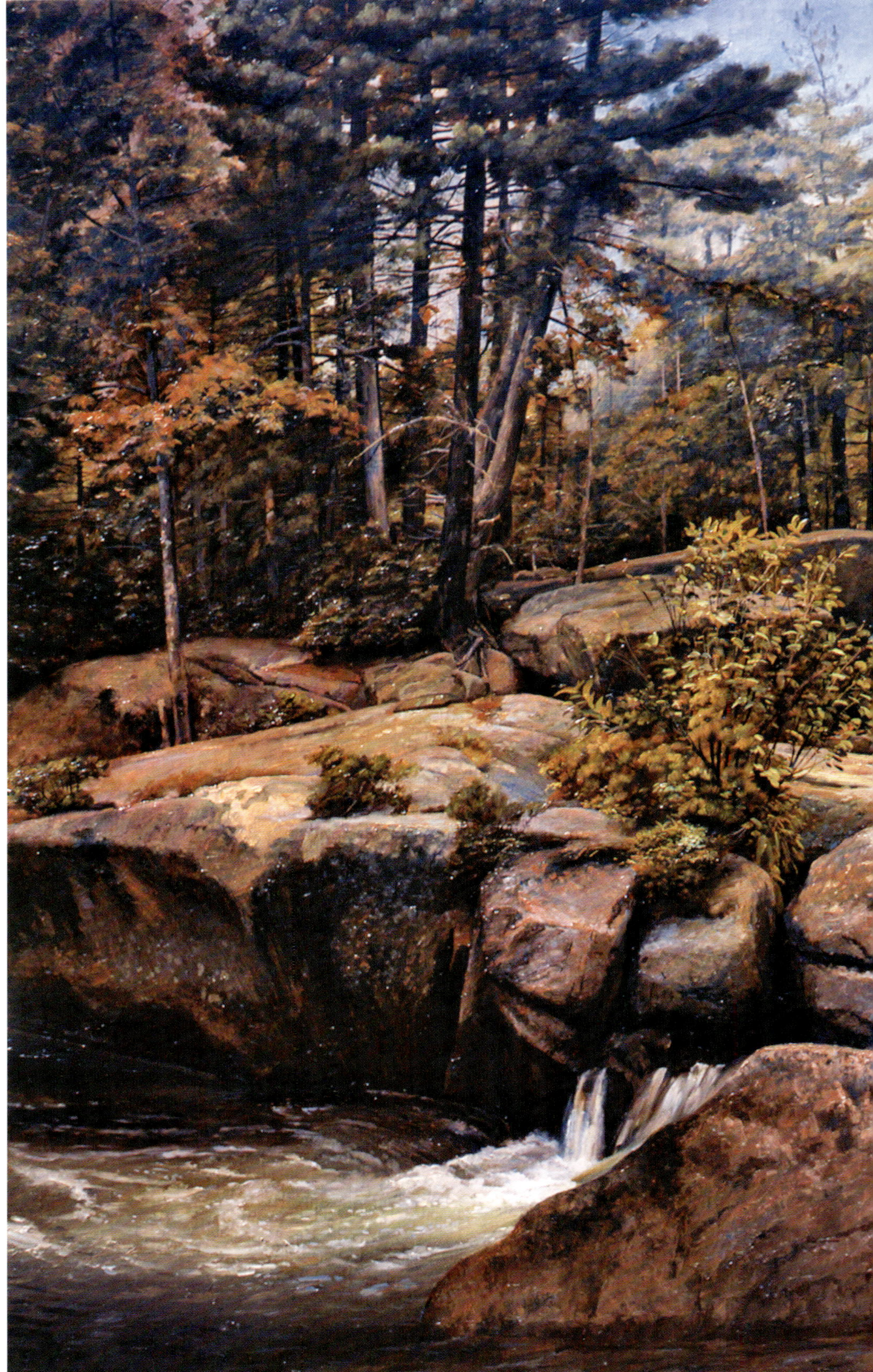

BIG NIAGARA, BAXTER PARK, 2000
OIL ON LINEN, 54 x 84 INCHES
PRIVATE COLLECTION

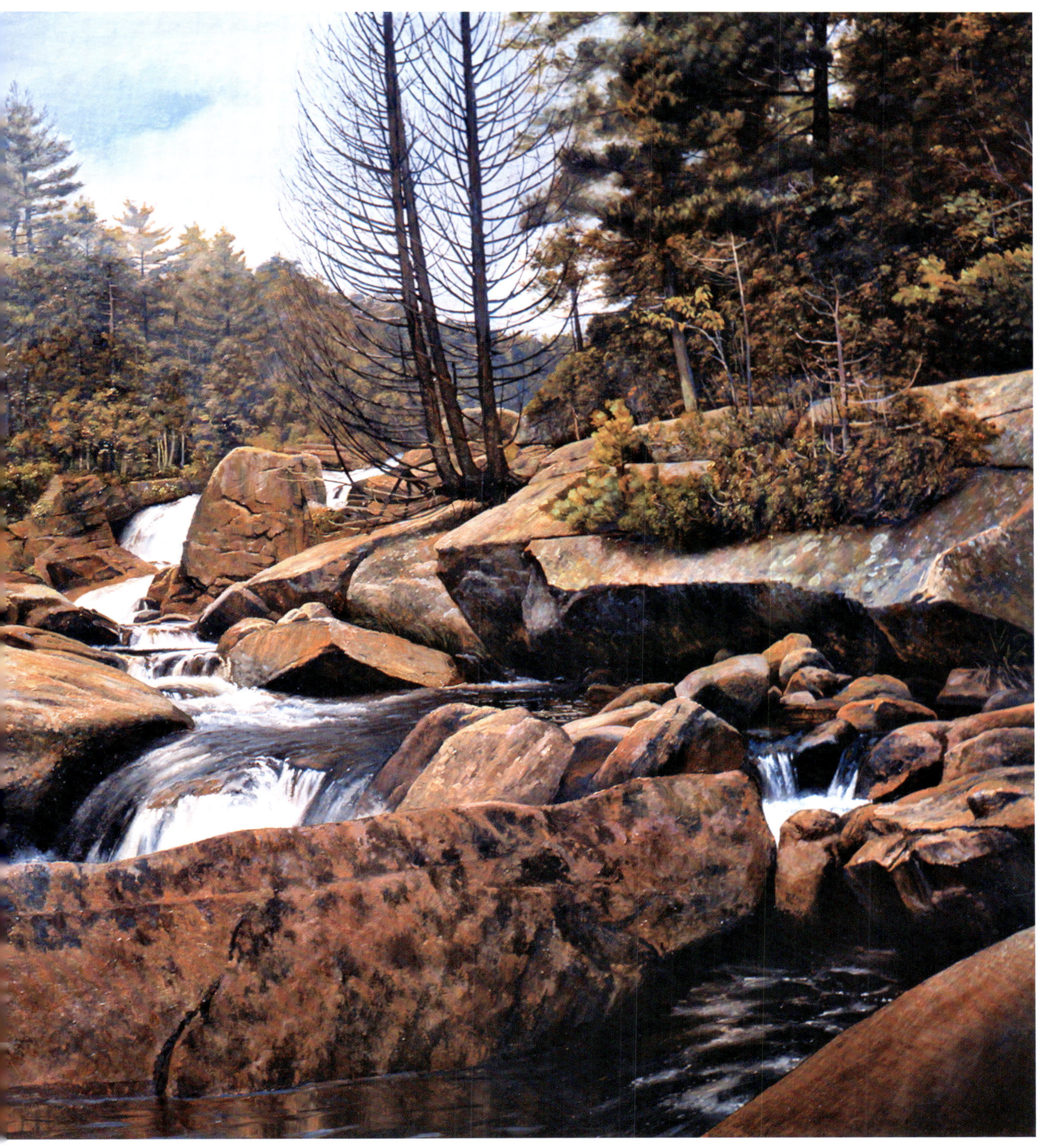

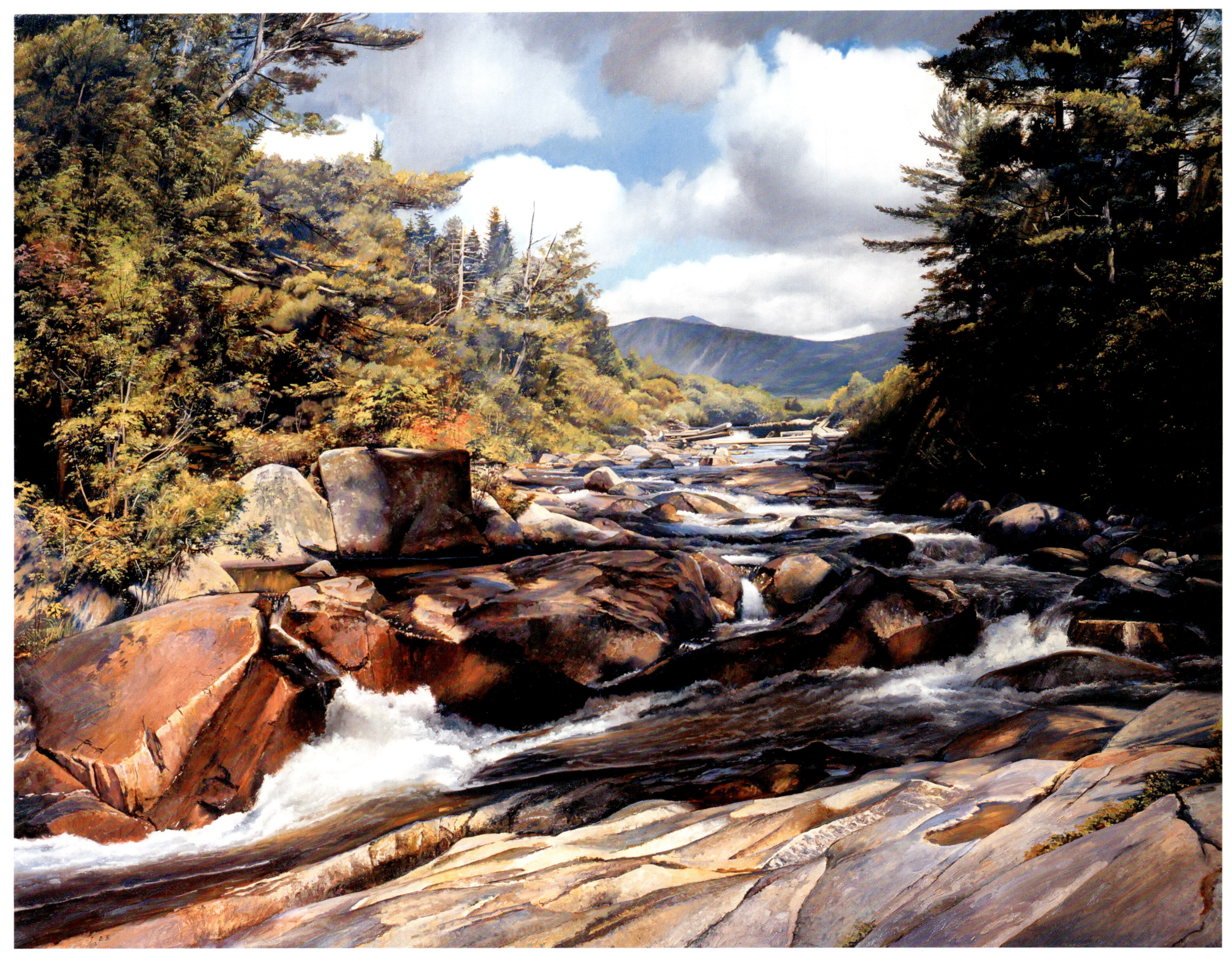

The Toll Dam, Baxter Park, Maine, 2004
Oil on linen, 48 x 60 inches
Private collection

Ruisdael, The Magalloway, 2010
Oil on panel, 18 x 15 inches
Scott L. Frey and Elizabeth Vose Frey

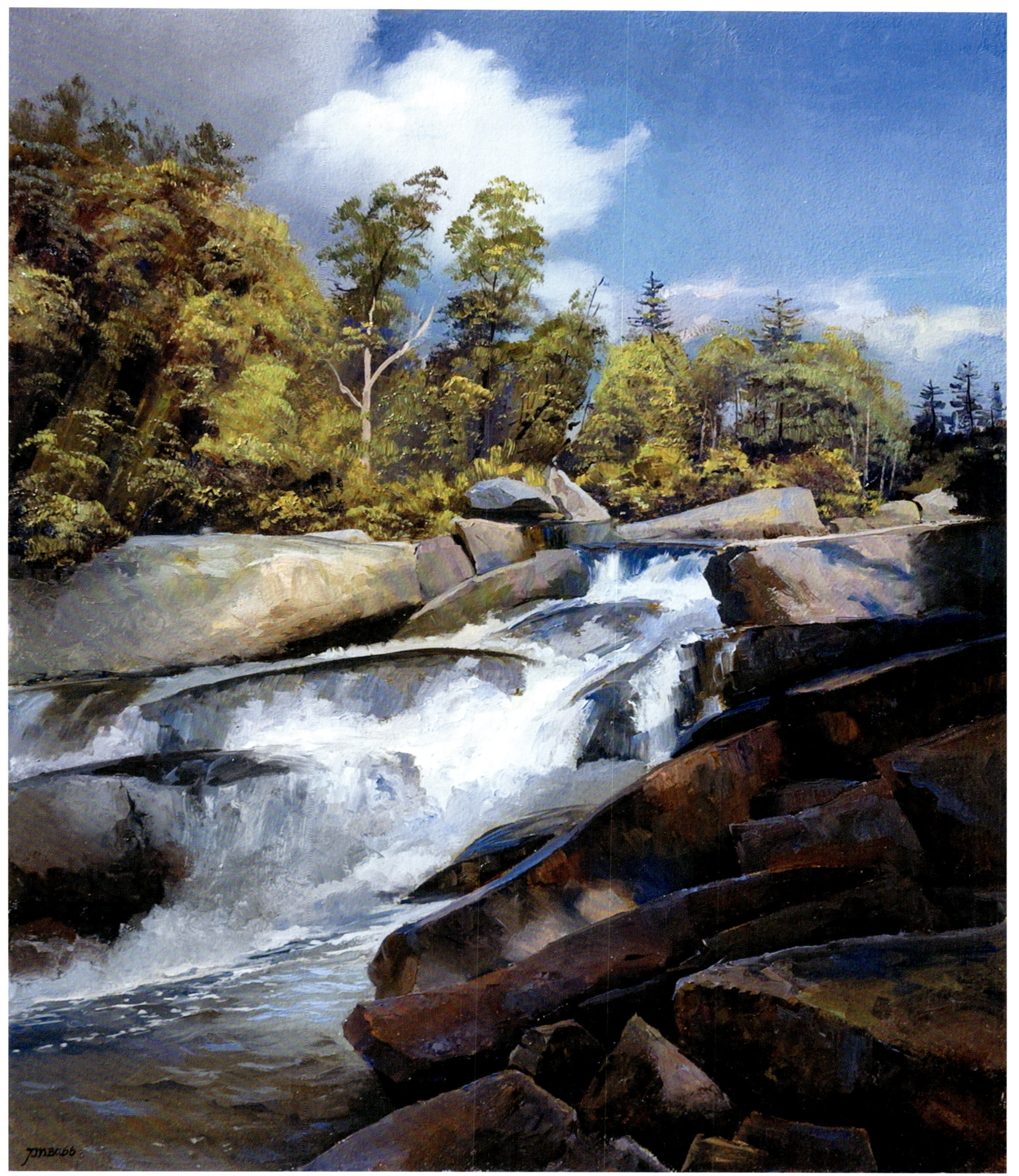

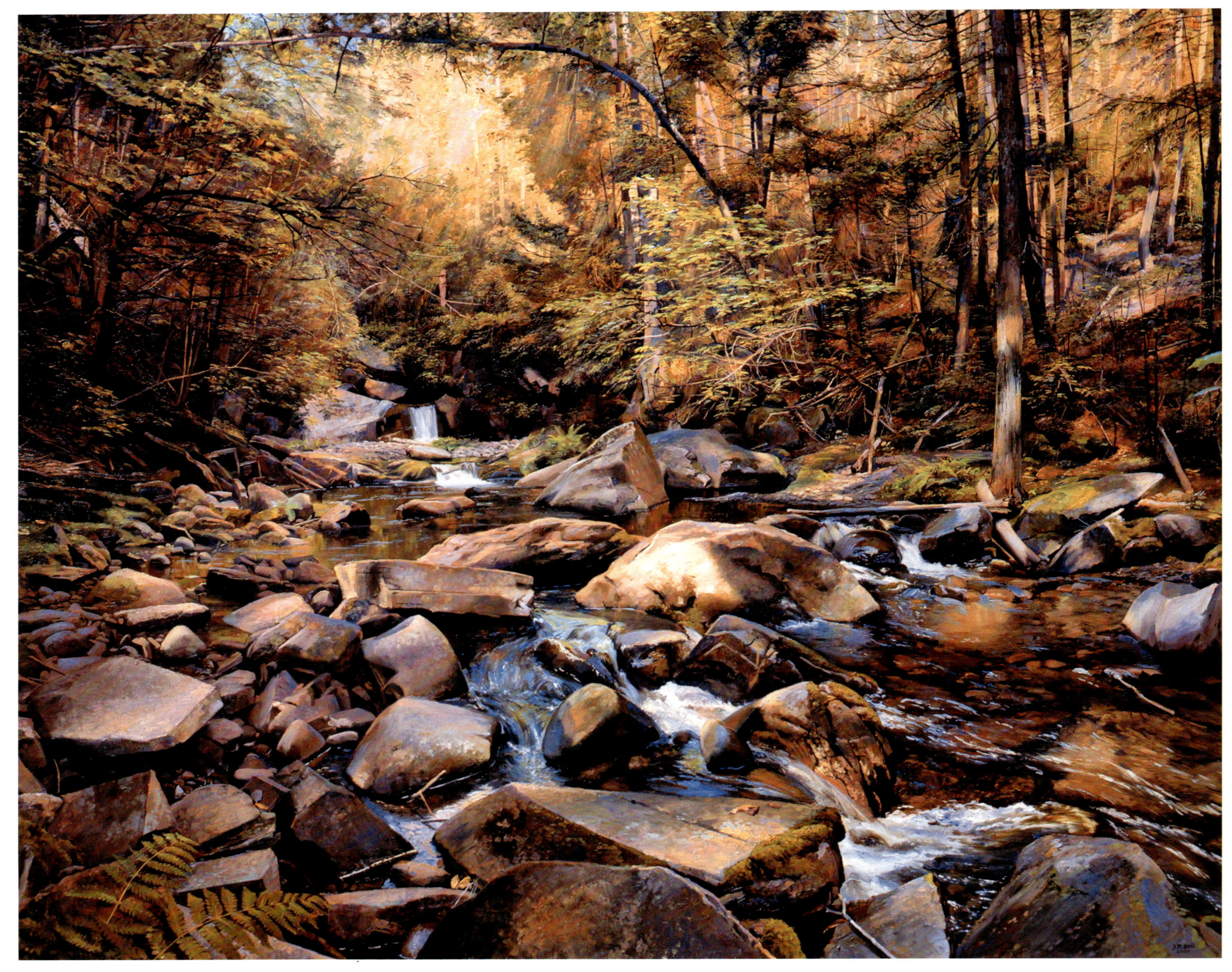

GULF HAGAS BROOK, MAINE, 2009
OIL ON LINEN, 58 x 72 INCHES, PRIVATE COLLECTION

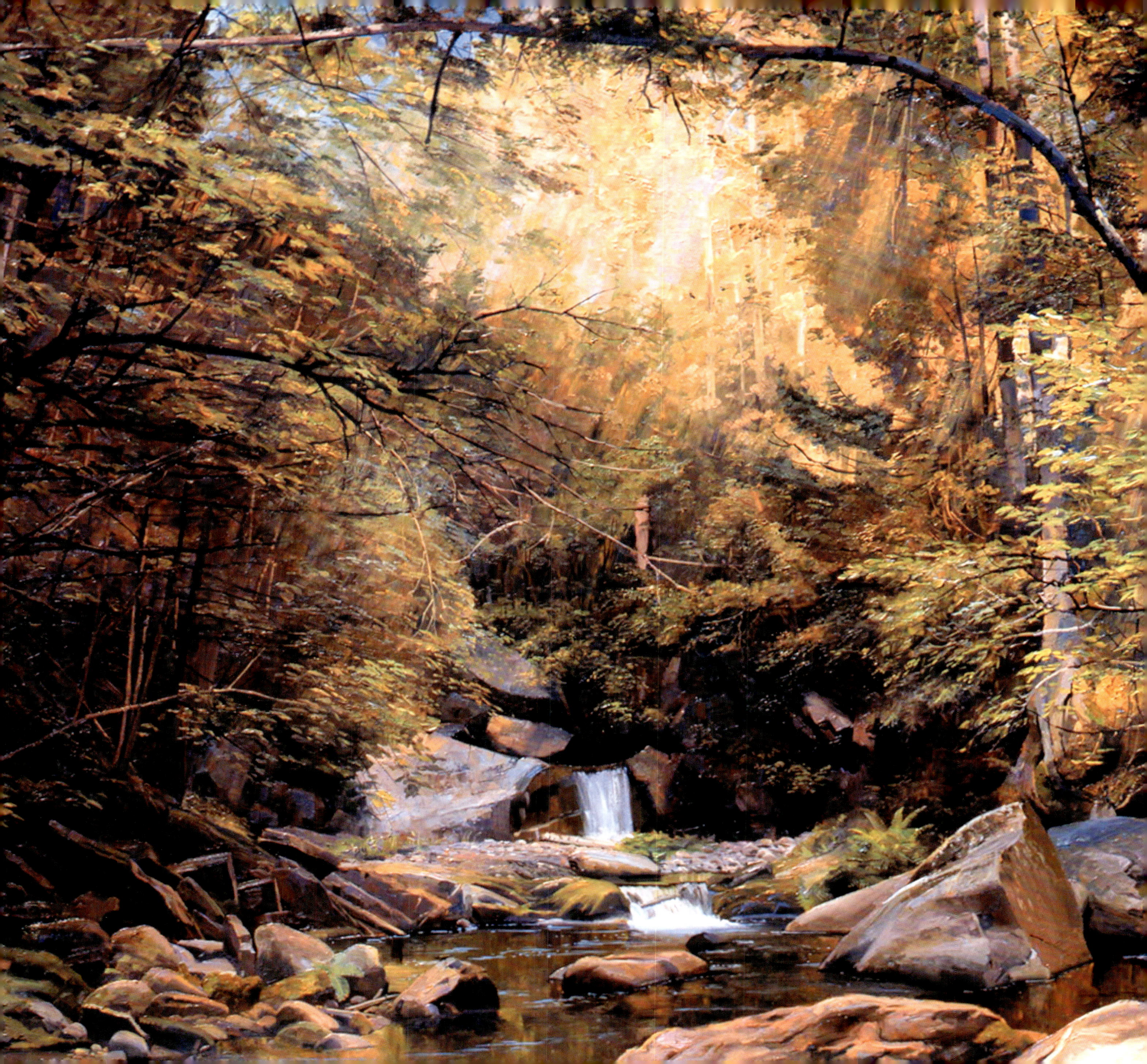

The Unnamed Brook, 2002
Oil on linen, 72 x 84 inches, Private collection

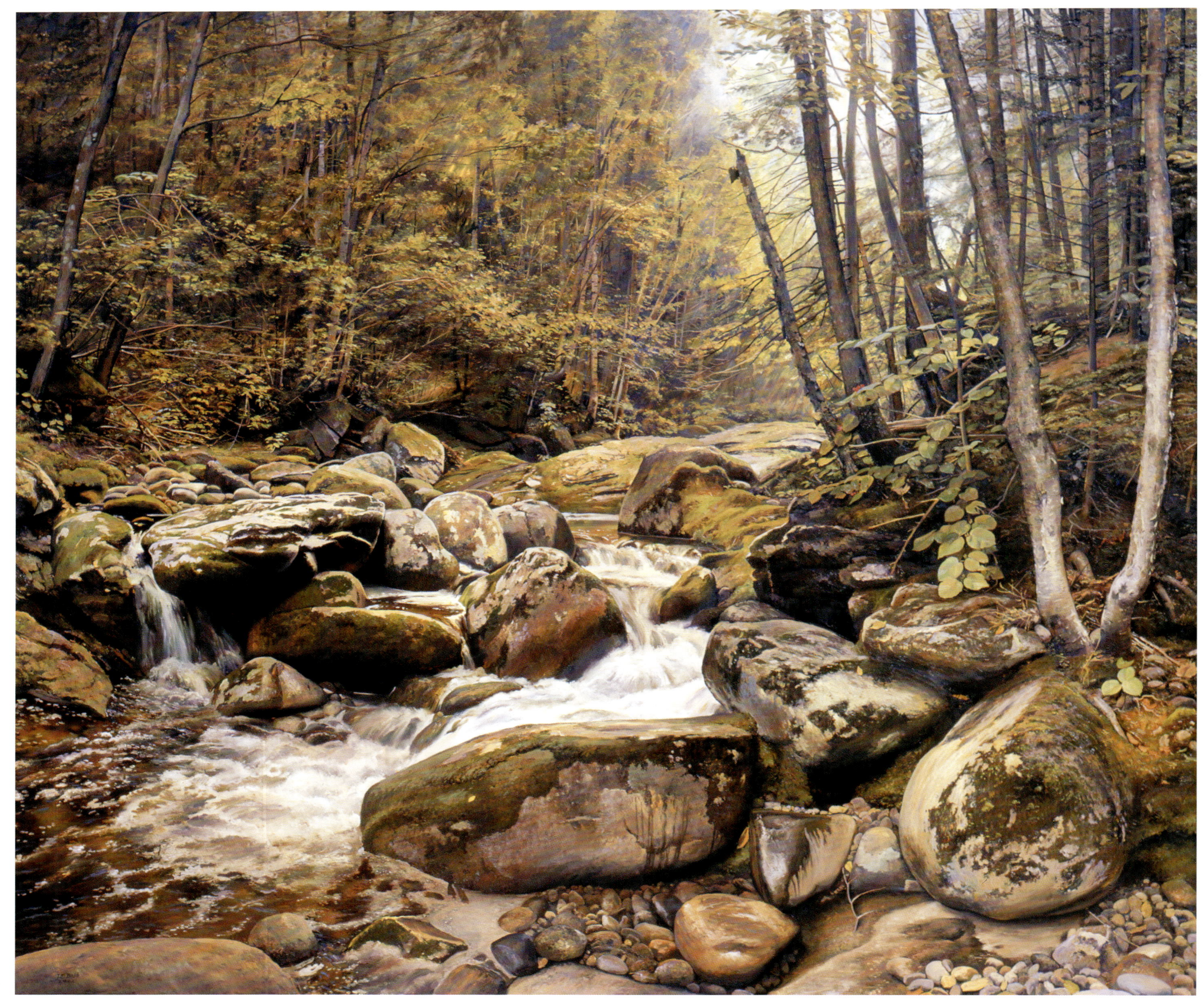

80

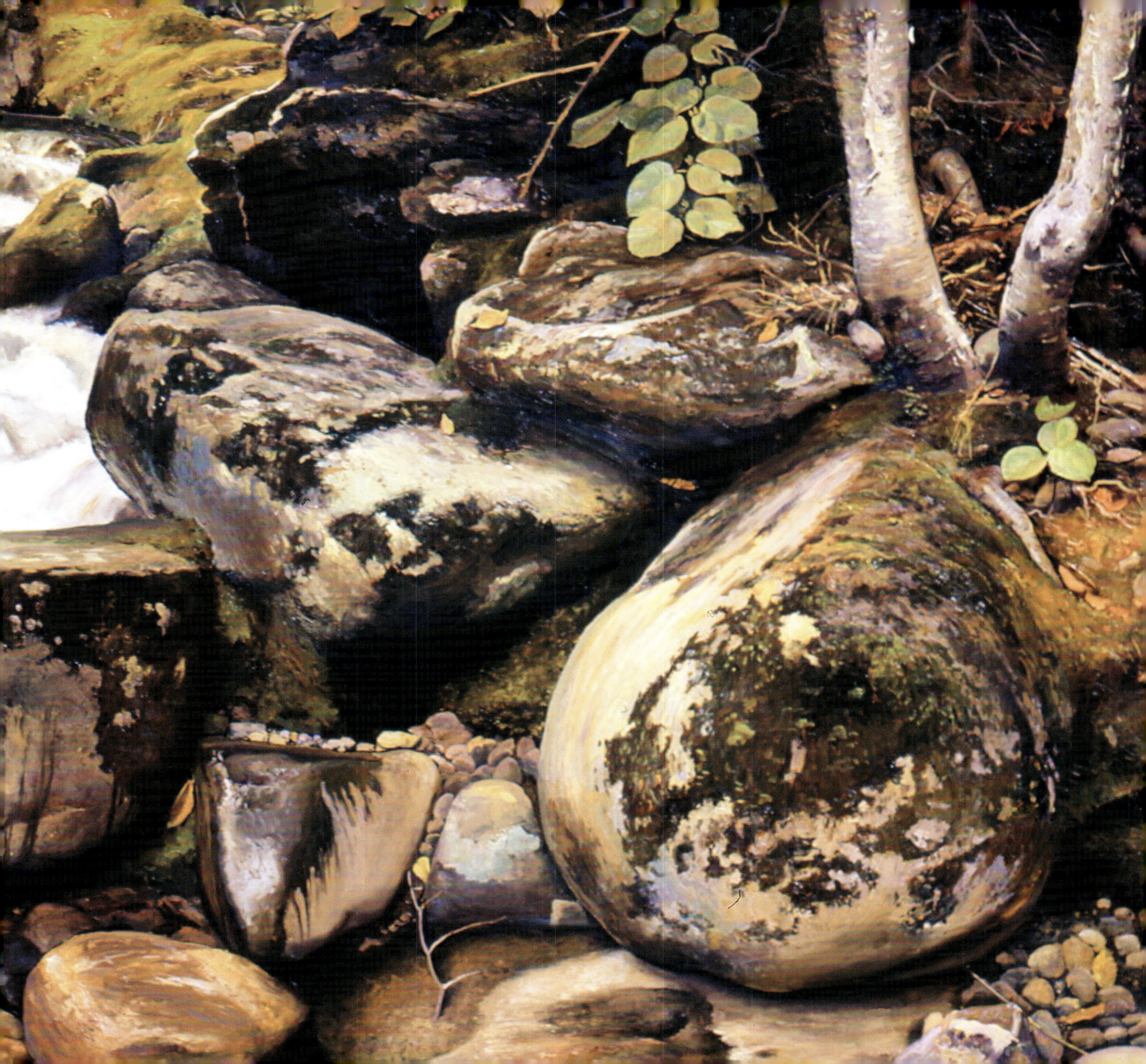

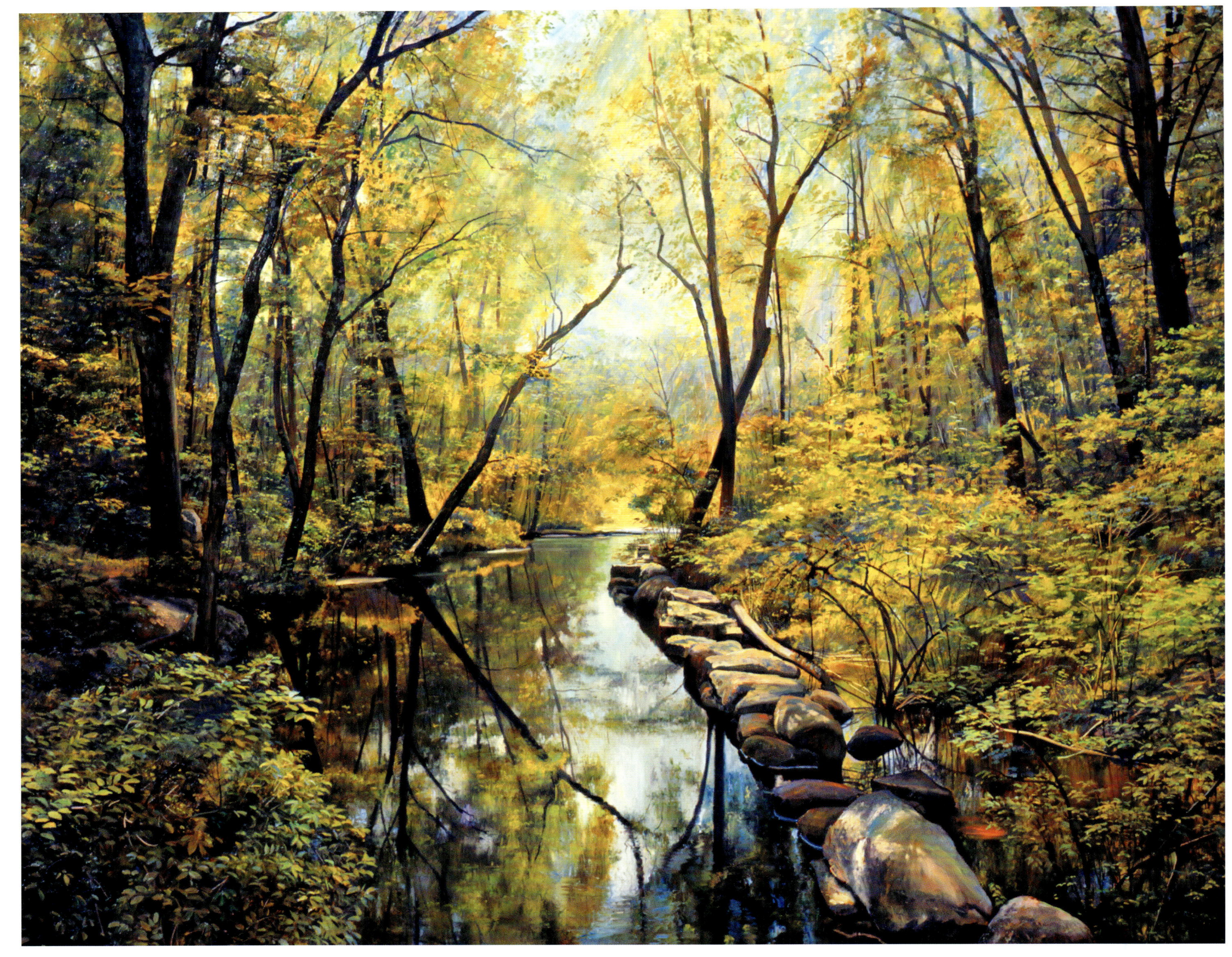

Nashoba Brook, Massachusetts, 2003
Oil on linen, 47 x 59 inches
Cambridge Savings Bank

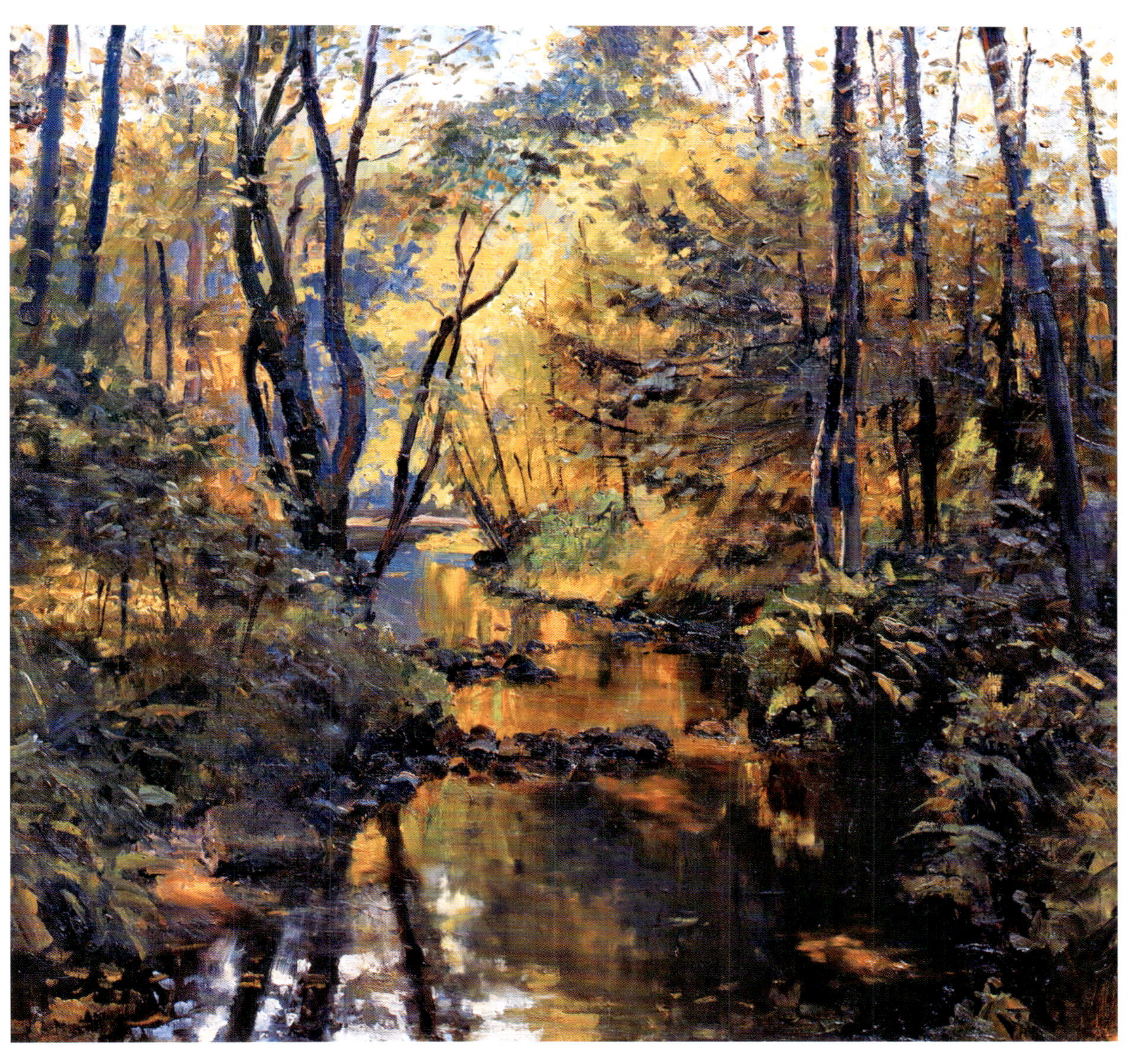

Our Brook by the Peru Bridge, 2001
Oil on linen, 32 x 34 inches
Private collection

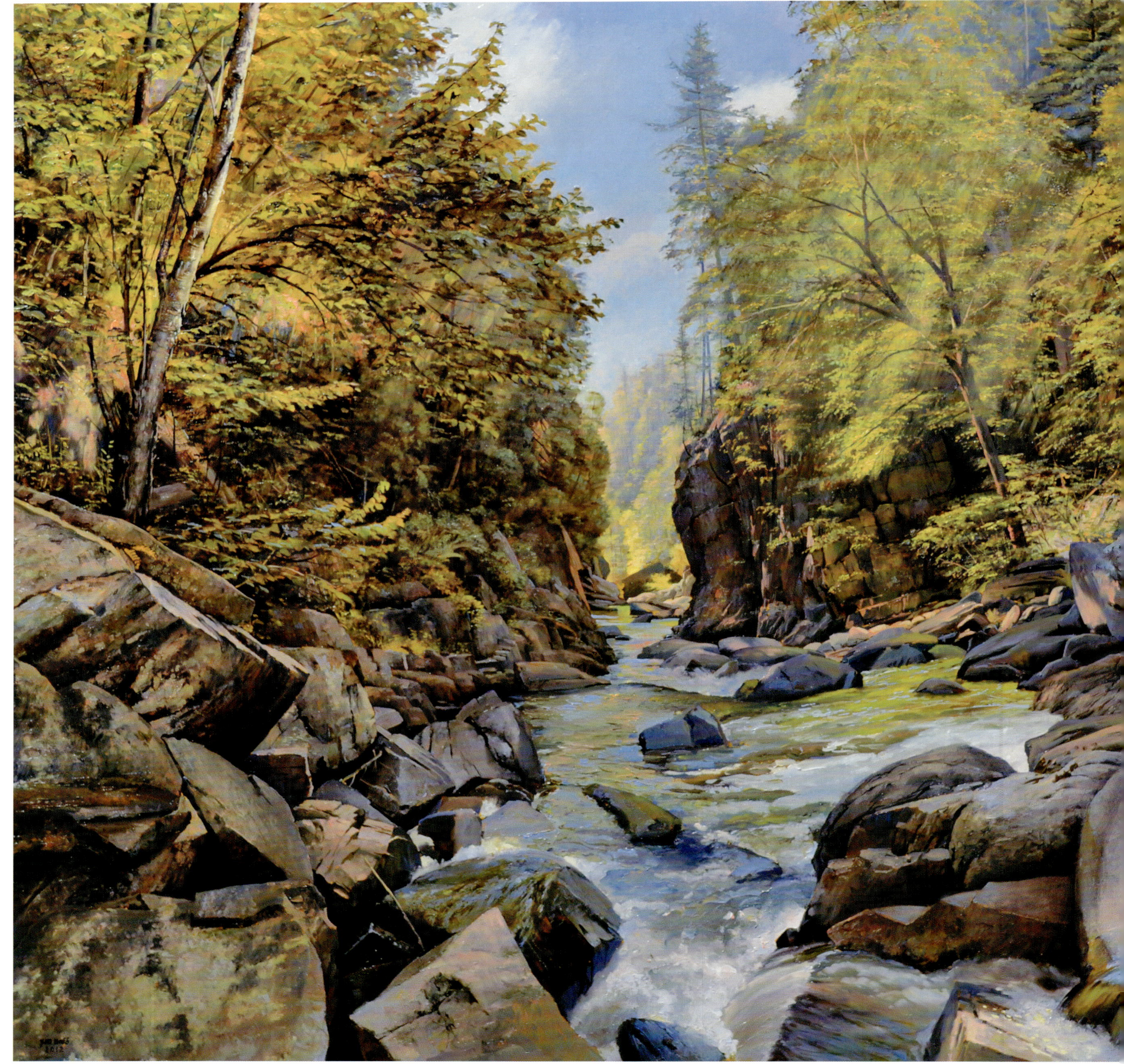

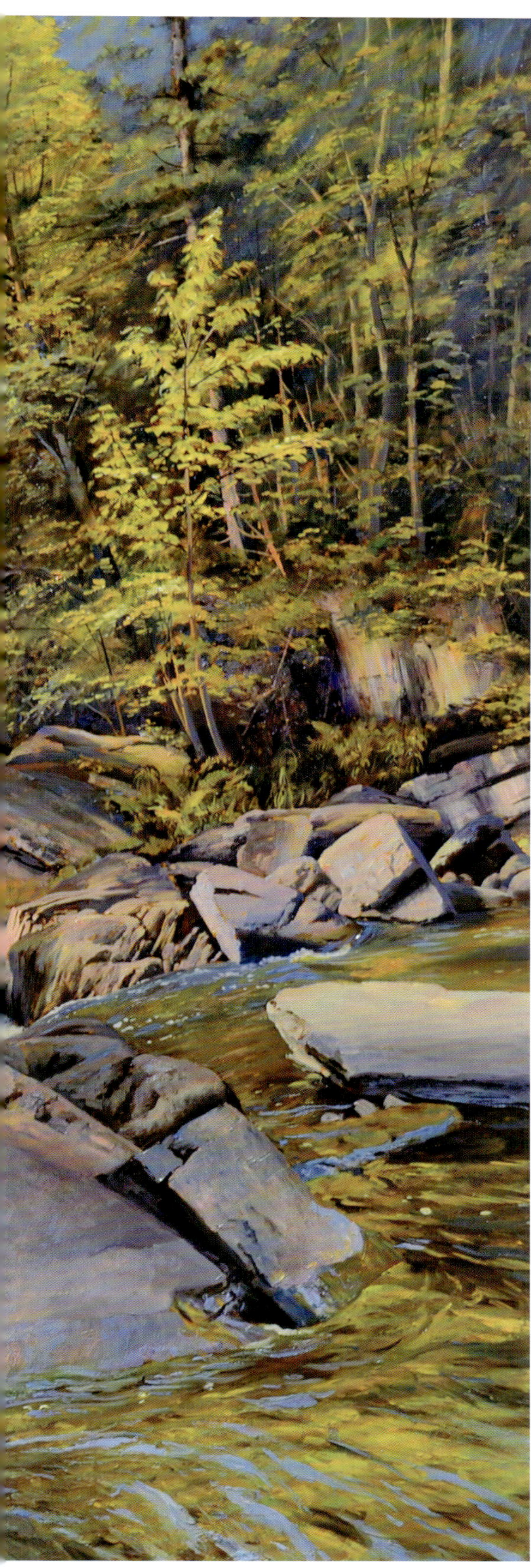

Gulf Hagas is a chasm deep in the Maine woods. The Pleasant River passes through it with many beautiful waterfalls. The Gulf seems to squeeze the distant view of trees in its jaws. Because of the depth of the gorge, little light makes its way down to the water. I made sketches and photographs one afternoon when the light was on the left side, and then came back the next morning when the light was on the right. Late in the morning the light began streaming down through the trees in a beautiful way. The final painting is a combination of all the impressions of the time spent studying there.

GULF HAGAS, MAINE, 2011
OIL ON LINEN, 45 X 64 INCHES
PRIVATE COLLECTION

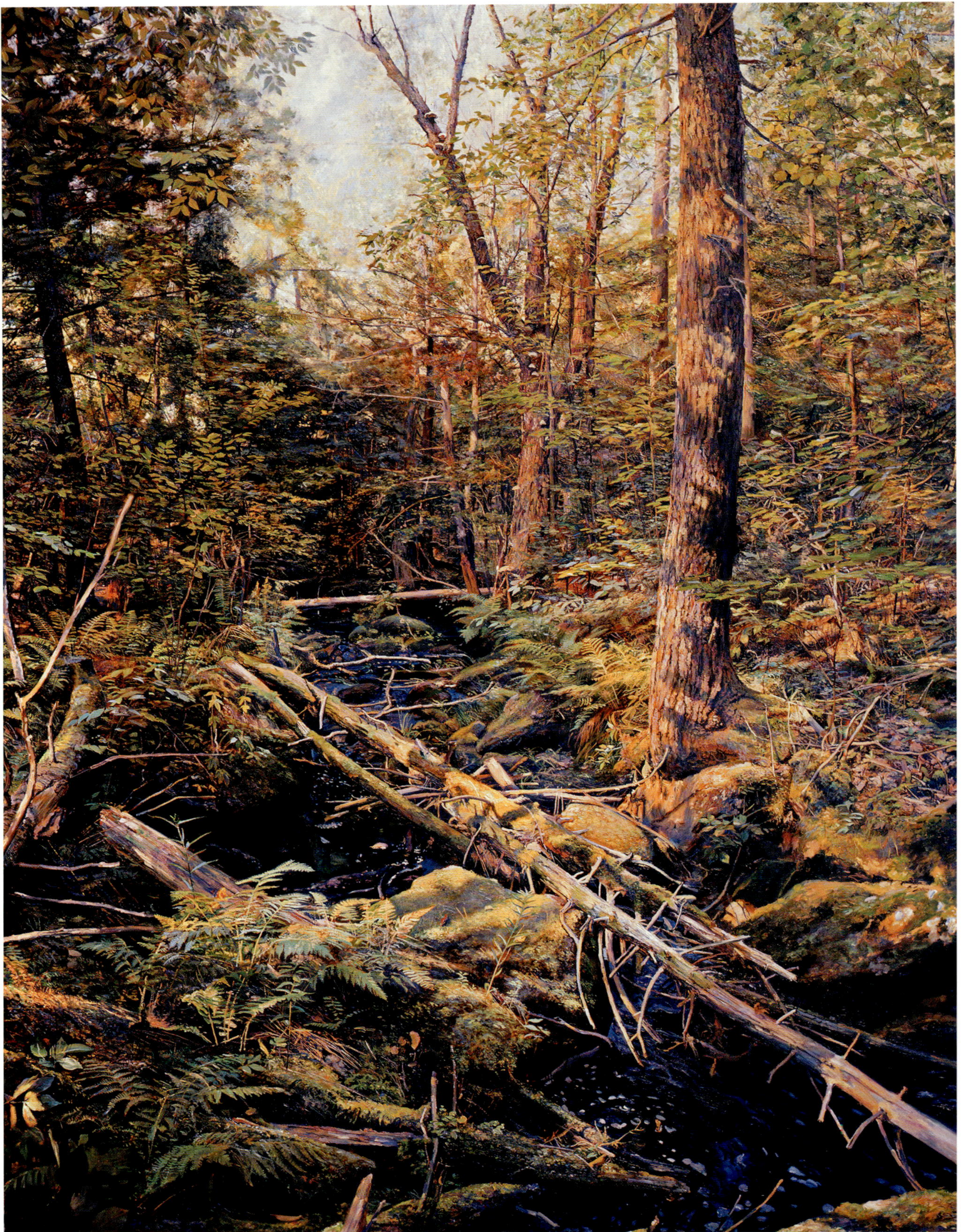

The dense visual tangle of the Maine woods is so different from the orderliness of a classical landscape. I draw the main lines of trees and branches in pencil, and then do an underpainting of transparent brown washes. This is the technique I developed in my studies of Baroque landscapes. Then comes the opaque overpainting of tints, which is more informed by Impressionist ideas of color and light— the new is built on a foundation of the old.

FOREST MURMURS
OIL ON LINEN, 82 x 62 INCHES
PRIVATE COLLECTION

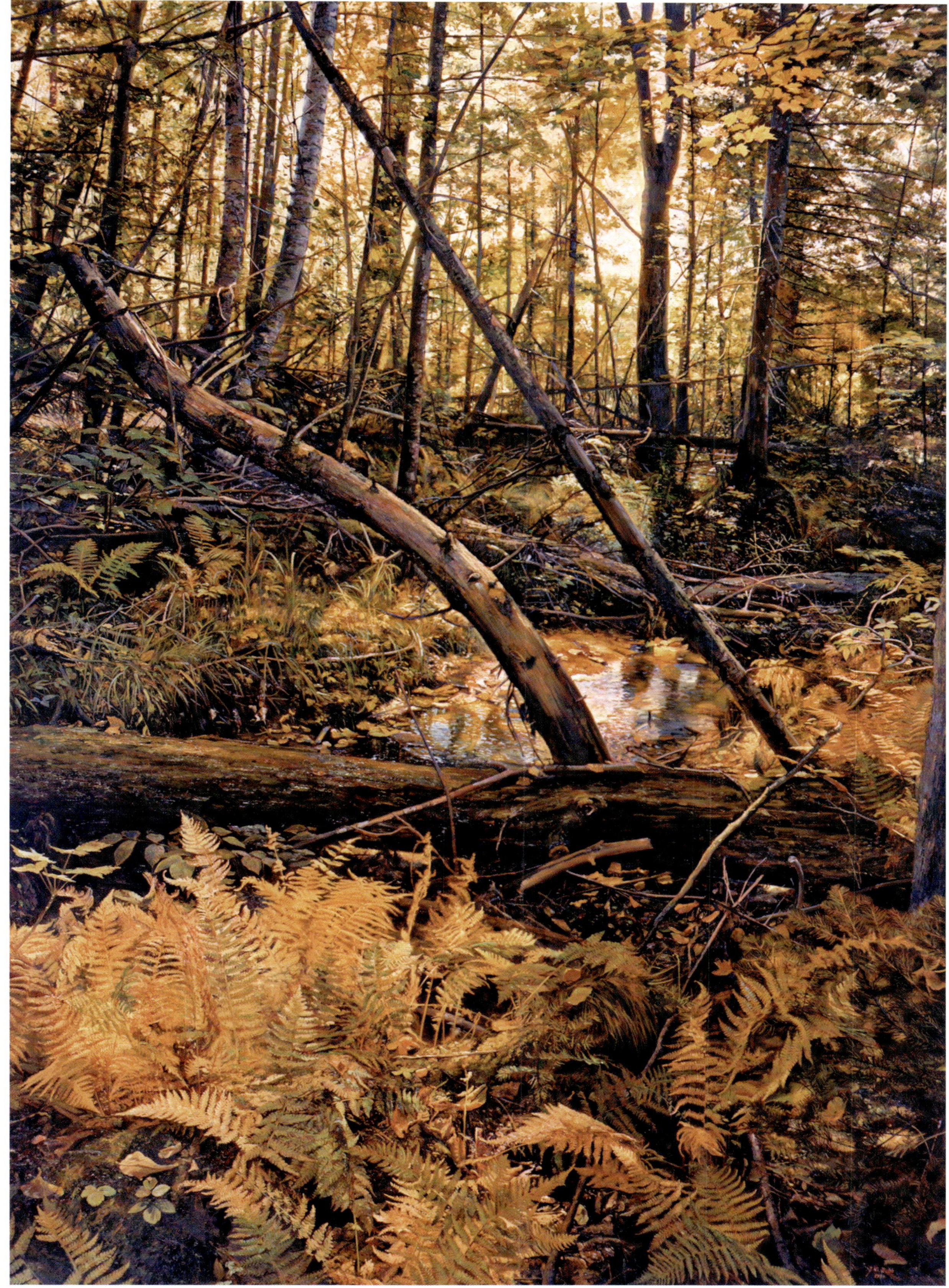

In THE GREEN FUSE *I began to think of how the woods are full of the energy of growing things, driven by the energy of sun which powers everything in the system. And yet the woods are full of aging forms—dying and fallen trees—which are not wasted but in decay become a source of energy for other smaller life forms. This reminded me of the lines of the powerful poem by Dylan Thomas:*

The force that through the green fuse drives the flower

Drives my green age; that blasts the roots of trees

Is my destroyer.

THE GREEN FUSE, 1995
OIL ON LINEN, 76 x 54 INCHES
DR. CHARLES DE SIEYES

87

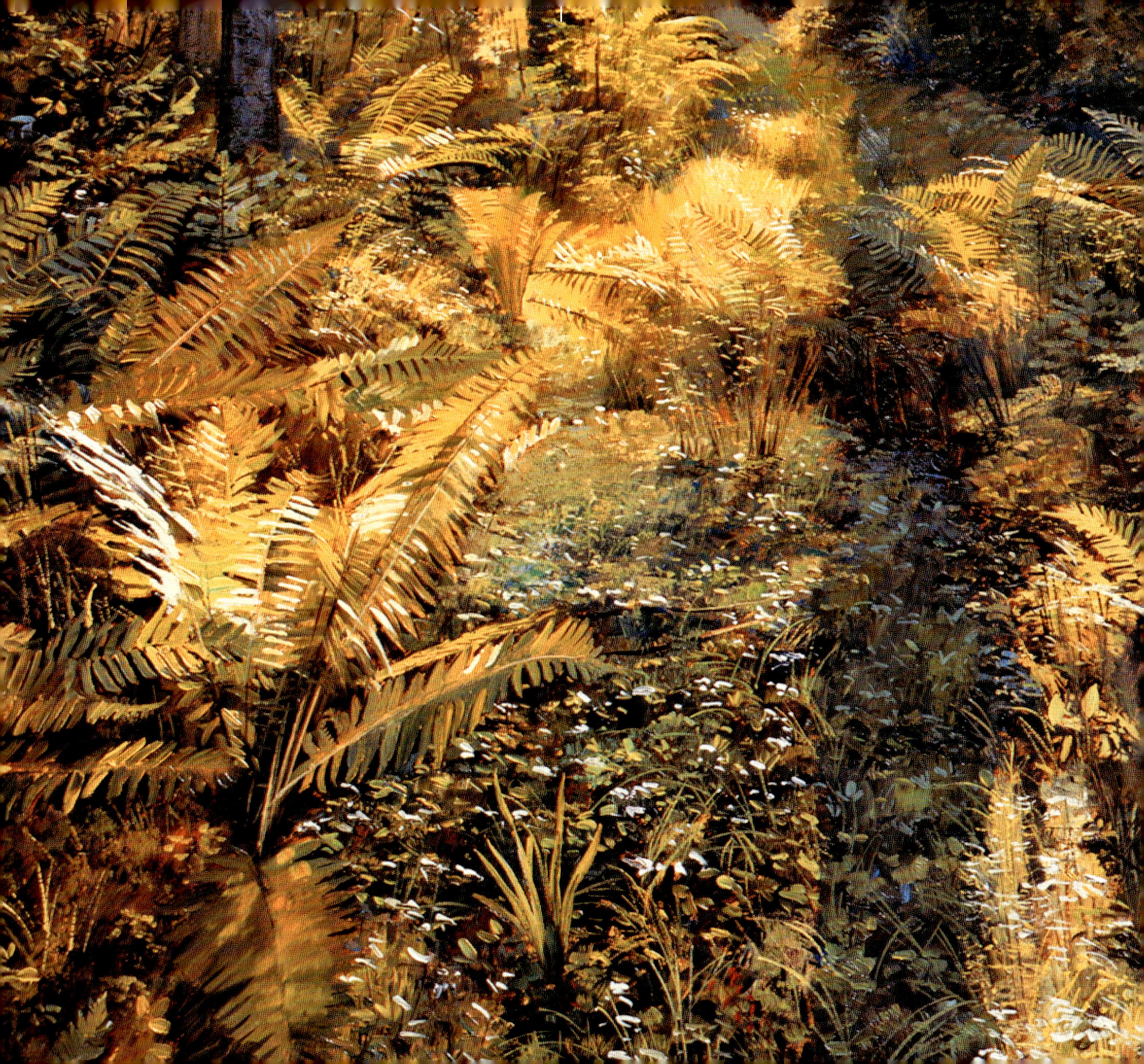

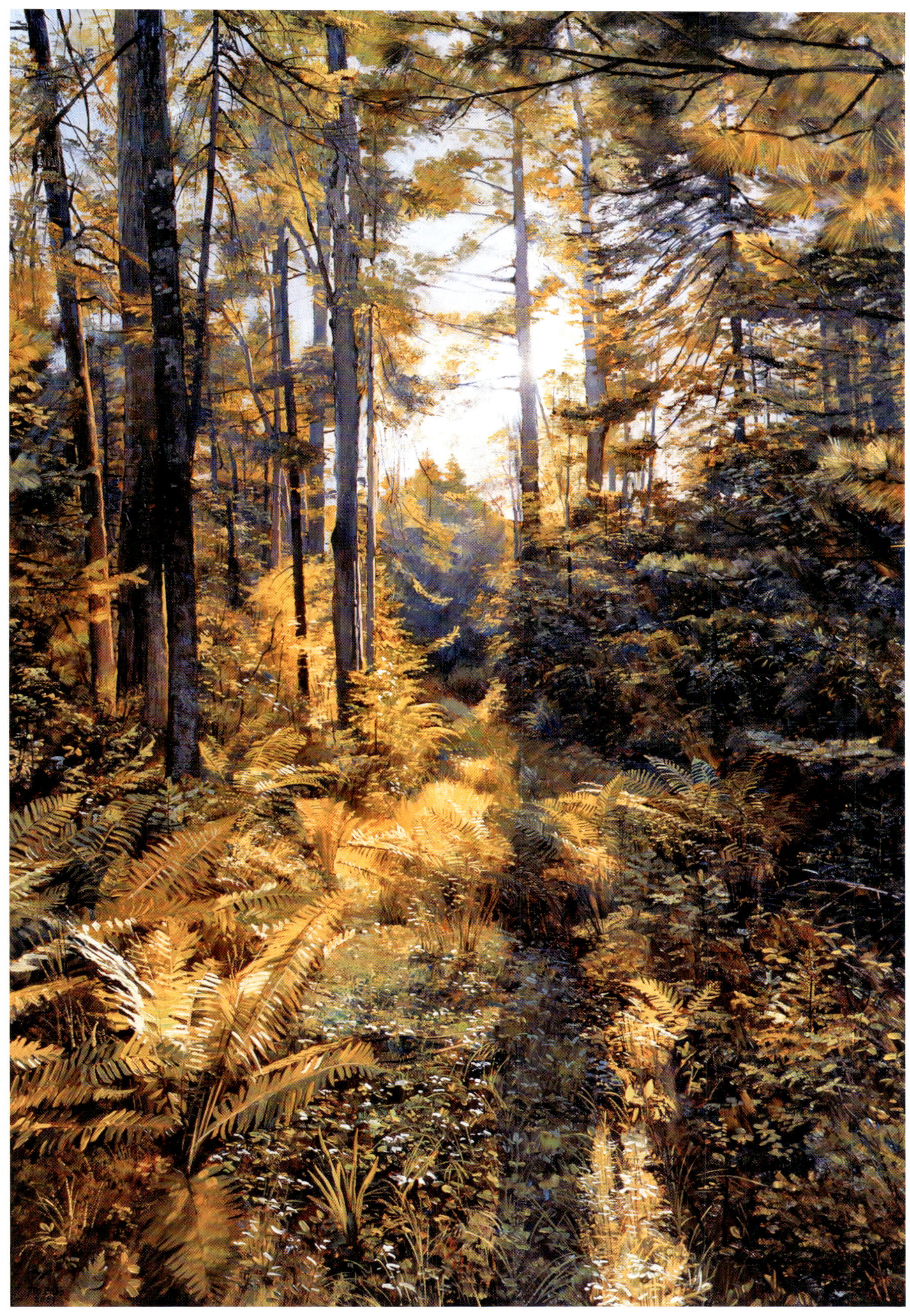

CARL'S PATH *shows the utterly transformative effect of light on a place. A view may be devoid of interest for most of a day, and then in the late afternoon for twenty minutes take on an almost miraculous appearance. There is a place in Ruskin's* MODERN PAINTERS *where he describes the appearance of leaves with the sun either shining through a leaf or reflecting off a leaf, as alternately an emerald and a torch. In* CARL'S PATH *the sunlight just behind a pine casts a long shadow, but the light shining through or reflecting off ferns and small leaves appears brilliant green or dazzlingly white. The path becomes a scintillating carpet and the trees incandescent with light.*

CARL'S PATH, 2009
OIL ON LINEN, 36 x 24 INCHES
CARL BENTON STRAUB

The large painting of a very low brook in autumn, filling with colored leaves as if a celebration of dying away, of seeming to go underground, suggested a connection with the feelings in one of the poems in SONNETS TO ORPHEUS *by Rilke. The sonnet talks about transcendence by joyfully accepting the fate of everything living in a world which is decaying and vanishing, and beautifully transcending it, like a ringing glass which shatters itself in ringing. Anyway, the painting is a meditation on the beautiful dying away of life as the leaves go down into the dark soil.*

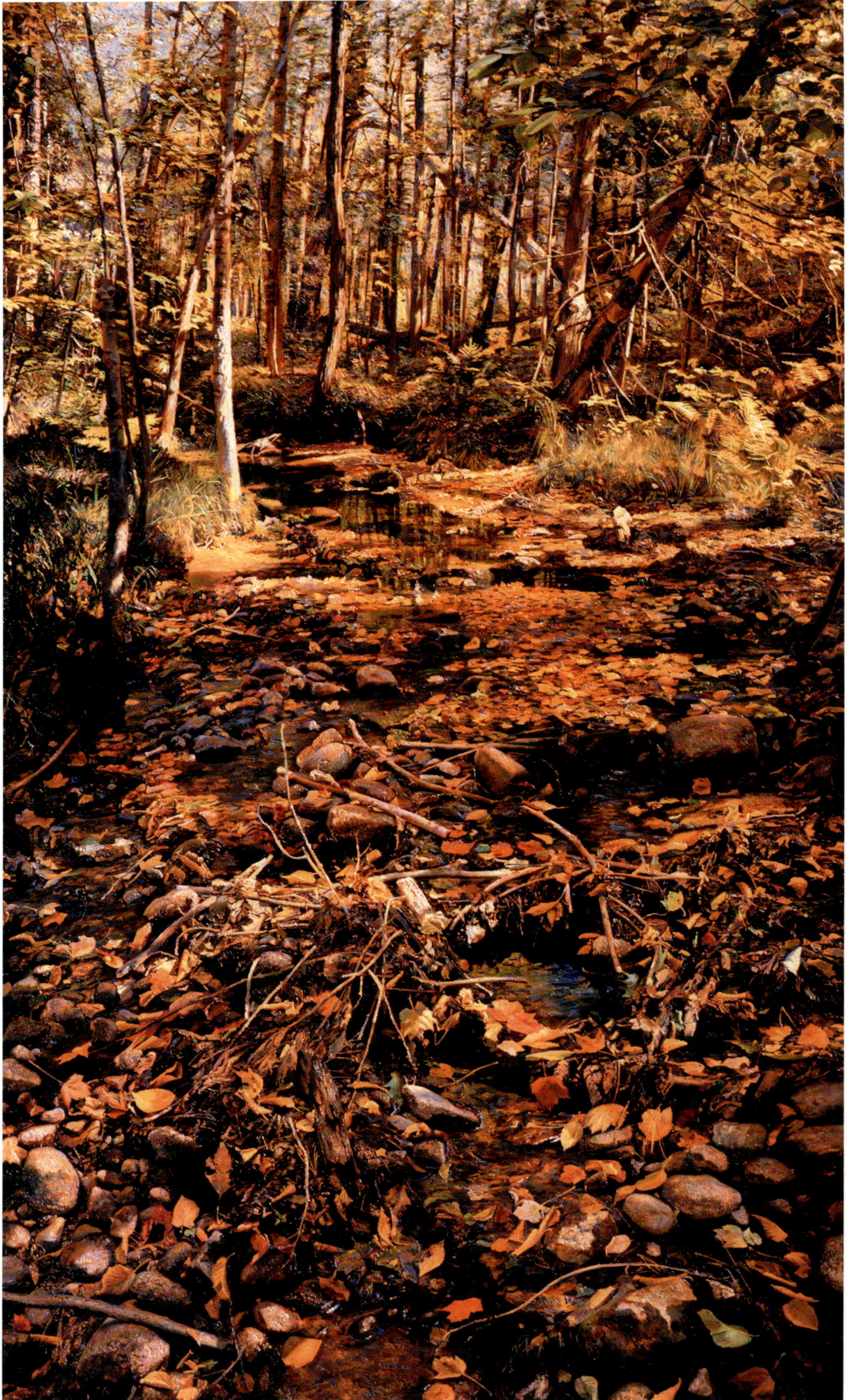

SONNETS TO ORPHEUS, 1990
OIL ON LINEN, 96 X 57 INCHES
PRIVATE COLLECTION

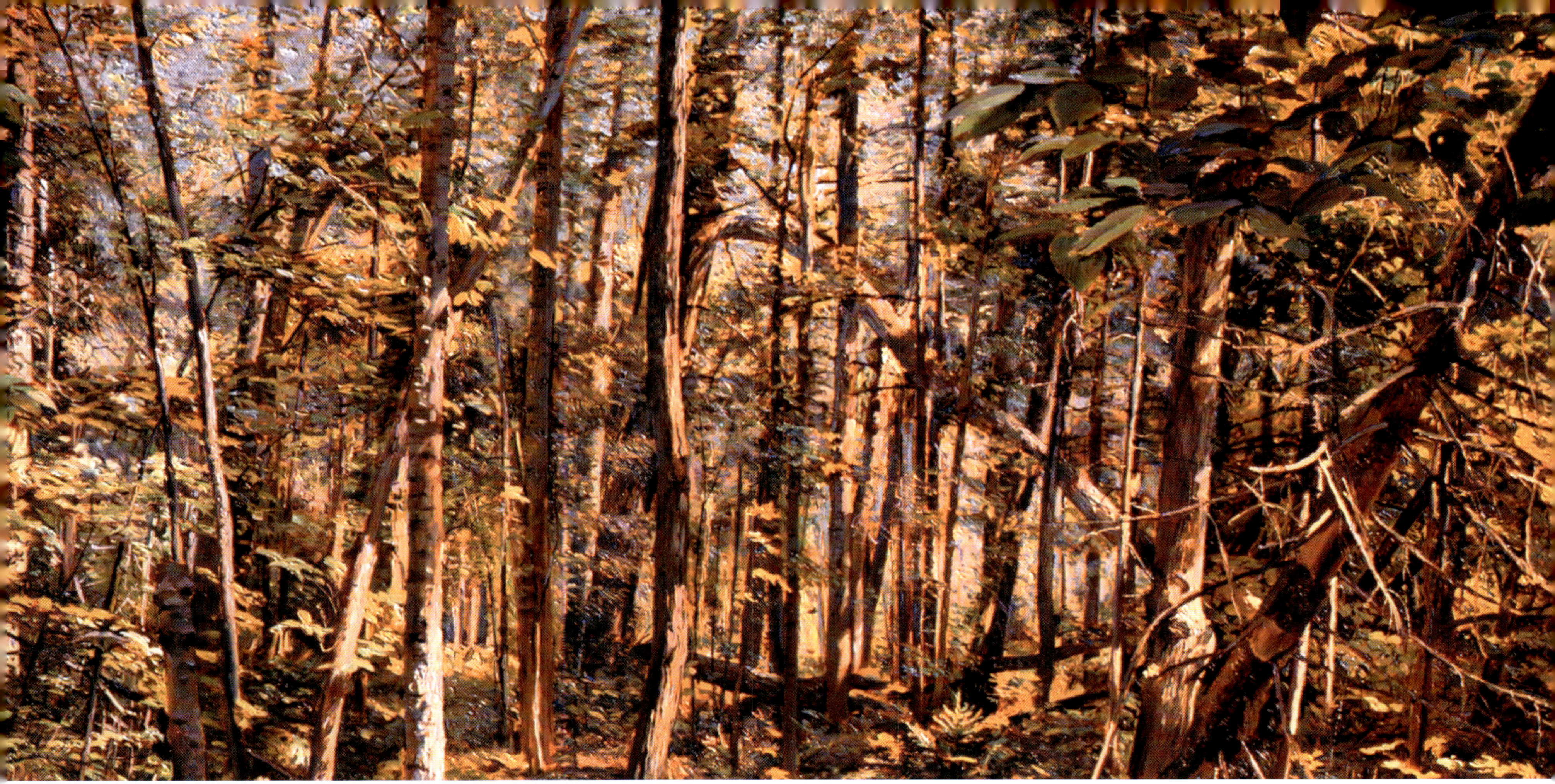

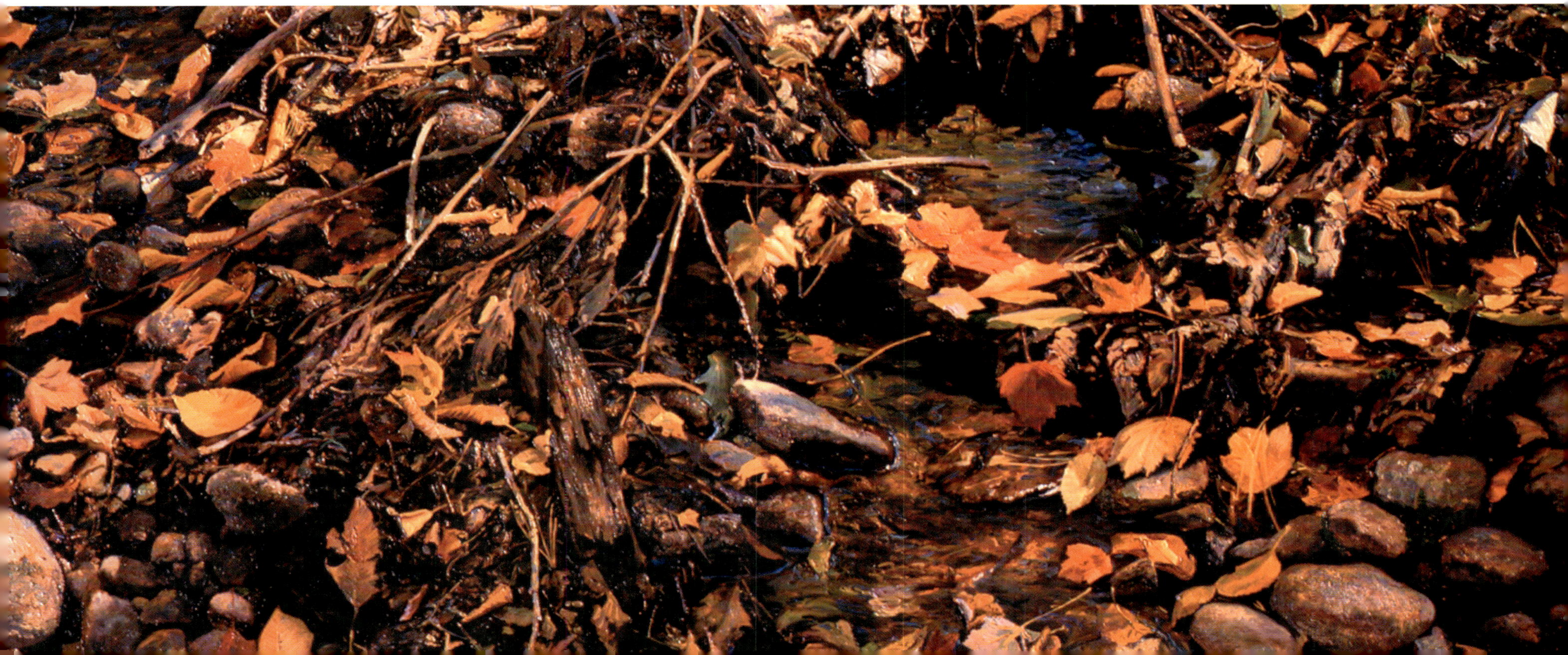

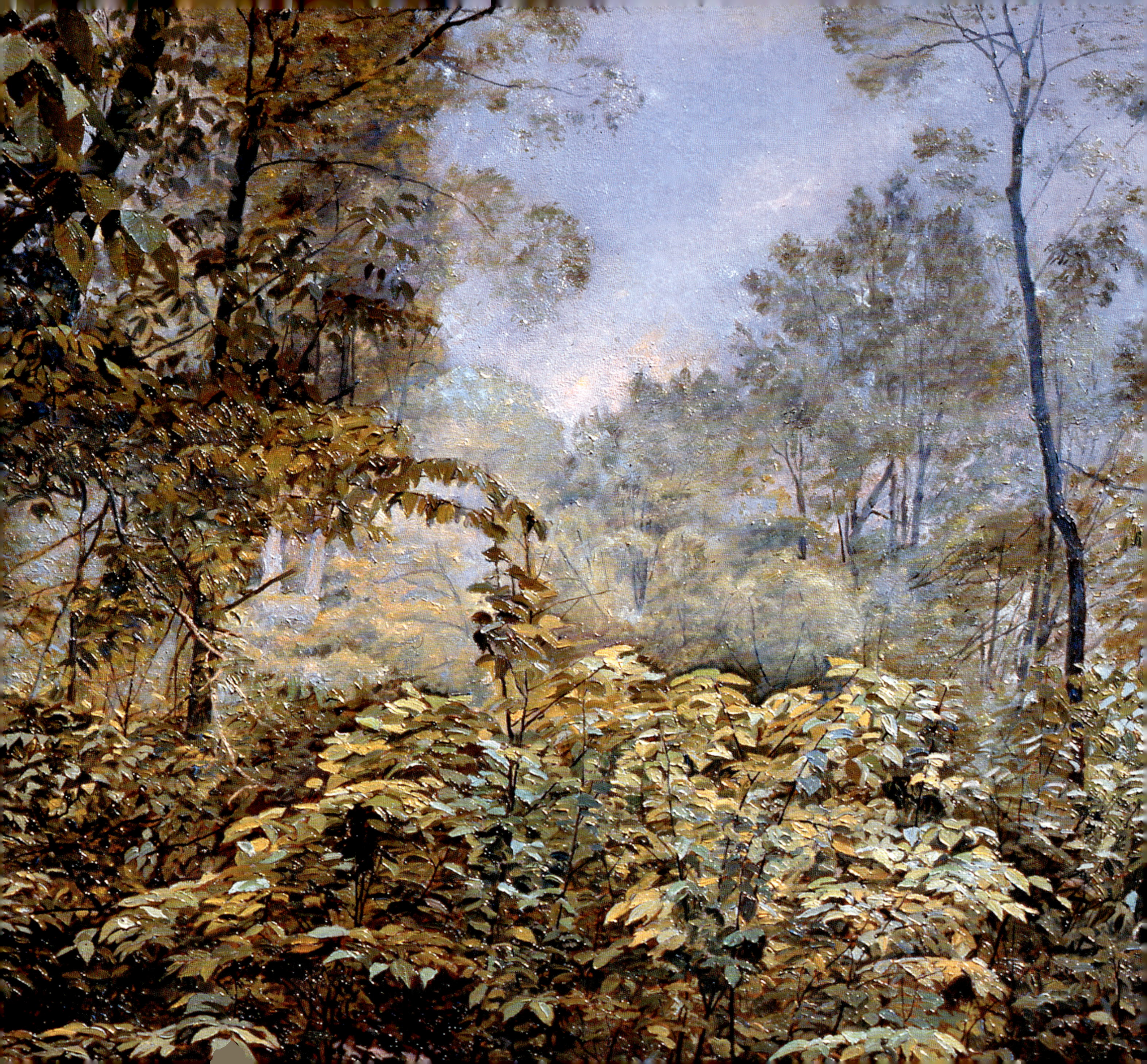

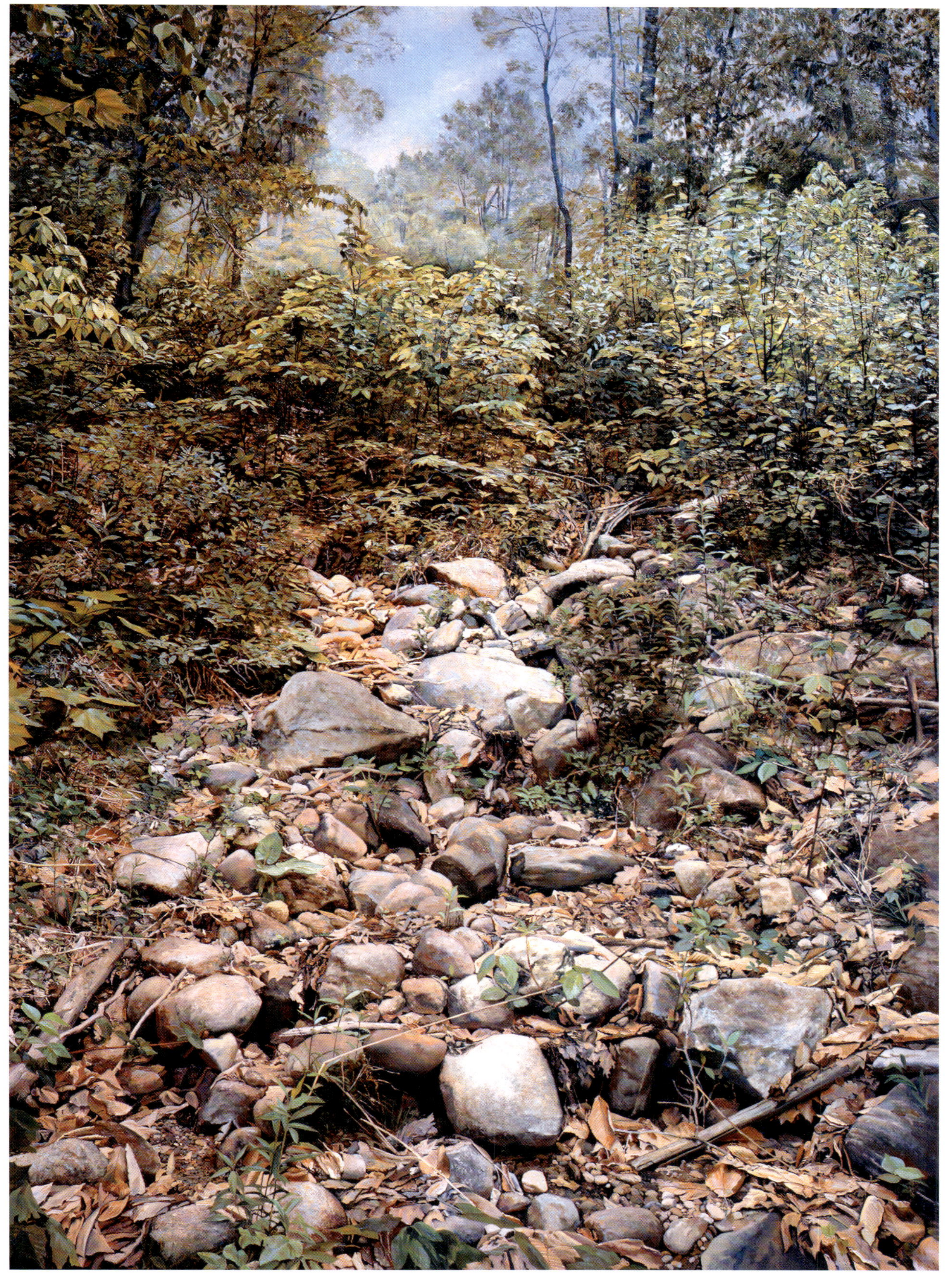

THE HOUNDS OF SPRING *embodies the return of life to a landscape in spring. New green is shooting up through the litter of last year's leaves. A washed out logging road is being reclaimed by the forces of nature, so life returns and nature reasserts her control. You have the feeling of being able to walk right into the scene and move up the hill into the distance suggested at the top. I love a landscape that allows one to travel through it in imagination. I like the idea of looking at small things from a sort of ant's eye view, and then moving up and away an order of magnitude to large and remote things: a microcosm contained within a macrocosm. The title refers to a poem by Swineburne with the lines:*

When the hounds of spring are on winter's traces,
The mother of months in meadow or plain
Fills the shadows and windy places
With lisp of leaves and ripple of rain;

THE HOUNDS OF SPRING, 1988
OIL ON LINEN, 96 x 68 INCHES
HARVARD BUSINESS SCHOOL

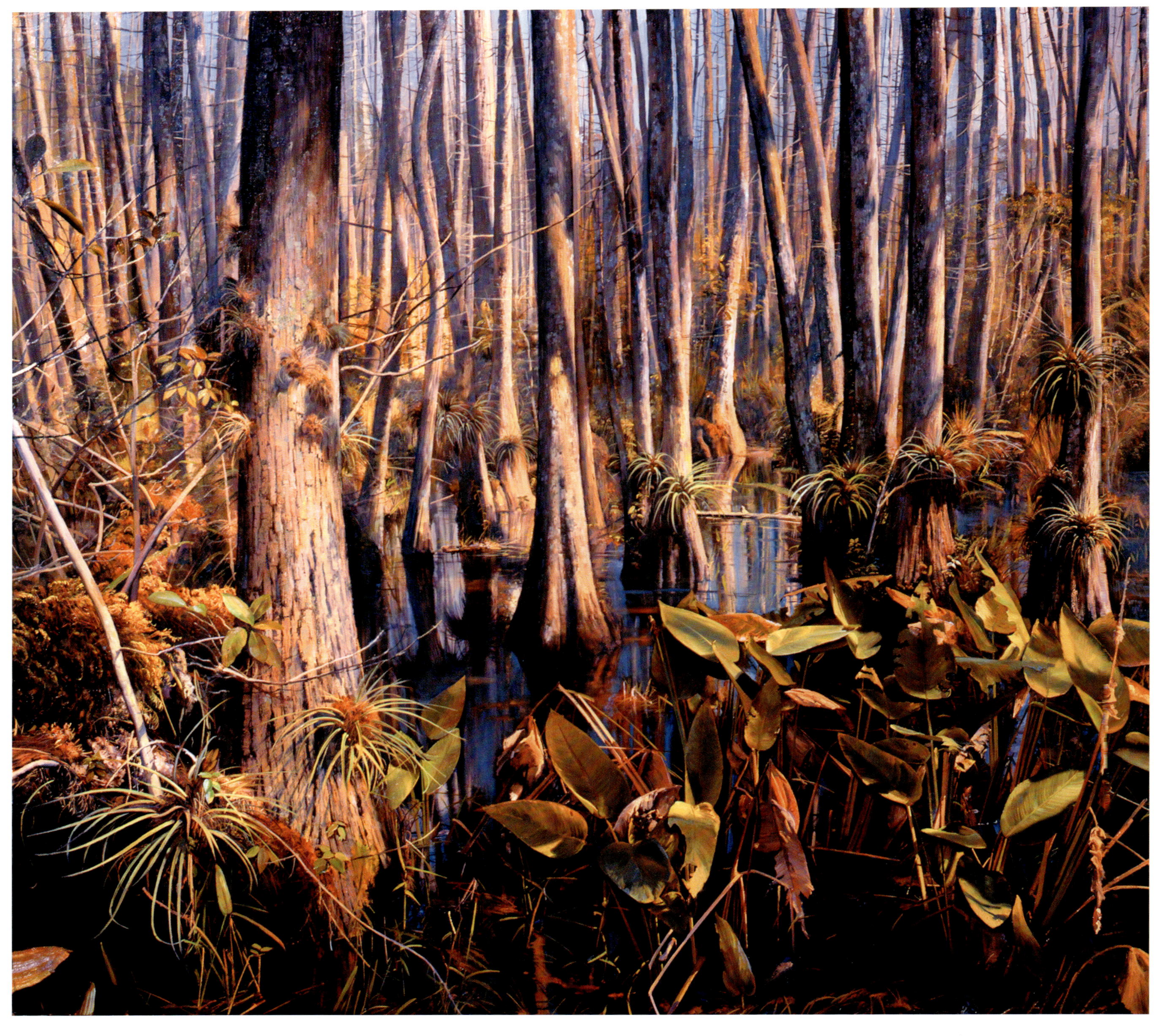

HEART OF A CYPRESS STAND, FLORIDA, 1999
OIL ON LINEN, 48 x 52 INCHES
PRIVATE COLLECTION

SANCTUARY, THE CORKSCREW SWAMP, FLORIDA, 1998
OIL ON LINEN, 41 x 42 INCHES
PRIVATE COLLECTION

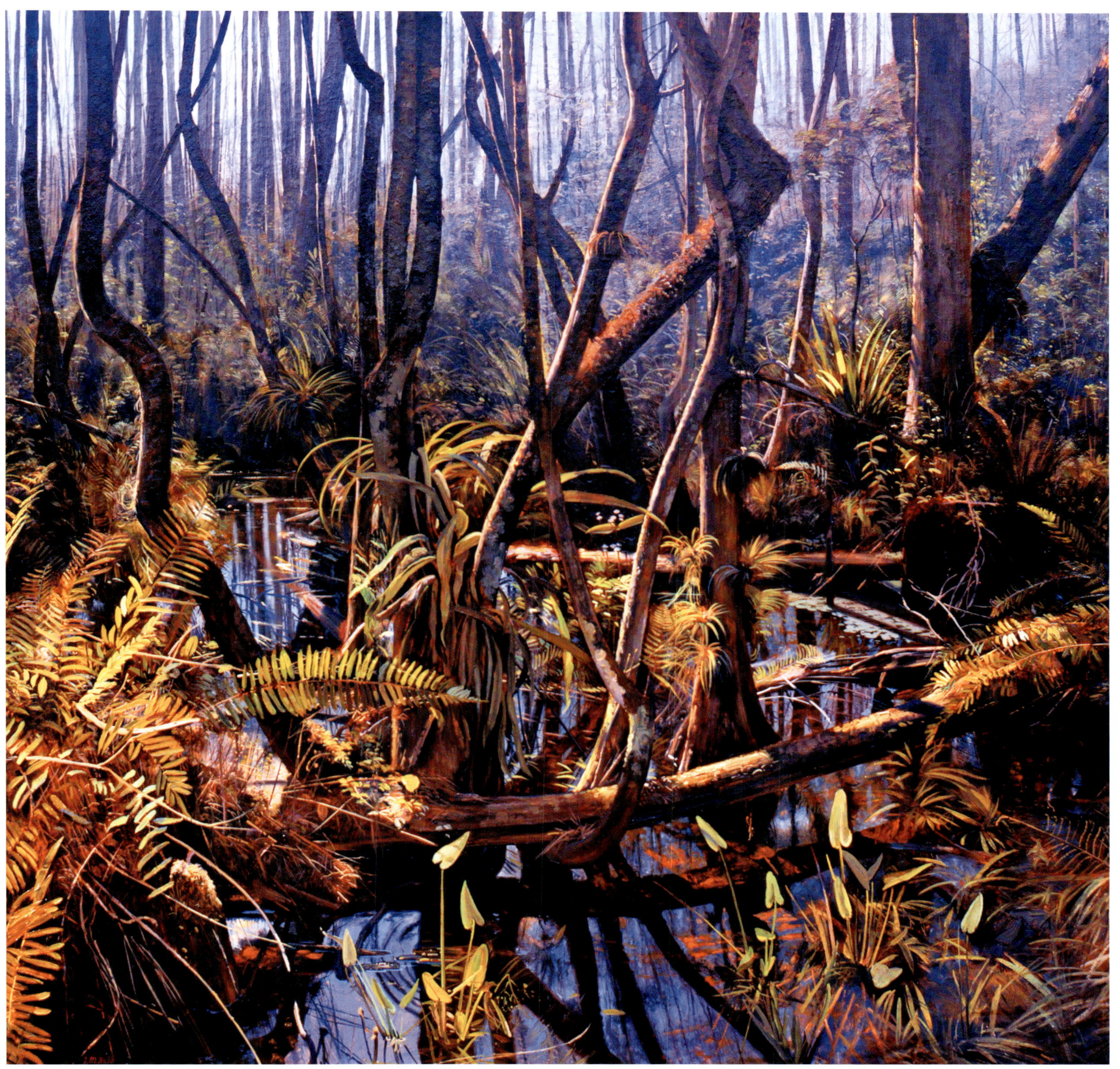

I painted a series of views of the Corkscrew Swamp, and the Big Cypress National Preserve in Florida. The landscape there is exotic and strange to someone accustomed to the northern forest, and it has an undeniable beauty and mysteriousness even in winter. The bottom is the hard chalky rock covered with a thin layer of black soil, but the water is pristine and flowing just perceptibly past your legs when you are standing in it.

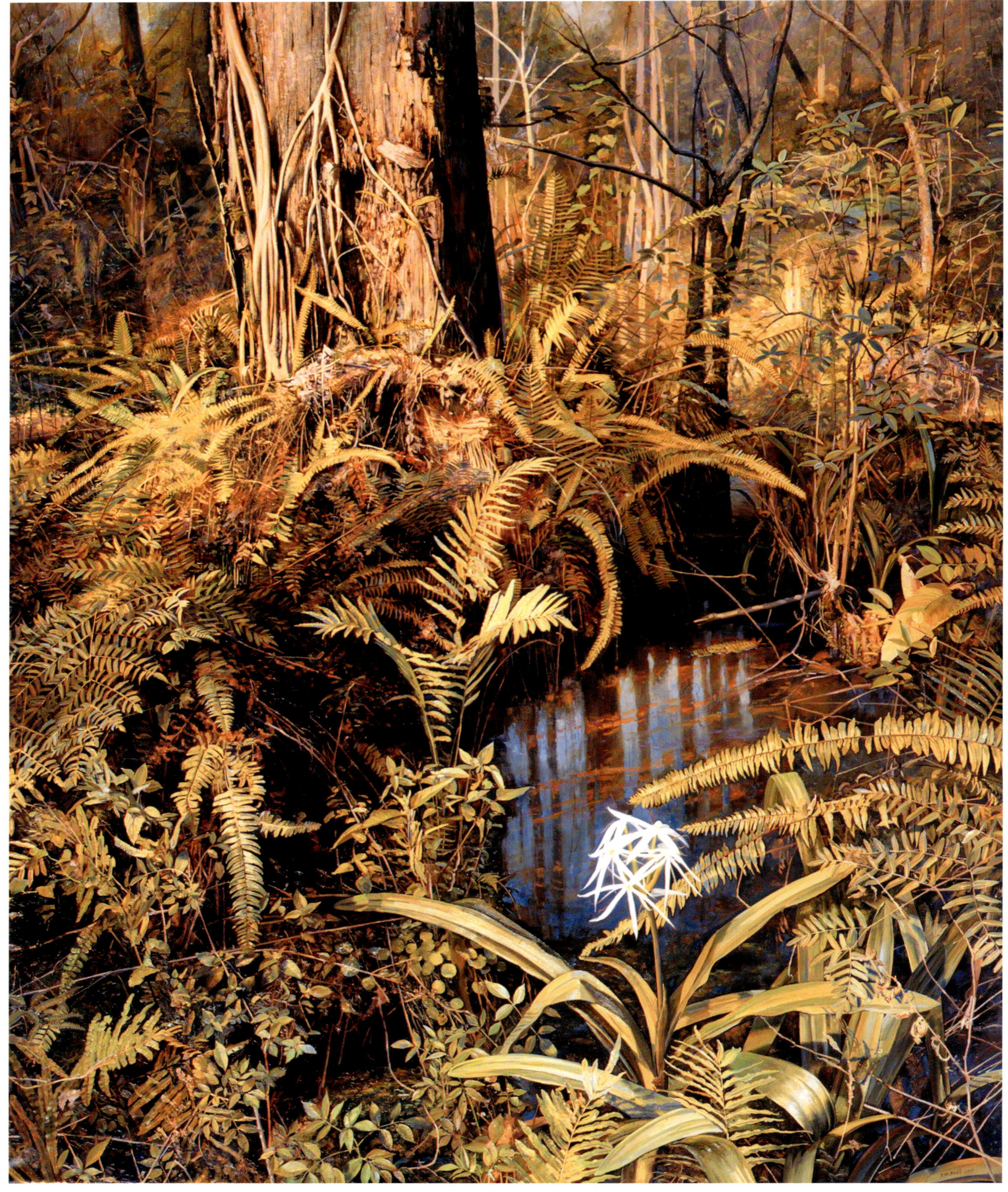

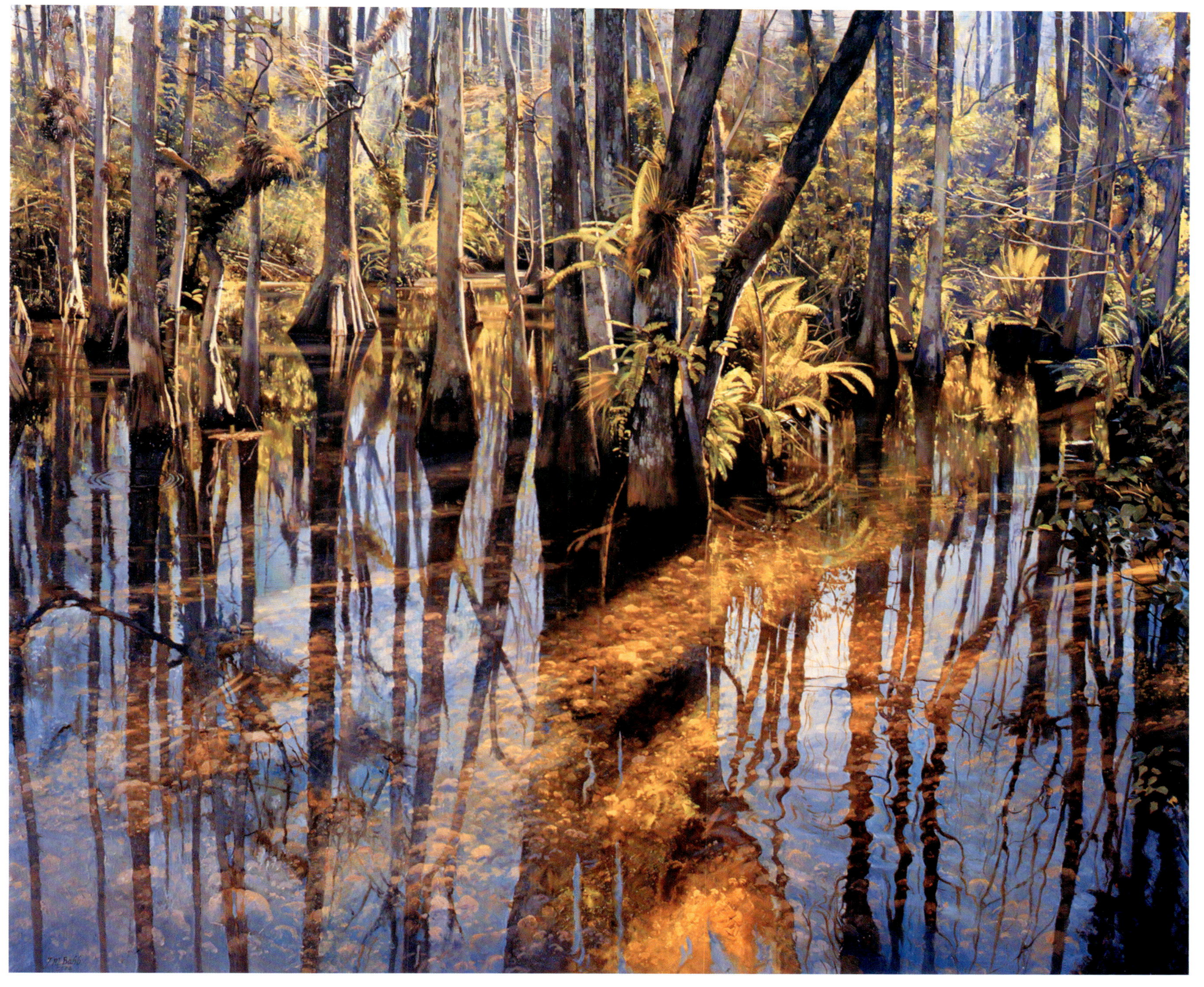

LILY AND CYPRESS, THE CORKSCREW SWAMP, FLORIDA, 2001
OIL ON LINEN, 78 x 64 INCHES, BARRY AND STACEY LABELL

CRYSTALLINE, 2005
OIL ON LINEN, 40 x 48 INCHES, ARTHUR AND SUSIE KURTZ

Babb traces his fascination with beaches to the period when he and his wife lived in Hull at the southern end of Boston harbor. Their apartment looked out over a park to Nantasket Beach and the open sea. The painter worked among the beach houses and at World's End—a preserve in nearby Hingham that had been designed by the landscape architect Frederick Law Olmsted and that featured lovely views toward Hull and Boston harbor.

Come Labor Day, Nantasket Beach was "literally blanketed with human forms," Babb recalls. Fascinated by this sea of humanity, the artist took photographs of figures while walking among them in his bathing suit. The first impulse, he notes, was to show a vision of the world so crowded with figures that "people had to battle for space to enjoy a little private recreation in the sun."[31] The theme of the crowded beach was explored in several paintings called *Real Estate,* an apt title evoking the territorial marking of one's place on the strand. Babb enjoyed painting the figure, especially in strong daylight. The beach is almost ideal for his purposes: the body "is in the light and air and in the water and visible to other people with less inhibition." Different body types, ages, and genders frequented the Nantasket shore, offering the artist a kind of cross-section of humanity.

Somewhat to the artist's surprise, response to the paintings proved positive. Babb went on to develop this theme at Old Orchard Beach on Saco Bay in southern Maine.[32] The composition and grouping of figures in these paintings derive from many separate photographs that had to be scaled to size to take into account the slope of the beach and the distance and height of the figures relative to the viewer's perspective. These horizontal pieces include a distant view of the five hundred-foot-long pier, which was rebuilt in 1980 after being destroyed by a blizzard in 1978.

Georges Seurat's masterpiece, *Sunday Afternoon on the Island of La Grande Jatte,* 1884–86, served as a model for Babb as he painted the Old Orchard Beach scenes. He had read William Innes Homer's *Seurat and the Science of Painting* and had enjoyed the historian's account of Neo-Impressionist color theory and technique. He had also studied Ogden Rood's *Modern Chromatics,* a treatise on color perception that had influenced Seurat and Camille Pissarro.

Babb's paintings of the Maine coast farther north and east provide a striking contrast to the beaches of southern Maine and Massachusetts. With a look over his shoulder at the paintings of Frederic Church, William Trost Richards, Alfred Bricher,

Homer, and other nineteenth-century American artists who depicted the New England coast—but also at certain Caspar David Friedrich works—he has produced a number of stunning views of the rock-bound edge of Maine.

In painting views of Schoodic Point, Otter Cliffs, Hardwood Island, and other locales, Babb prefers to spend as much time as possible on site, studying the elements. The light changes, the tide goes in and out—one must be in place to seize the moment. For his painting of Eggemoggin Reach, he spent an entire week making watercolor sketches and drawings and taking photographs of the setting. "In that whole week," Babb recalls, "there was one moment when cirrus clouds drifted by. They were there for fifteen minutes or so and then they were gone, but they made the whole painting."

Babb has on occasion tackled other coastal motifs. A view of Port Clyde is full of the charm of that fishing village from whence one takes the ferry to Monhegan Island. By contrast, his paintings of the Bath Iron Works capture this renowned shipbuilding complex in all its industrial glory. *Leviathans—The Bath Iron Works,* 1994, now hangs at the Maine Maritime Academy in Castine, a perfect setting for this symbol of sea-going America.

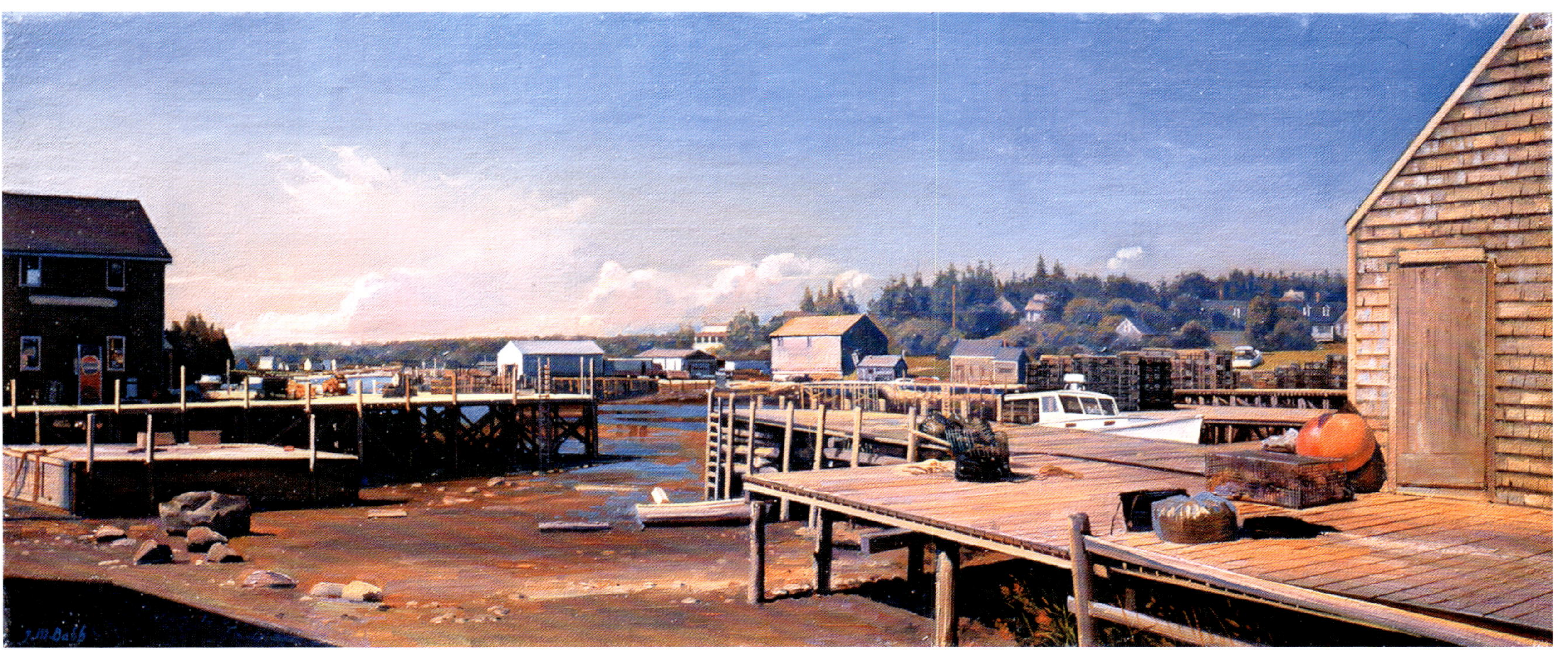

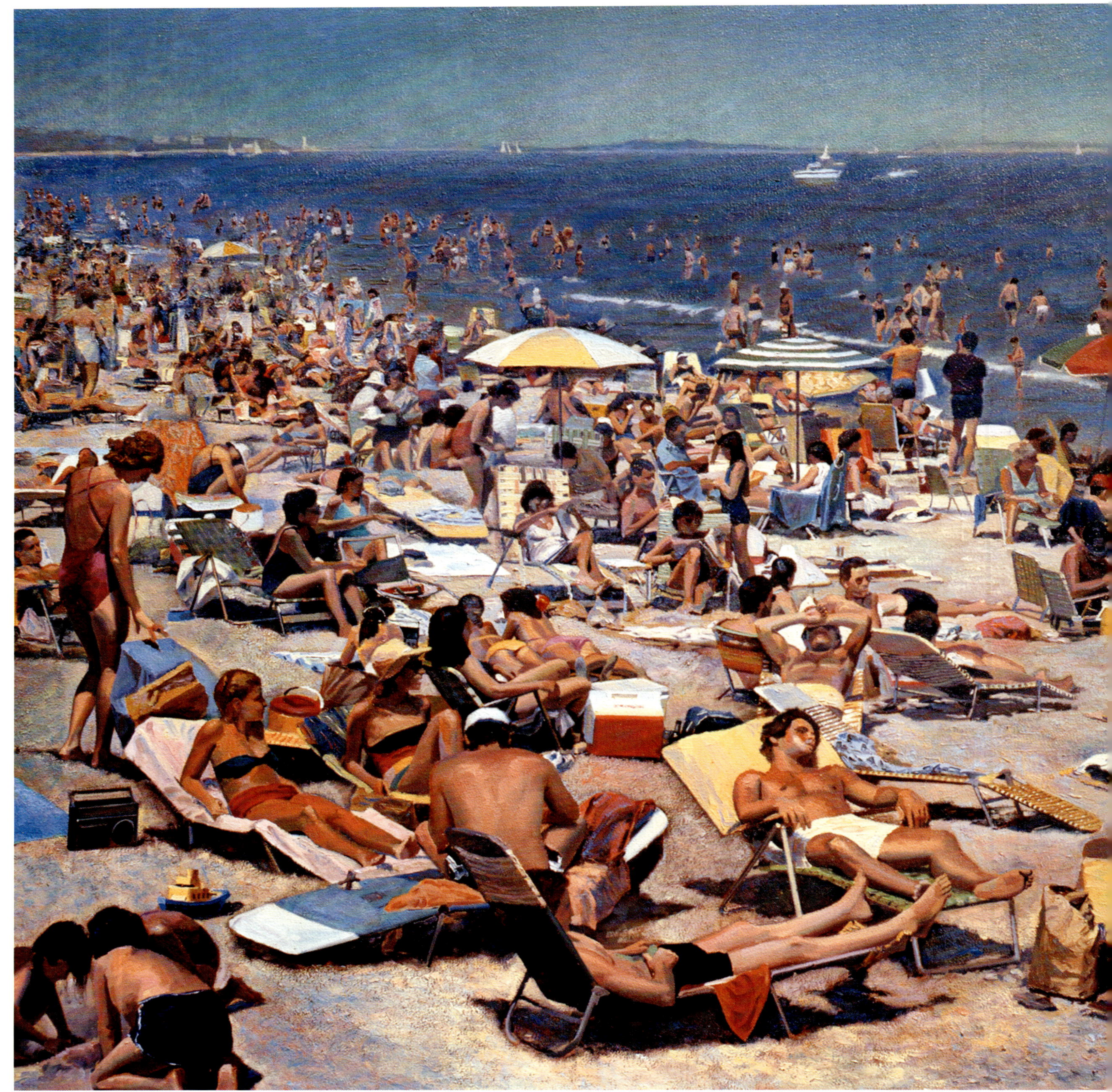

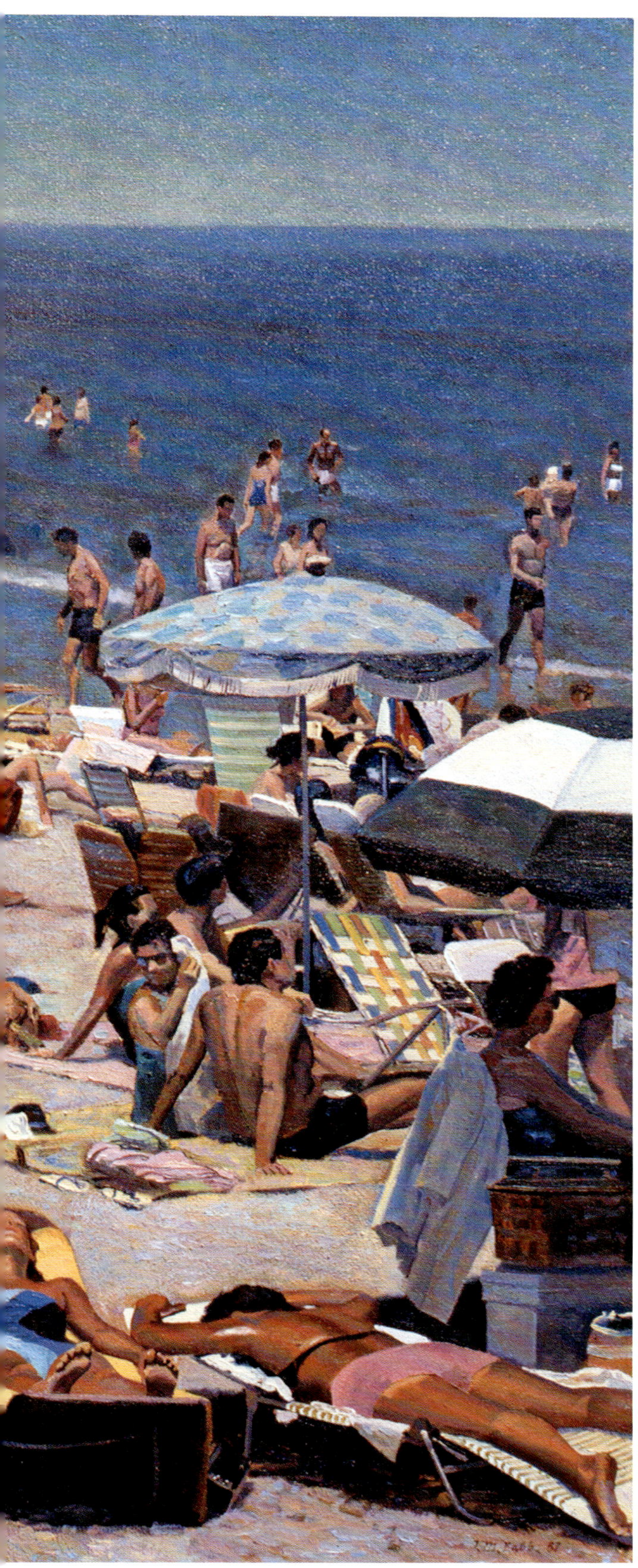

I had painted an anti-classical landscape composed of nothing but cars in a parking lot, and I imagined the first of my series of beaches as a similar comment on crowded urban modernity. But the beach scenes took on a joyful aspect from all the figures having fun in the elements. They are figure paintings, but they are also landscapes, in which the atmospheric perspective works changes on human bodies with distance until real people dissolve into a pattern of far off, colored specks. Of course to those far off people, I seem just a remote colored speck. There is great natural beauty in empty beaches, but something elemental in the equalizing regression when everyone, all ages and types, goes to the beach to enjoy the sun and air and water together.

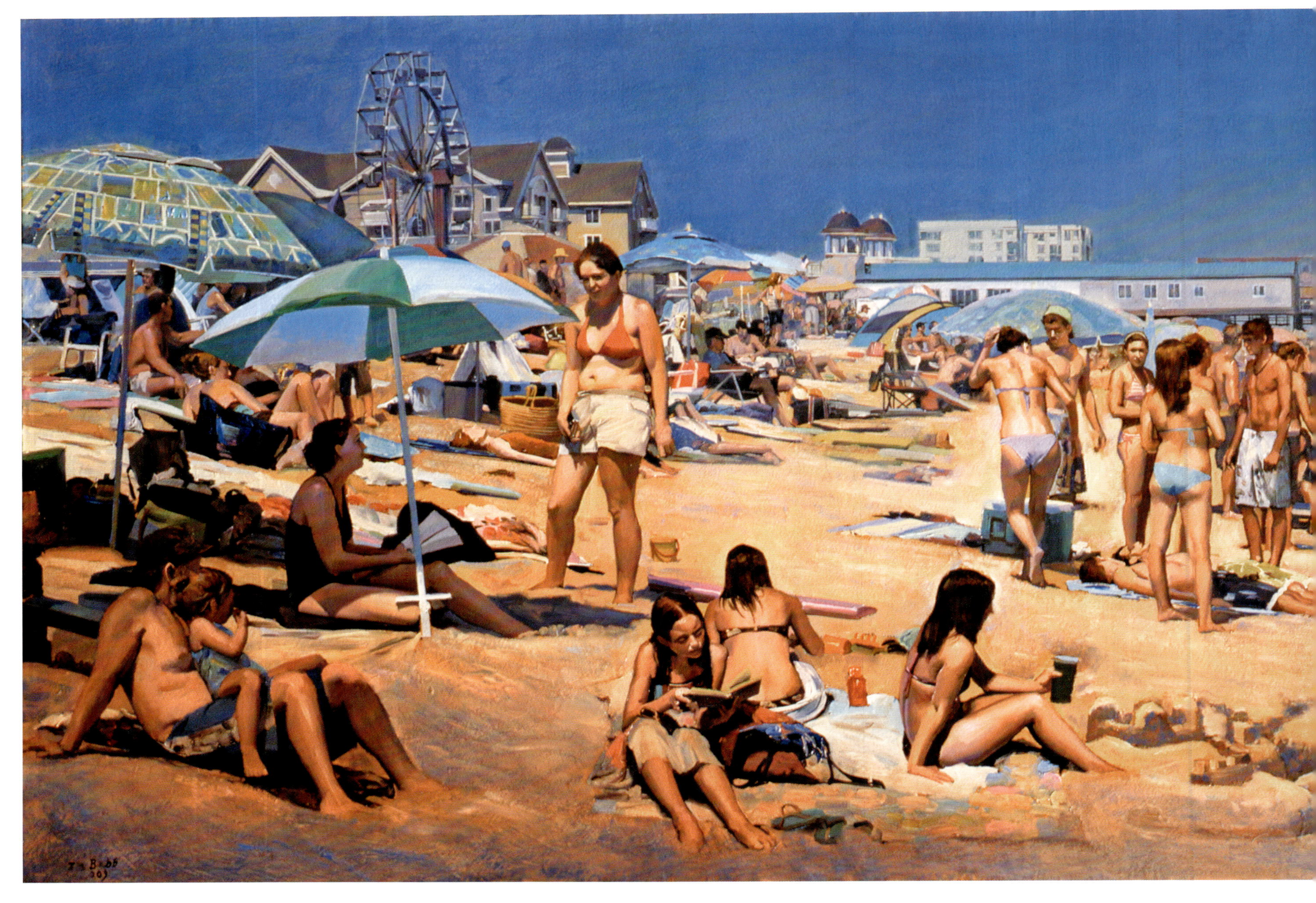

Beach Panorama, Old Orchard, 2009
Oil on linen, 22 x 66 inches
Private collection

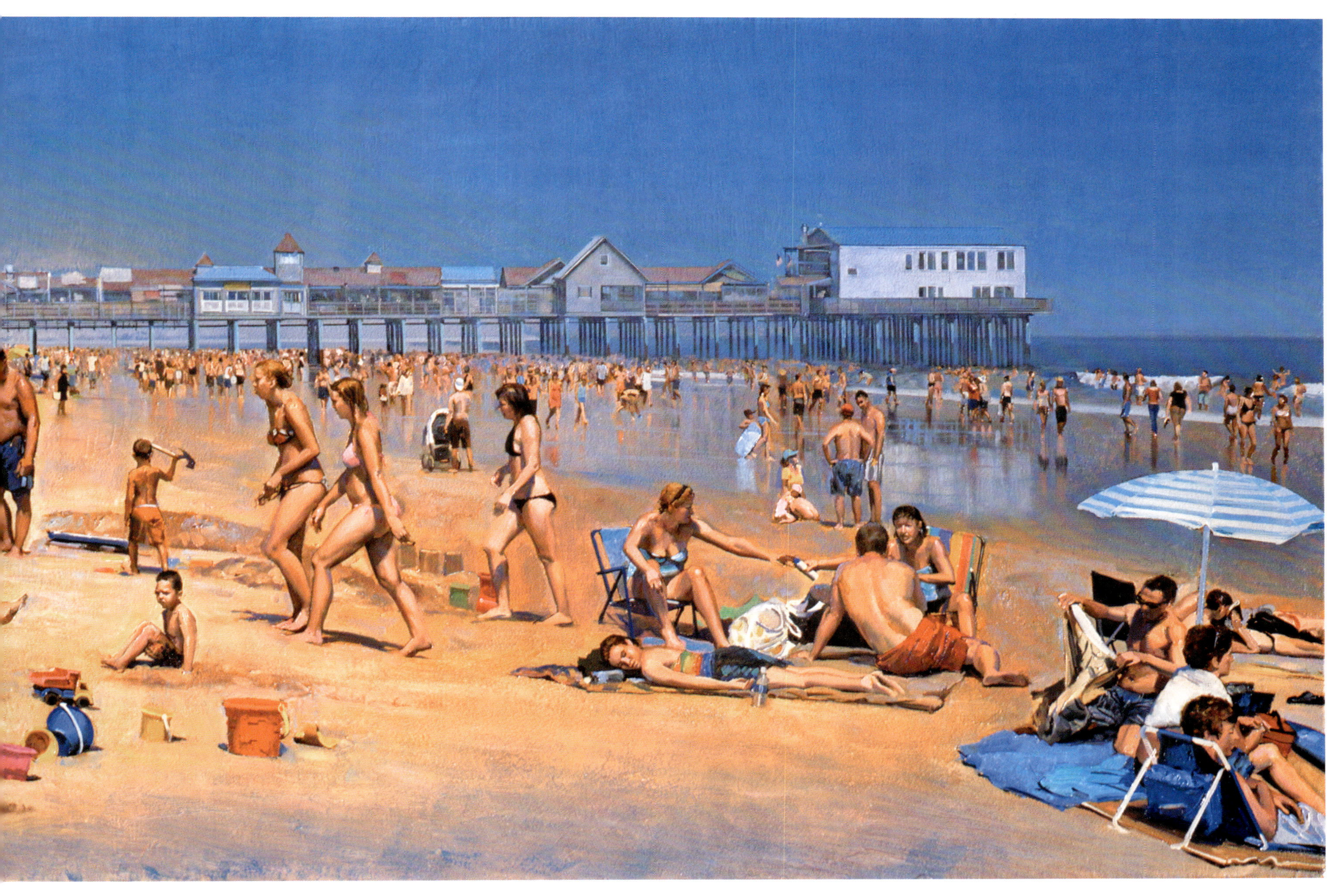

We lived for several years on Nantasket Beach south of Boston, where miles of beach were completely deserted in winter, but in hot summer filled with vast crowds. Old Orchard Beach in Maine attracts thousands of Canadians, and every summer I am attracted down from the woods to enjoy the spectacle of so many people playing at the beach.

A Return to Rome

When Babb first visited Rome in 1969–1970, he sketched the city but did not paint. He was there as a student, "looking at everything Roman, mediaeval, renaissance, and baroque," and he succumbed to the spell of the classical style. An exhibition he saw in 1996 at the Brooklyn Museum inspired his eventual return to Rome with a new agenda. *In the Light of Italy* centered on the French artist Camille Corot and other painters of his generation who worked in Rome in the nineteenth century. Where earlier visitors had focused on studying classical monuments with the idea of producing history paintings in their studios, Corot and company painted views of the city and surrounding countryside outdoors en plein air, representing a radical shift in approach to the old-world landscape.

Eight years after viewing this exhibition, Babb and his wife, Frannie, revisited Rome, renting an apartment near the Piazza Navona for the month of March. Babb continued his explorations of the city again in 2005. His idea was to find sites that Corot had depicted and "sort of sit shoulder to shoulder with him painting." Babb admired the simplicity and "apparent modesty" of Corot's style but recognized, and was humbled by, the masterful way in which he treated the landscape.

Although the landscape of Rome has undergone changes since Corot's time, in comparing his views with Babb's one recognizes the city's essential continuity. Though the Tiber River has been walled and its island transformed by surrounding construction, the major landmark elements of the French painter's view maintain their presence in Babb's versions.[33] At the same time, the semi-rural character of the Rome of Corot's time has all but disappeared. Indeed, Babb has found it difficult painting in the city, with traffic and people often interrupting the scene. On his last trip to Rome, he ended up painting by the river in order to escape the crowds. As he stated in an interview, "there is an industrial strength tourism which scours away the last vestiges of the pleasant bucolic idyll that existed here and there among the ruins."

These Rome paintings combine the immediacy of plein air with Babb's eye for line and structure. The bridges arc, the columns stand straight, the domes of the churches curve against the sky. Some paintings display the impressionistic qualities of Corot and Cézanne; others are tightly conceived. The canvases are more than souvenirs of a Roman holiday: Babb has refreshed our vision of this ancient city, from the river to the rooftops.

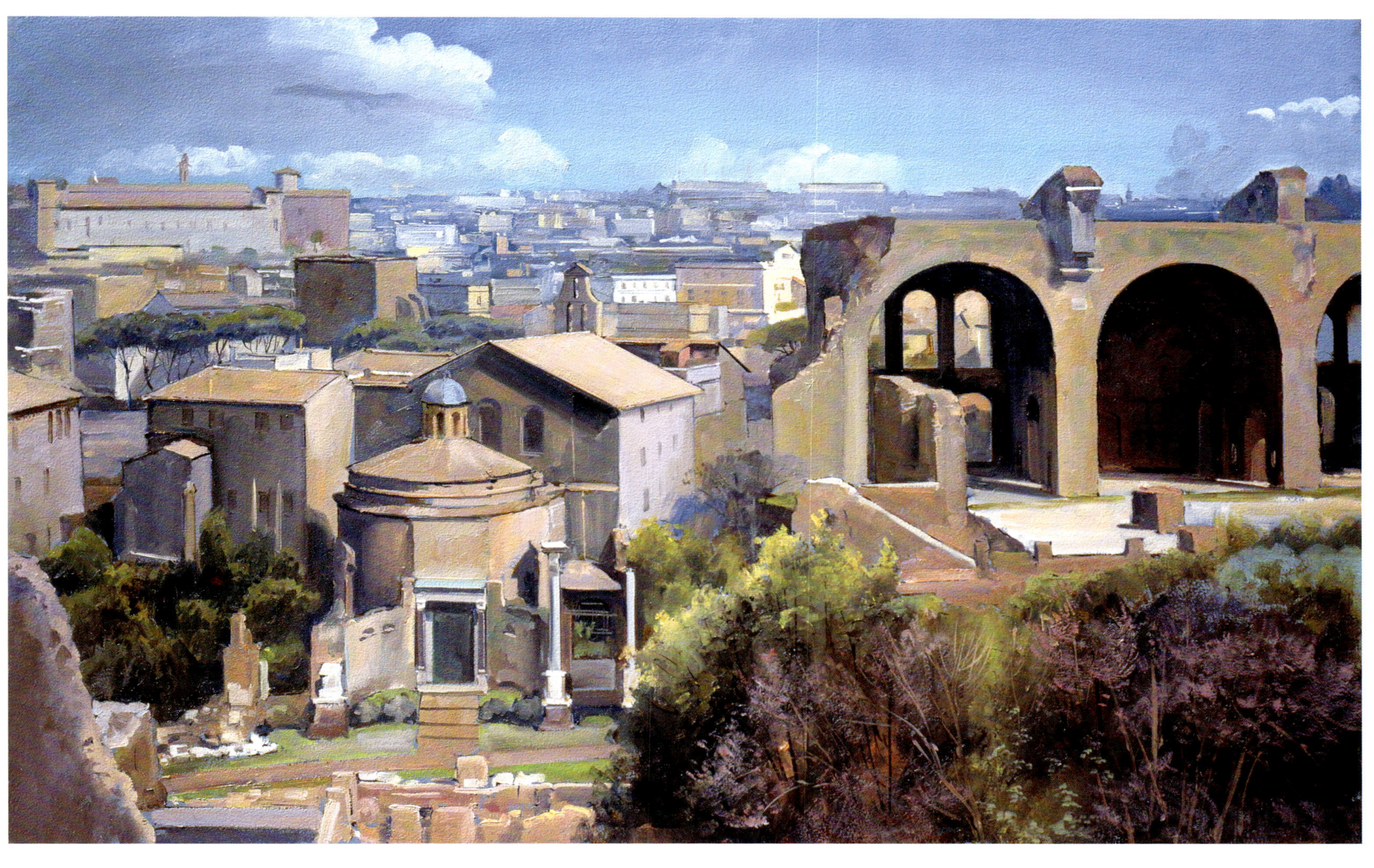

BASILICA OF MAXENTIUS, 2004
OIL ON PANEL, 15 X 24 INCHES
COLLECTION OF THE ARTIST

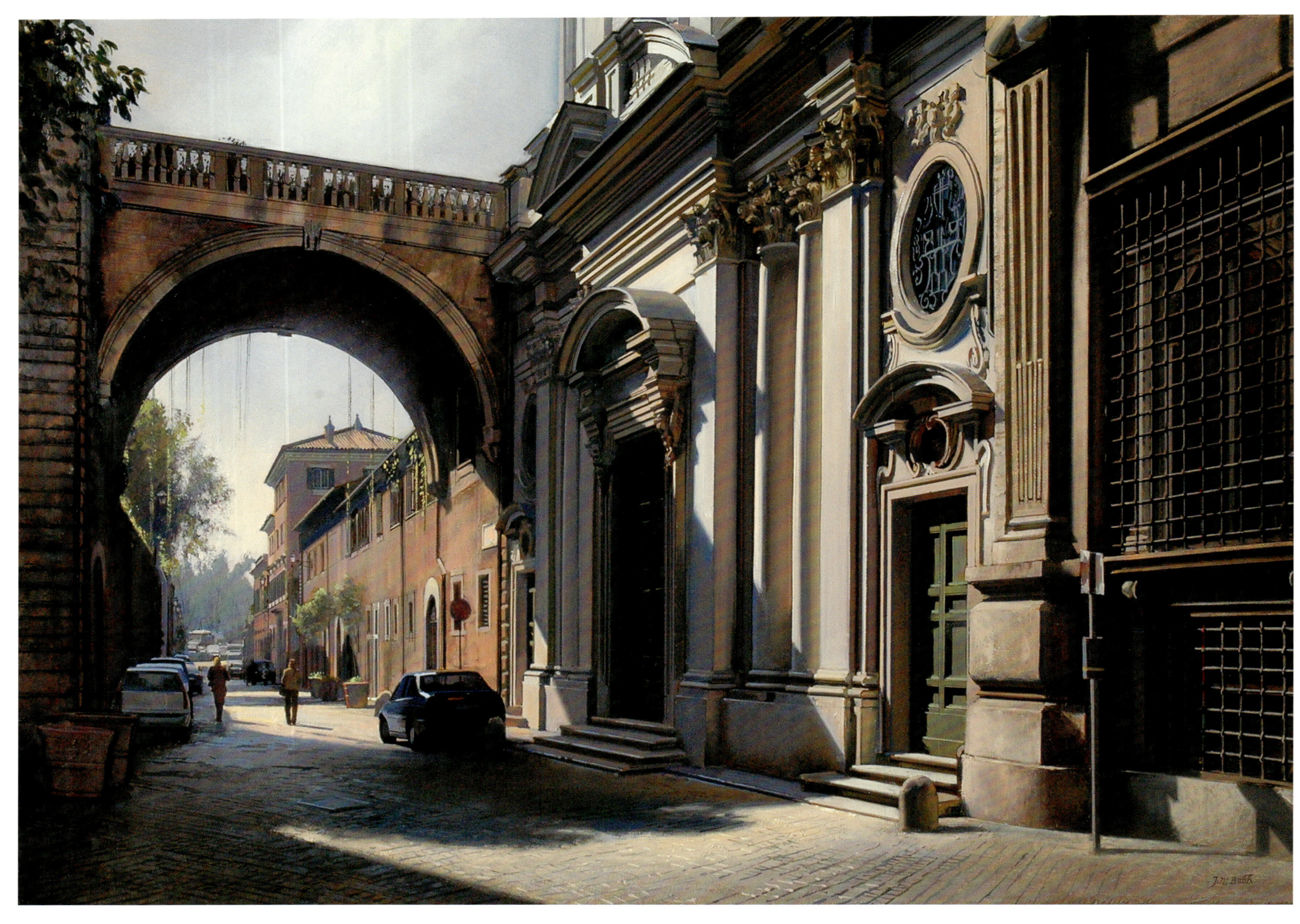

On The Via Giulia, Rome, 2005
Oil on linen, 20 x 28 inches
Elizabeth C. B. and Paul G. Sittenfeld

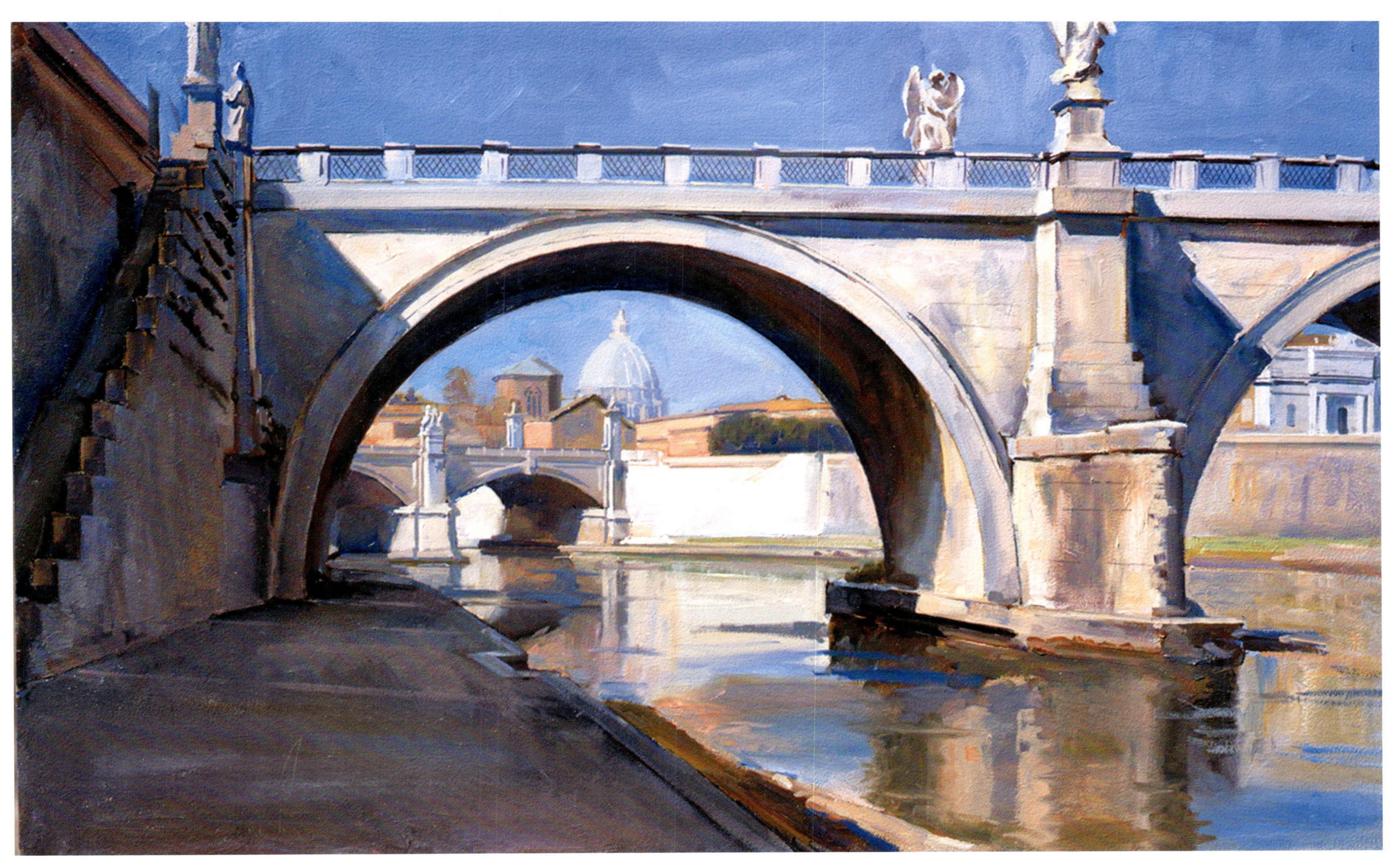

ANGELS BRIDGE AND ST. PETER'S, ROME, 2003
OIL ON PANEL, 15 x 24 INCHES
PRIVATE COLLECTION

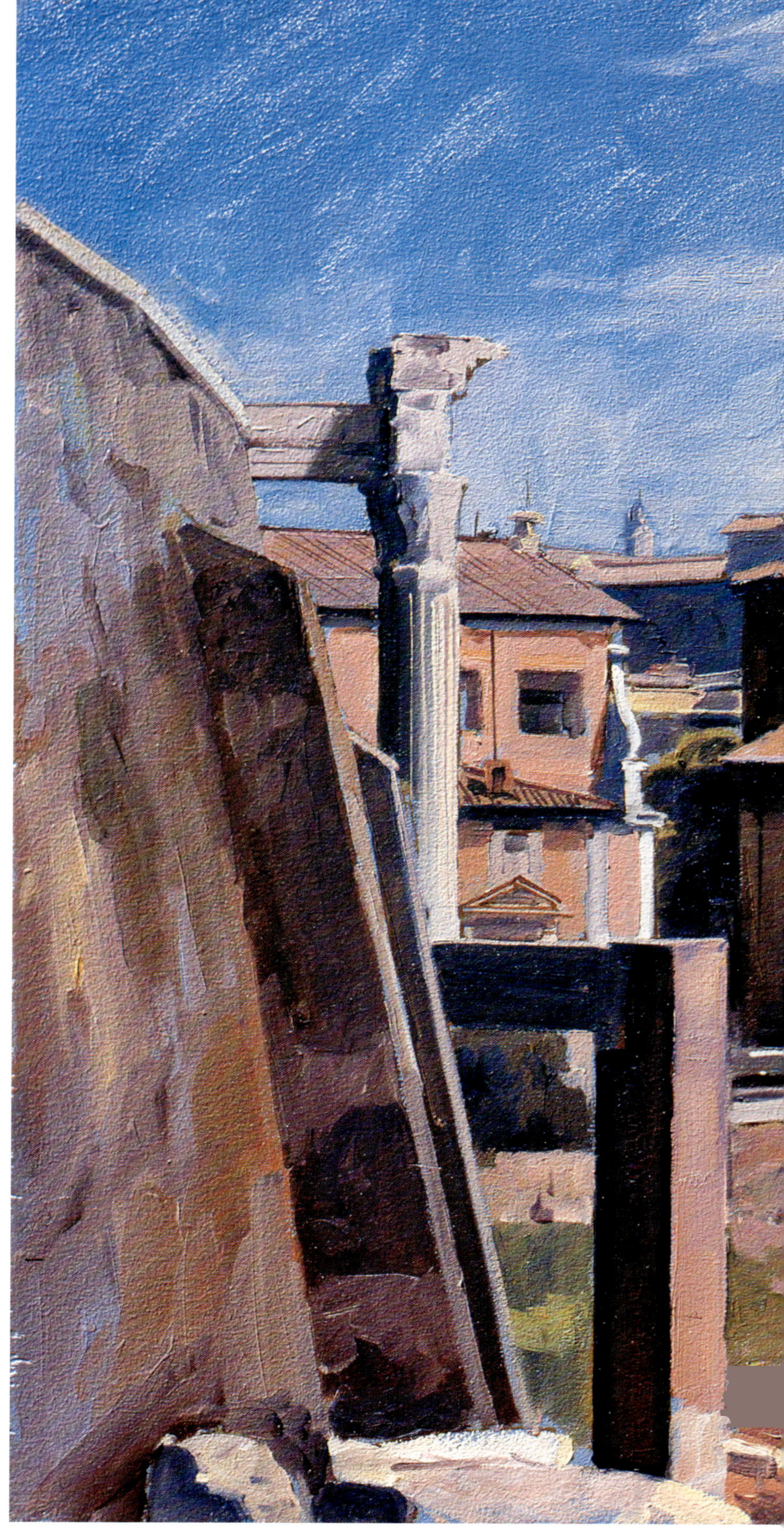

At one time all artists were attracted to Rome as the essential city for art, and then
at some point Paris became the attracting city. I've found myself in sympathy with
the earlier traditions of Rome. I always found it impressive to be in front of a statue
in the Vatican that inspired Michelangelo's style, or was copied by Rubens, or that
Joshua Reynolds took note of; or to be in the garden of the Villa Medici and possibly
see the wall and gateway that Velazquez painted when he was living there, before it
became the French Academy. In Rome you fall under the spell of the classical style,
but also the Renaissance, Baroque, and Neoclassical versions of it.

TEMPLE OF SATURN AND FORUM, ROME, 2004
OIL ON PANEL, 15 X 24 INCHES
PRIVATE COLLECTION

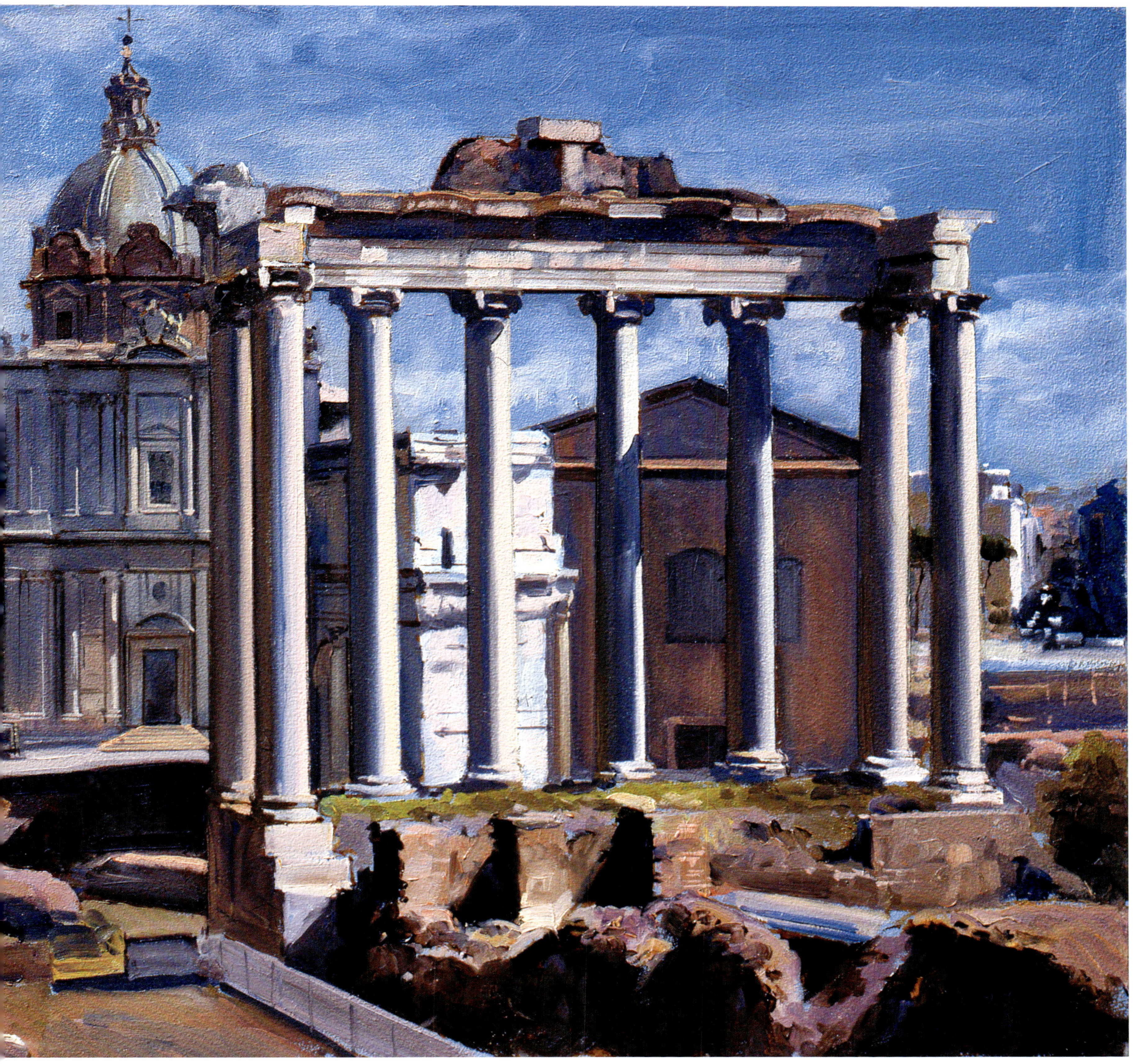

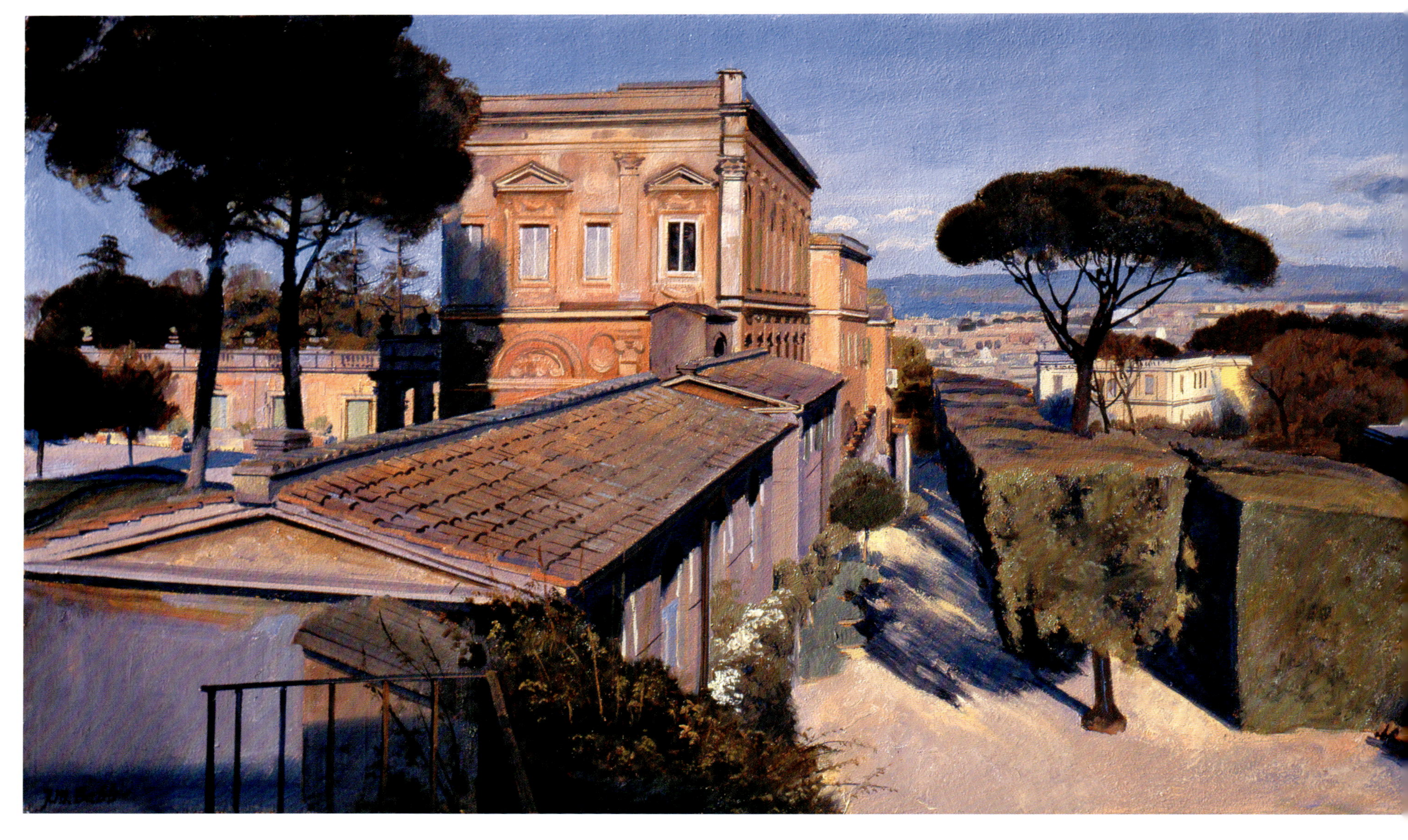

In the Villa Aurelia, Rome, 1998
Oil on linen, 12 x 25 inches
Jim and Sallie Spence McGregor

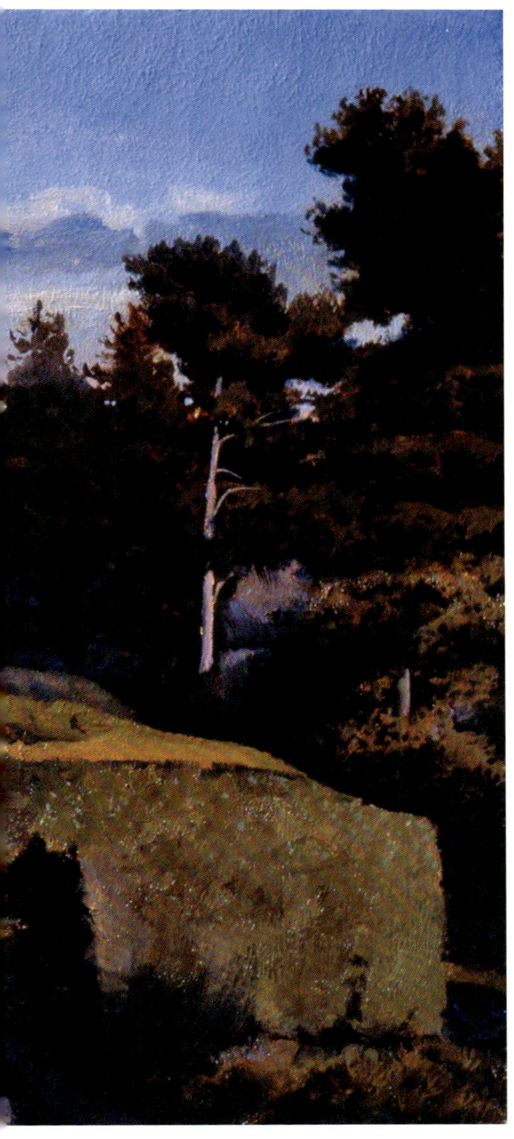
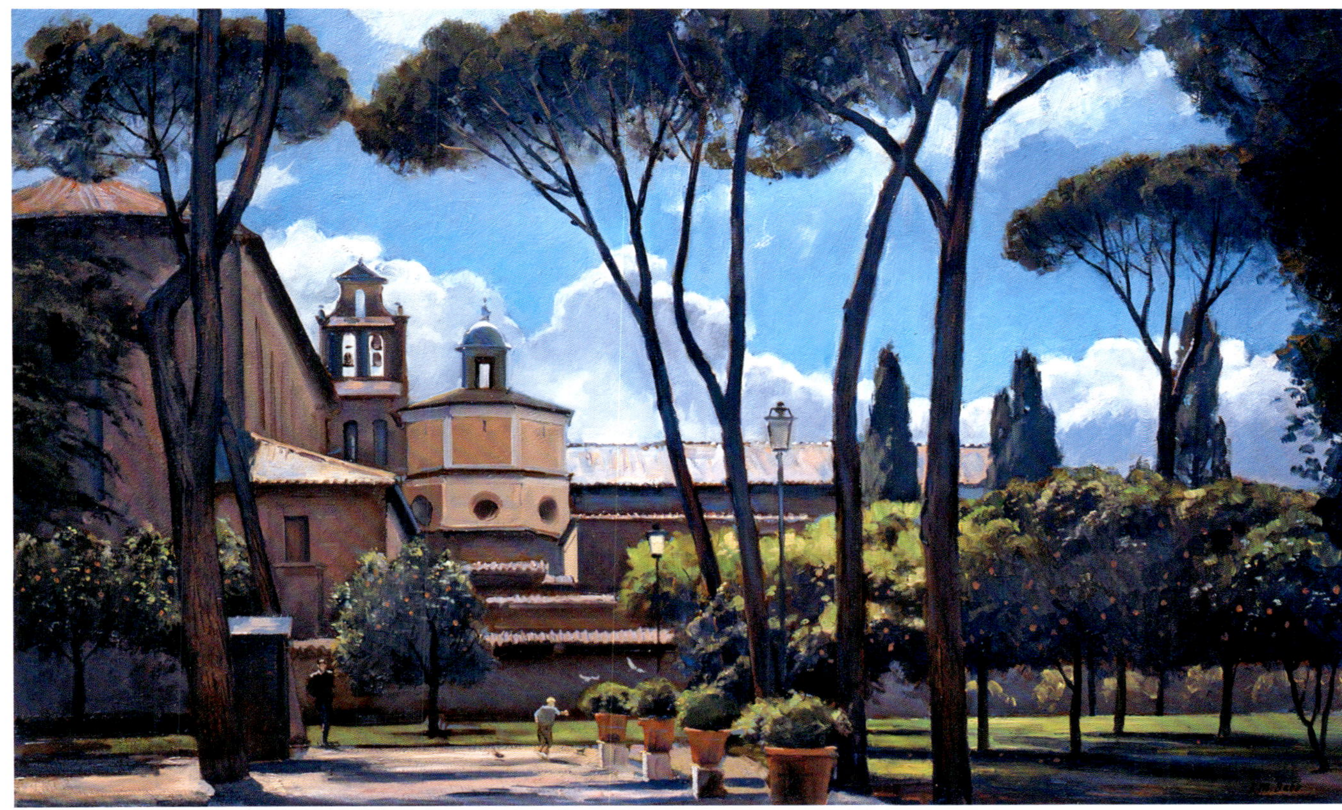

Santa Sabina and Parco Savelli, Rome, 2004

Oil on panel, 15 x 24 inches

Bob and Jackie Laskoff

The Ponte Rotto, the broken bridge, is the remains of a
Roman bridge. It was used for over a thousand years but
finally collapsed in the flood of 1598. This view of the
remaining arch and Tiber Island was painted more than
once by Corot in his Italian period. The view has been
much changed by the building of high walls along the
river, but the island is still served by two Roman bridges.
One is much used by ambulances to reach the island's
busy hospital. I sought out views painted by Corot in the
1820s and had a feeling of painting shoulder to shoulder
with him—which is humbling because of his great but
deceptively simple mastery.

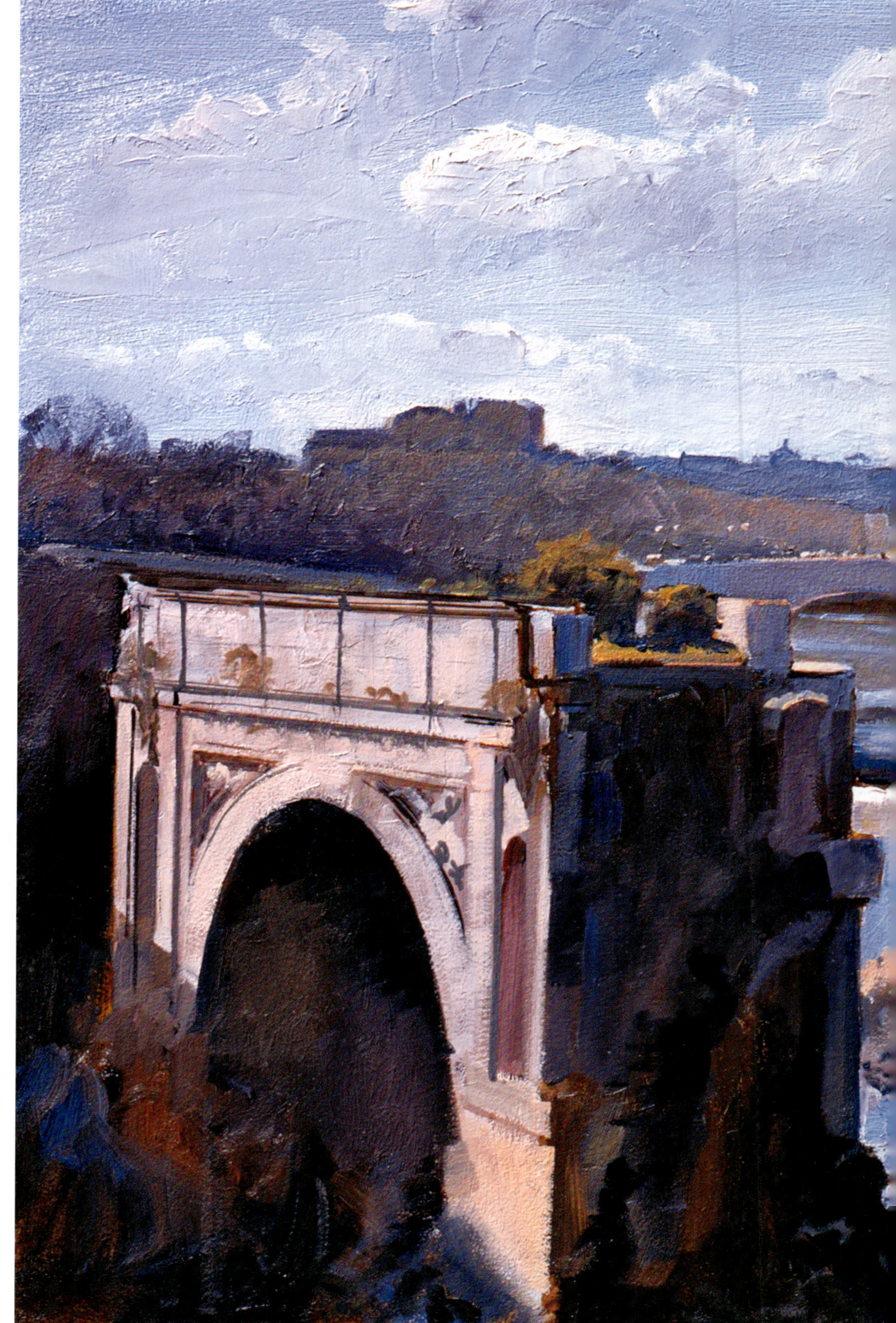

PONTE ROTTO AND TIBER ISLAND, ROME, 2003
OIL ON PANEL, 15 x 24 INCHES
JIM AND SALLIE SPENCE MCGREGOR

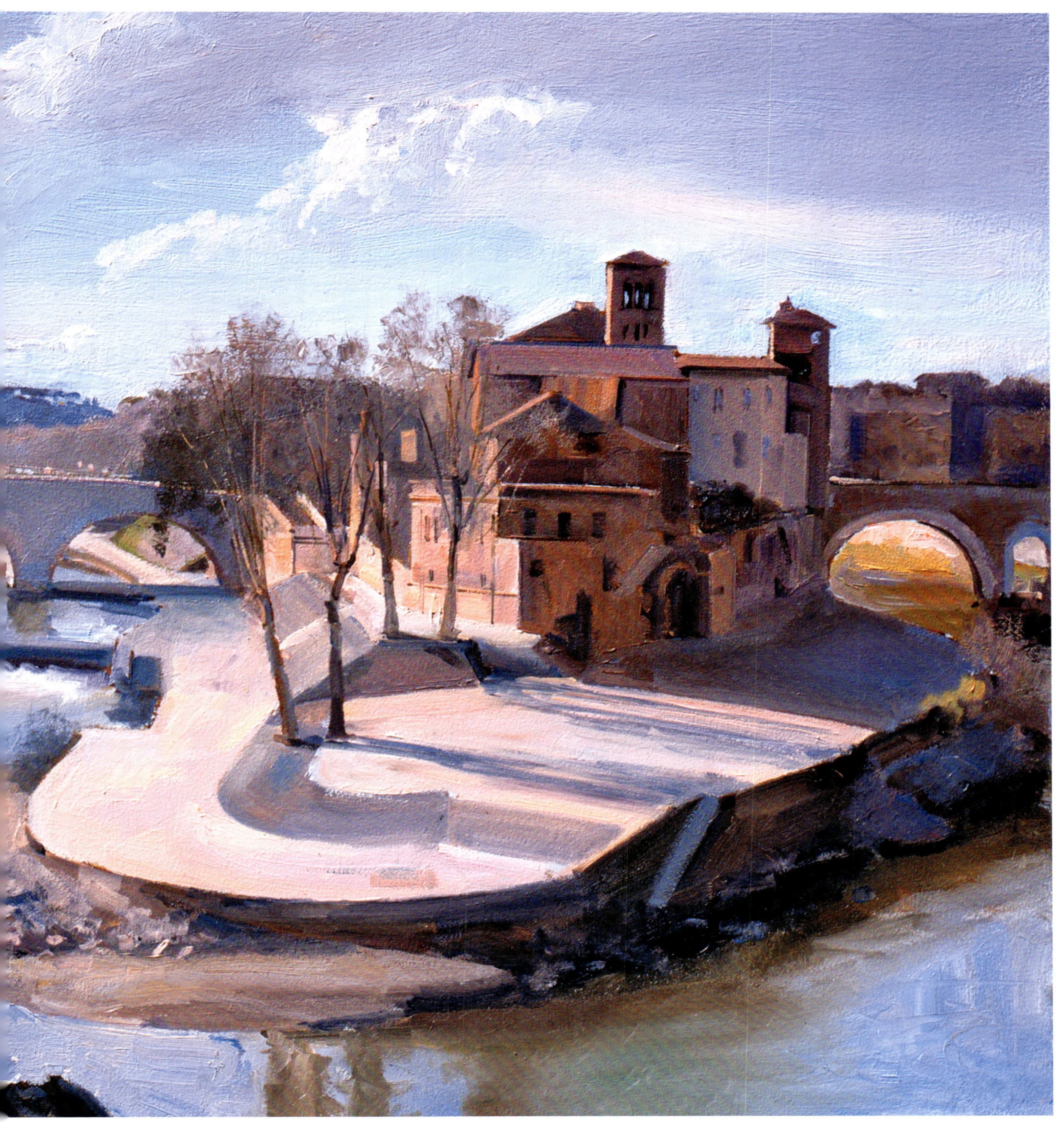

Early in his career, Babb painted a handful of portraits, including that of William Appleton Coolidge, a well-known art collector and a trustee of the Museum of Fine Arts, Boston. He also made a portrait of the Polish composer Frédéric Chopin. Commissioned by Leonard S. Coleman, former president of the National League of Professional Baseball, the likeness is based on the 1849 photograph of Chopin by Louis-Auguste Bisson. Babb had to invent the color and the background, helped in part by a photograph of a piano that belonged to the composer.

Although he had no desire for a career in portraiture, Babb went on to paint a number of commissioned portraits over the years, including those of five renowned Boston-based doctors. These portraits, displayed in the Countway Library of Medicine at Harvard, were painted from historical photographs either because the subjects were deceased or because it was desired that they be represented by younger likenesses. Since many of the photographs were black and white, Babb was obliged to improvise the color. The last of these portraits, and among the most memorable, is that of Dr. Abraham Stone Freedberg, a Harvard cardiologist and pioneer in the study of ulcers who had died in 2009. Babb worked from a series of photographs of the doctor taken by a *New York Times* photographer in the study at Freedberg's home in Jamaica Plain.[34]

Babb's approach to portraiture is similar to that of his landscapes: he relies on both photography and sketches from life. Over the years, the directness of drawing and painting from the nude has lent a fresh energy to his figurative work, much as painting from nature has enhanced his appreciation of light and the vitality of the natural world.

One of Babb's most ambitious portraits involved a group of doctors in the act of performing the first successful organ transplant. The painting was commissioned by three of the physicians, Drs. Joseph Murray, Francis Moore, and Leroy Vandam, who participated in the groundbreaking operation performed at Brigham and Women's Hospital in Boston on December 23, 1954.

Though generally chary about taking on a project falling outside his interests, Babb had several reasons for accepting this particular commission. A central one was his curiosity about the process of developing a history painting. Once the highest form of art in the hierarchy of Western painting, the genre is rarely considered by contemporary artists. A second reason was personal: at the age of thirteen, Babb had undergone an operation to correct a congenital defect between the atria in his heart. The procedure

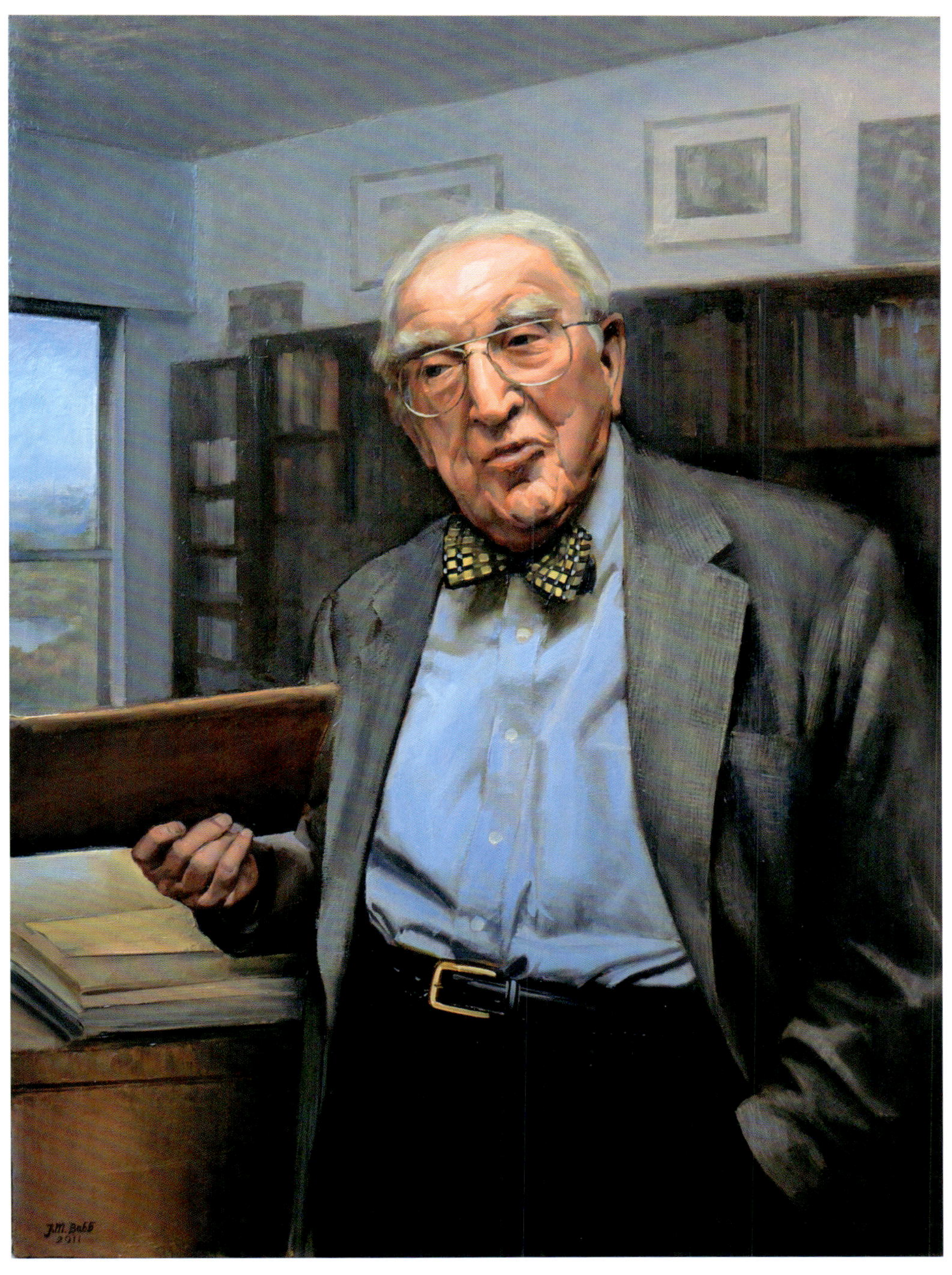

Dr. A. Stone Freedberg, 2010
Oil on linen, 36 x 42 inches
Countway Library of Medicine, Boston

had been a significant event in his childhood. He looked on this painting project as a way both to explore the world of surgeons and to confront the trauma. Finally, the commission offered many challenges, not the least of which was re-creating the scene of the famous operation. In addition to a mock-up of the original operating amphitheater, Babb worked from vintage photographs and the memories of the doctors.

Over the course of the eighteen months Babb spent painting the scene, he held several viewings and invited members of the medical school faculty to make suggestions on the work in progress. In addition to adding a scrub room between the two operating rooms, Babb learned that there had been large windows on one side of the room, which required him to adjust the light in the painting. He also obtained a glass brick in order to study the patterns of light as they might have appeared in the wall that divided the two rooms.

The First Successful Organ Transplantation in Man was unveiled on December 20, 1996. The painting hangs in the Countway Library at the Harvard Medical School, directly across the way from Robert Hinckley's *First Operation under Ether, 1882–1894*, of which it was conceived to be a pendant (Babb made the figures in his painting the same size, as a visual complement).[35]

After the successful completion of the commission, Babb asked Dr. Moore if he could return to the hospital to take photographs for a contemporary surgical painting. Through arrangements with Dr. Elof Erikson, a surgeon, he was invited to witness a coronary bypass operation. From the photographs he took, Babb made two large drawings, which he held on to for ten years before finally finding the opportunity to paint the picture. Composed from the perspective of the anesthesiologist, *Coronary Bypass,* 2007, is an extraordinary representation of the operation, a tour de force of illusionism in its masterful rendering of the many instruments and machines. The image has an immediacy to it—as if the surgeon might turn to the viewer to request assistance. In a manner of speaking, Babb performed his own operation—with brush and paints— in producing this tribute to modern medicine in all its detailed glory.

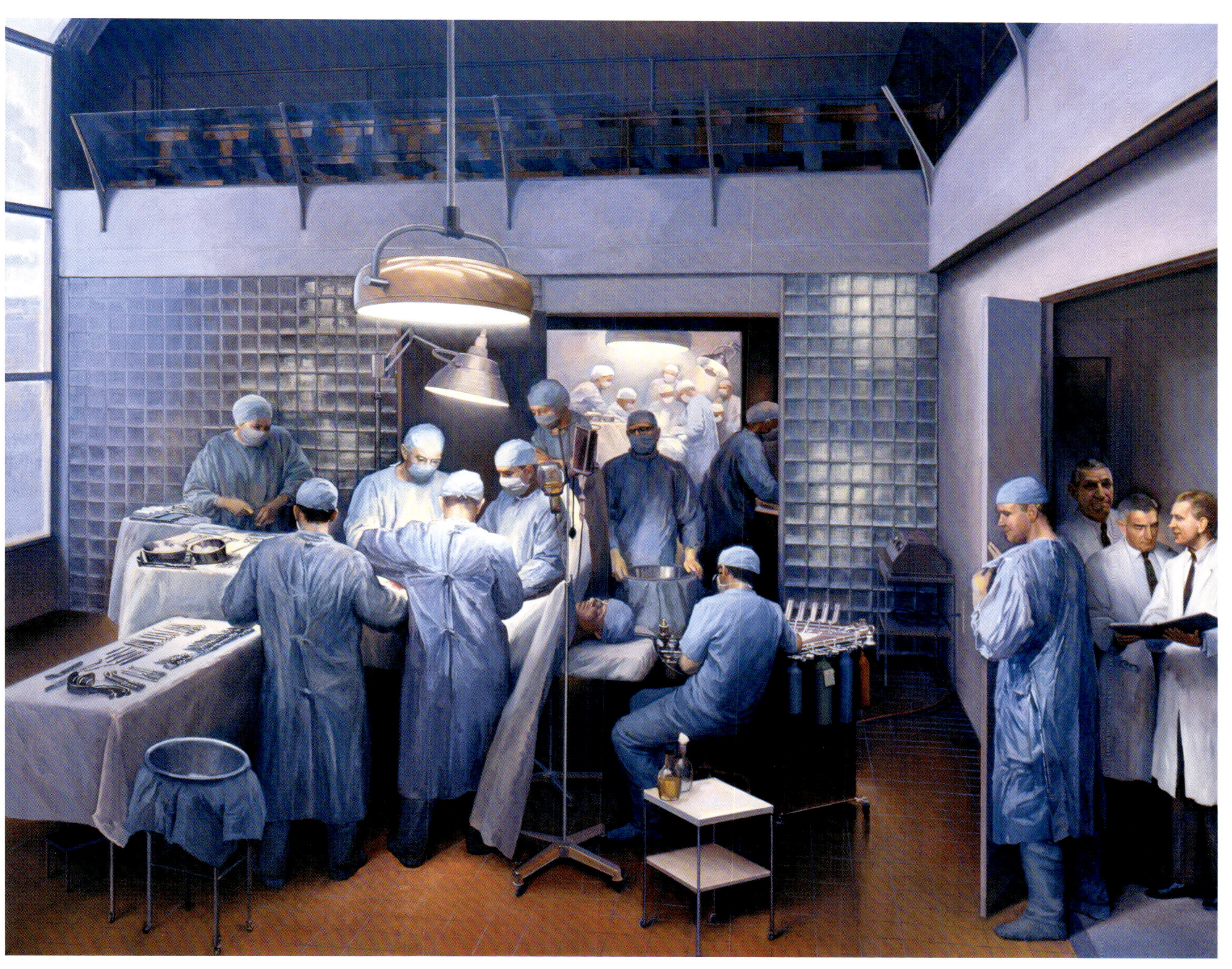

THE FIRST SUCCESSFUL ORGAN TRANSPLANTATION IN MAN, 1996
OIL ON LINEN, 70 x 88 INCHES, COUNTWAY LIBRARY OF MEDICINE,
HARVARD UNIVERSITY MEDICAL SCHOOL, BOSTON

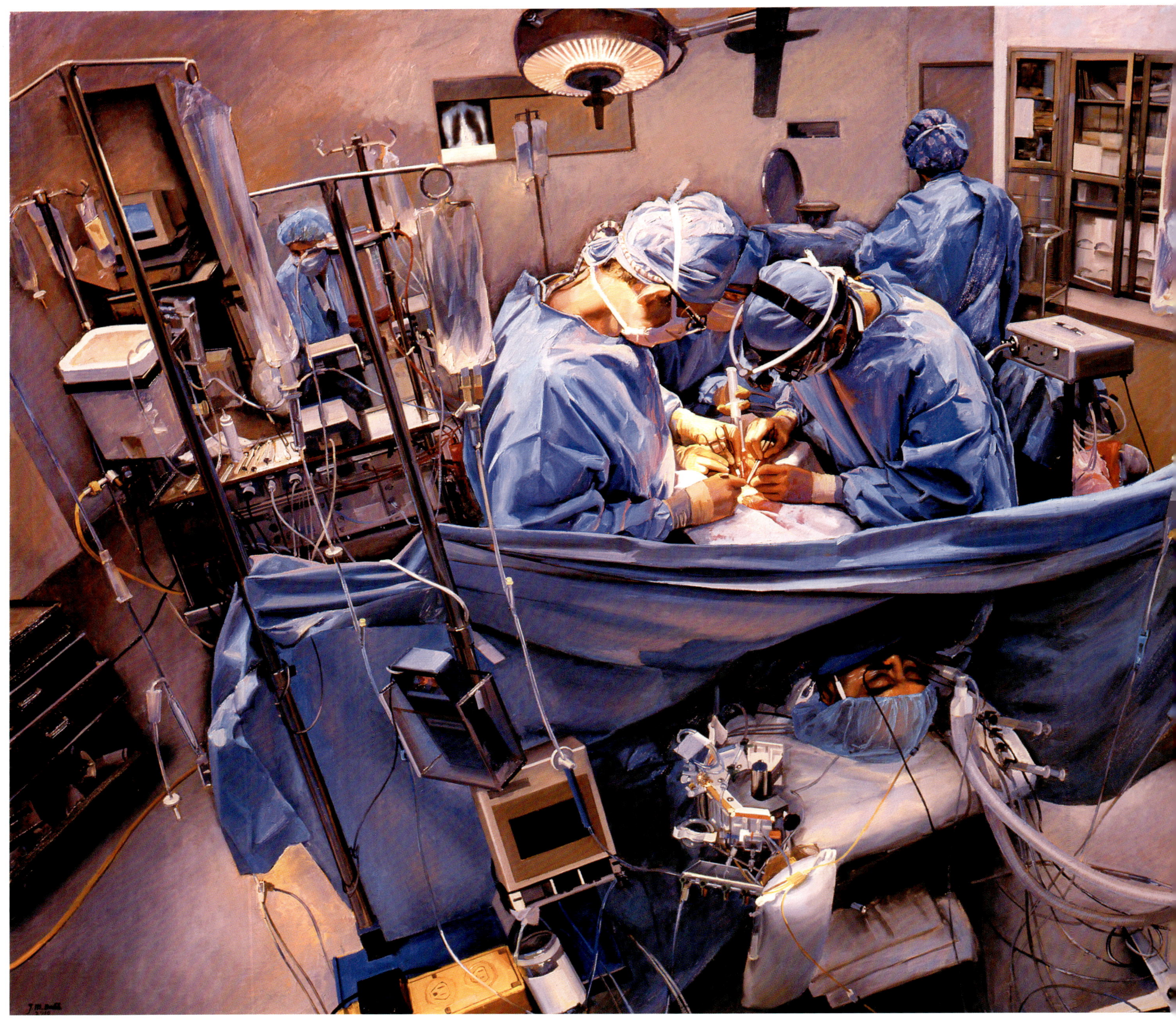

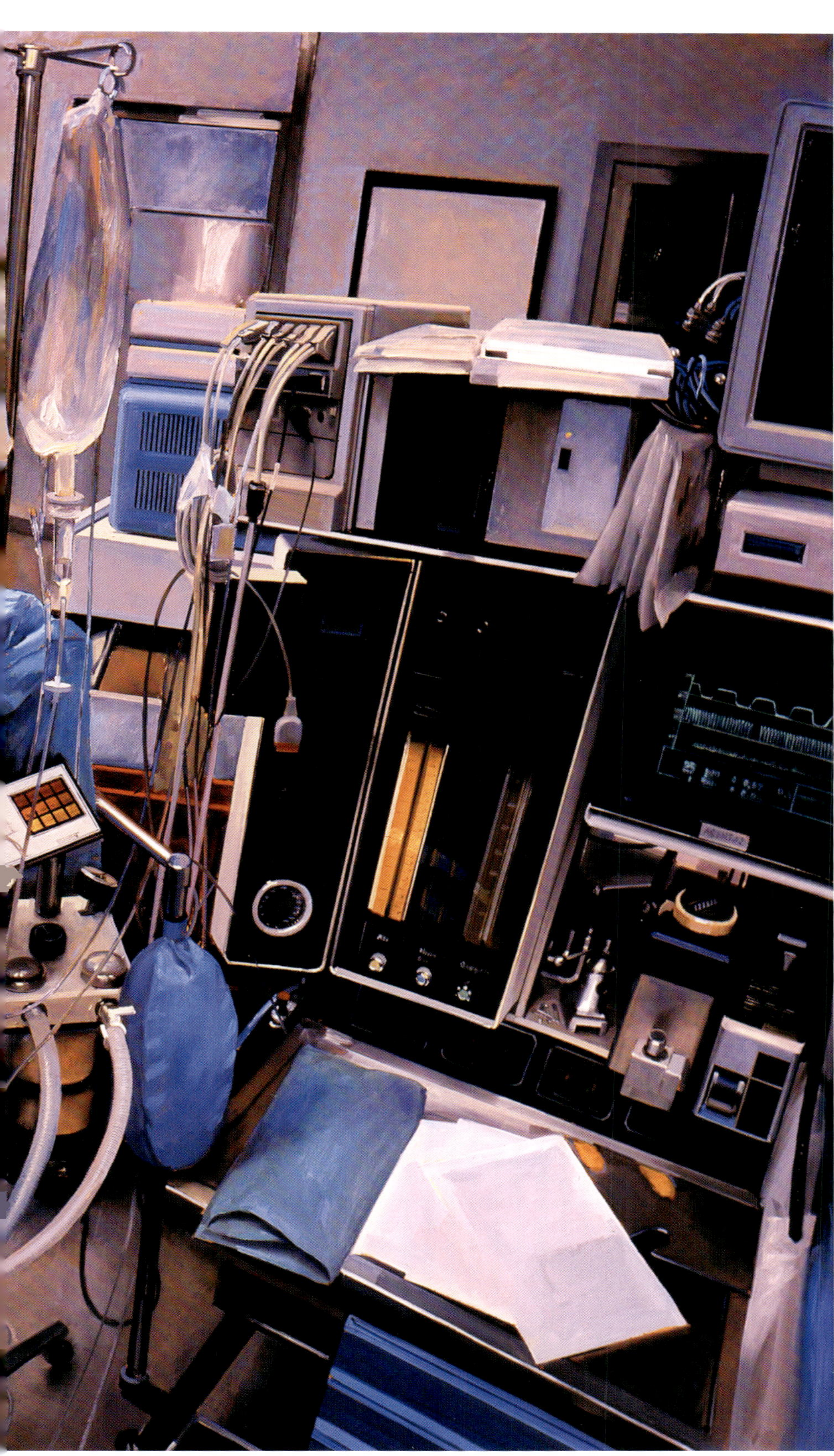

A Coronary Bypass Graft Operation
at the Brigham and Women's, Boston, 2010
Oil on Linen, 40 x 70 inches
Collection of the Artist

To PURSUE HIS PHILOSOPHY OF SEEING, Babb moved against the prevailing currents of contemporary art and the sometimes doctrinaire attitude of art schools. The decision to retrieve the past as a means for representing the present was not an easy one, and the painter experienced those dark nights of the soul that accompany such a quest.

The year 2013 marks a decade since Babb left teaching to paint full time. The wisdom of that move—and the good fortune for all of us that it was made—is borne out in the canvases that are being created in that studio in East Sumner.

With his images of Boston, Babb takes his place alongside his contemporaries Richard Estes, Rackstraw Downes, and a handful of others as one of the foremost city painters of his time. His images of the New England landscape also belong in the pantheon of artists that stretches back to the Hudson River School in the nineteenth century. Looking at the span of Babb's work, from *Early History*—an imaginary view of Rome executed in his thirties—to, say, *Boston from the Hancock Tower*, 2008, we witness an amazing transformation that nonetheless reflects a constant desire to create the world anew. And the world according to Joel Babb is a wondrous place that needs to be painted.

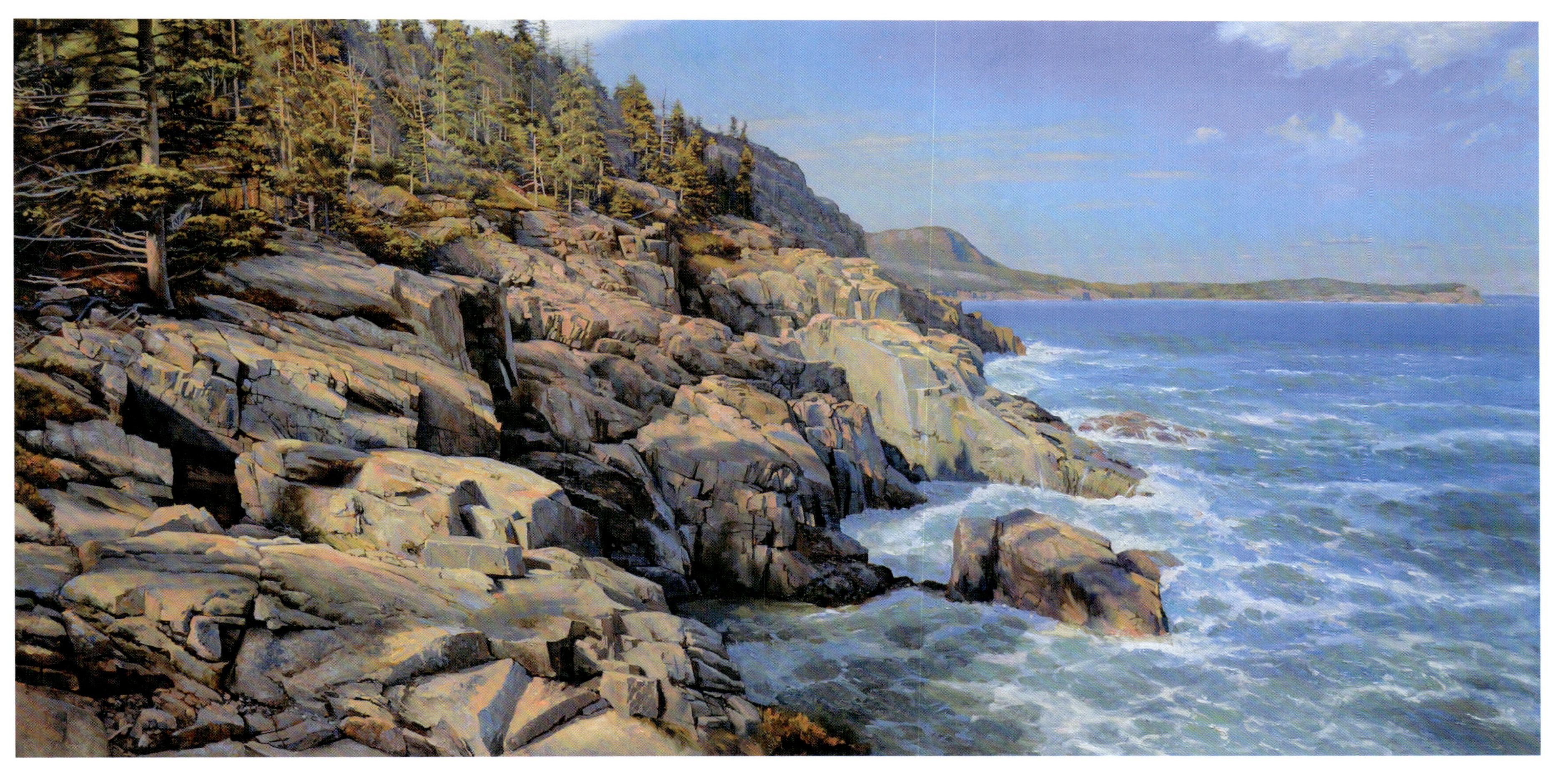

The Maine Coast, Mt. Desert, 2011
Oil on linen, 42 x 84 inches
Collection of the Artist

NOTES

Unless otherwise noted, citations from the artist in the text and footnotes are drawn from Joel Babb's unpublished "Notes on a Review of My Work," written in fall-winter, 2011–2012, and from interviews with the author over the same time period.

1. Babb said, "I realized why all the Impressionists had houseboats. It's incredible: the light on the water, being able to move around to get a different composition."

2. Edgar Allen Beem, "At Home In Maine." Camden, Maine: *Down East,* March 2002, p. 65.

3. The profile of Dickinson appeared in the February 10, 1961, issue of *Time* under the title "Defying Time and Fashion."

4. The image of a Baroque church "invaded by untrammeled light," which was on the cover of one of the classical albums, led to an appreciation for these old world edifices Babb would later visit in Germany and Italy.

5. Babb recalls finally viewing Dickinson's painting at the Metropolitan Museum of Art later in his life. "It was like seeing the Acropolis for the first time."

6. "There was no major [in studio art] and the Creative Arts Program was just beginning."

7. Babb recalls that Ortman at the time "was constructing his large paintings by fastening together many small independent pieces with mending plates and screws on the back."

8. The studio was in an elementary school that the university had purchased to house its art programs. As part of the fellowship, Babb served as a research assistant in the Princeton University Art Museum making condition reports on artworks in the university collection.

9. Seeing his prodigious production, one day Ortman asked in wonder how Babb had found the time to do so much painting while keeping up with academic work. "I guess it should have been obvious to me that painting was more important than being a good student," the artist notes in retrospect.

10. "I developed a habit of taking long exploratory walks, some of which turned into familiar ritual passages: to the Princeton Theological Seminary, through the grounds of the Carpenter Gothic house of the president, down Mercer Street past Einstein's house, to Marquand Park where I often sketched, or to the woods of the Institute for Advanced Study."

11. "One of the figures [in my installation] had a Coffee-mate jar for a vagina with a spoon sifting a white powder into a cup of steaming coffee. Segal saw this and cautioned against trying to be too strange because in New York City there were those who could outdo the strangest….His warning stuck in my mind as important, but it seemed odd at the time coming from an artist whose works were unusually innovative and part of the scene of new art in the 60s, which was provocatively experimental."

12. "…When I had become familiar with Rome, in preparing to see the [Carracci ceiling] frescoes again, I read [John Rupert] Martin's book [on the Farnese Gallery] with the benefit of years of experience, and I was struck by the magisterial quality and elegance of the book…. I couldn't help thinking how much he had been wasted on us as undergraduates [at Princeton]."

13. "I'm reminded of the vertical precipices of Chinese mountains when I wander between Black Mountain and Tumbledown Dick, the hills near my house [in East Sumner]."

14. Princeton University Press published MacGregor's landmark study *The Discovery of the Art of the Insane* in 1989. MacGregor also wrote a major book on the outsider artist Henry Darger.

15. Some years later, after finishing his MFA degree, Babb spent almost a year focusing on drawing with pen and ink and wash in imitation of Claude Lorrain's drawings and also of J.M.W. Turner's sketchbooks, with the idea that oil paintings "might be done in the studio from the sketches, the way they did."

16. Goldwater, Robert, and Marco Treves. *Artists on Art.* New York: Pantheon Books, 1947, p. 156

17. John Joseph Burns (1918–2010) taught at the School of the Museum of Fine Arts for thirty-six years.

18. Painter and photographer T. Lux Feininger (1910–2011), son of artist Lyonel Feininger and younger brother of the photographer Andreas Feininger, "represented a bridge of experience to the great early modernists, who had great understanding and training in art and established a new tradition of their own." Babb, "Notes on a Review of My Work."

19. "Joel Babb: A Dialogue with Nancy Allyn Jarzombek," in *Illuminated: Boston, Maine and Rome.* Exhibition catalogue. Boston: Vose Galleries, 2006, p. 26. Babb had left teaching by this time and expressed pleasure at being "simply an artist."

20. One is reminded of the mythological paintings that Bryson Burroughs set on the island of North Haven in Maine or of some of Thomas Cornell's modern-day allegories set in New England landscapes.

21. Babb points to a long history of the use of devices for reproducing the world, from the camera obscura to digital cameras. "Van Deren Coke's *The Painter and the Photograph* is eye-opening about the degree to which photography began to enter the painter's practice."

22. The cars in the painting have become less contemporary over time; Babb foresees the day when the picture will become "quaint and historical," a fate that many paintings endure, realist or otherwise. The effect of motion is akin to that found in some of Robert Birmelin's street scenes.

23. This new take on the world reminded Babb of the book *Flatland: A Romance of Many Dimensions* by the mathematician Edwin A. Abbott. The painting was

moved later from the lobby to the third floor of Cambridge Savings Bank. The move required taking out the window on the third floor and hiring a crane to hoist the picture to its new location.

24. *Copley Plunge* was selected by the critic Theodore Wolff for the landmark exhibition *On the Edge: Forty Years of Maine Painting, 1952–1992* at Maine Coast Artists. Babb's painting was one of only a handful that was not directly Maine-related.

25. "….The habit of looking at paintings came from the tradition of connoisseurship I encountered at Princeton, grafted onto my own early experiences of painting at imaginative experience." Babb, "Notes on a Review of My Work."

26. Babb had studied two Canaletto paintings in the Museum of Fine Arts, Boston collection and had concluded that the painter had used a T square device and a compass to delineate the structures in his views of Venice. The Metropolitan Museum of Art exhibition caused Babb's reappraisal of the artist: the Venetian painter was much more "varied and imaginative" than Babb had previously understood him to be.

27. In what may be a personal record, Babb worked from forty-five different photographs in producing the remarkable *Fan Pier, 2007.* Marcia I. Vose, "Process: A Babb of Our Own," in *Joel M. Babb: Enlightened Perspectives*. Exhibition catalogue. Boston: Vose Galleries, 2009, p. 16.

28. "'Homesteading' in a field, building a place to live and work without a mortgage, enabled me to put most of my time into painting. I put down roots, and though I often paint the city, the mountains and streams are my real home." Joel Babb, cited in Theodore Wolff, *On the Edge: Forty Years of Maine Painting, 1952–1992.* Exhibition catalogue. Rockport, Maine: Maine Coast Artists, 1992, pp. 161–162. Babb reiterated those sentiments in *Sumner: Portrait of a Small Maine Town, 1798–1998,* by George Healey and Mark Silber, published on the occasion of the town's bicentennial.

29. "Joel Babb's first exhibition at Vose Galleries in 2006, in which he presented thirty-one paintings of New England cityscapes and landscapes, was so successful that the artist was able to enlarge his small clapboard house in the woods of East Sumner, Maine, and build a proper studio next door." Marcia L. Vose, "Process: A Babb of Our Own," p. 2.

30. Stephen May, "Old Influences, New Approaches." *American Artist,* March 2004, p. 69.

31. Babb originally visualized this painting having a pendant based on a "severe traffic jam on the Southeast Expressway," the highway by which he and Frannie commuted to Boston. He actually took photographs of tie-ups while driving in, "steering while looking through the viewfinder of the camera."

32. The American modernist Marsden Hartley also painted at Old Orchard Beach, focusing on bathers.

33. The sky, too, differs. Babb notes that his skies are cooler and bluer than Corot's "warm golden atmospherics." Having painted in Rome primarily in March, in a relatively cooler part of the year, Babb wonders if the quality of the sky is not related to season.

34. After retiring from the research faculty at Harvard Medical School, Dr. Freedberg went into clinical practice for another twenty-five years. Babb met him on a number of occasions when he was in his late nineties and still practicing medicine.

35. The artist likes to say that his career as a painter peaked when Harvard Medical School took down a large John Singleton Copley portrait to hang his painting in the lobby of the library.

Joel Babb:
The Essence of What Is

Bernd Heinrich

It may seem odd that a scientist with no formal training in art should dare to venture thoughts about art and an artist. My excuse is that I have been both a practicing scientist and a visual artist most of my life. I believe art and science come from the same wellspring. Neither originated from the utilitarian and both spring from the aesthetic. As the French philosopher of science Henri Poincaré famously said, "The scientist does not study nature because it is useable; he studies it because he delights in it, and he delights in it because it is beautiful." The scientist seeks to reveal its beauty by elucidating its patterns and then presenting them. Most of us attempt to grasp at least little bits of nature, and perhaps unconsciously we see nature as the standard of what is or can be beautiful. To grasp beauty, however, means to see and seize the real, or "truth," which is, as the poet John Keats said, "beauty."

It takes both skill and knowledge to see, capture, and reveal the often hidden beauty of nature that the scientist seeks and the artist shows. In *A River Runs Through It*, Norman Maclean said, "…All good things—trout as well as eternal salvation—come by grace and grace by art and art does not come easy."

I get the same pleasure from art that I do from science, and the same displeasures. Pleasure comes mainly from excellence and coherence revealed, which make previously irrelevant, uninteresting details important and endowed with new meaning. The first criterion on whether or not it can teach or touch is therefore whether or not it is real.

I suspect that the aesthetics that determine beauty, in both science and art, come from the same source as all our senses, tastes, urges, and perceptions. As in all animals, it's from our biology. Aesthetics are a way of perceiving and grading quality, through feeling and emotion, of what is and has been important in our lives throughout evolution, when for millions of years we had been attuned to what enhanced our welfare, our survival. We can assume that what enhanced survival would evolve to engender positive emotions and attraction. On the other hand, that which was associated with risk encoded repelling, perhaps eventually by logic but fundamentally, more indirectly, by fear, disgust, and aversion. Beauty was that which was ultimately constructive and life promoting. Conversely, the ugly was the aversive, the destructive, the chaotic.

Few of us are close enough to nature now to appreciate the practical connection between beauty and our ancient life-giving stimuli, many of which became enshrined in our culture and art. Earlier in our evolution, when we lived directly in the nature we evolved in, culture and art coincided with the natural world as we knew it. As we became distanced from nature, art may have started to lose its grounding.

A painting is the product of the eye, mind, and hand. The mind has to be transported into the scene, then captivated by certain features of it, for the "truth" of it to shine. Thus, when we see a painting of a brook, we are consciousness-sharing with the artist. We are seeing not only a brook but also what has entered a person's eyes and has been processed and executed to be reproduced into a recognizable facsimile of the real. The painting also represents a human caring. It shows what the painter values and appreciates. It is the visible proof of that consciousness and caring.

Some other animals can also infer what is in the minds of others (technically referred to as "theory-of-mind" capacity). But we are unique in being capable, in varying degrees, of expressing it symbolically. In the artist as well as the scientist, this capacity allows us to continue to focus and accumulate sights and insights over time that may encompass generations. We see the essence of what is or has been relevant in ever-greater sharpness and focus, and that allows us to approach what we ultimately perceive as "truth." It is thus also a record of human consciousness, of what we hold or have held noteworthy and important.

Babb shows me what is now, at least to me, important and familiar, but in a new light. He sat down on a chair in the middle of my long-familiar Alder Brook and, with a brush dipped in paints, magically captured it on canvas. He brought it home for all to enjoy—those who had never been there and who would likely never be able to venture to that sprite of water in the woods of western Maine.

Babb's art speaks to me of consummate skill, focus, caring, and a seemingly infinite patience to process what he has seen and transferred through the mind and hand, and to distill the essence of it on canvas. As the images in this book amply show, Babb is skilled to portray any object, scene, or thing, but I would argue that the one thing he portrays that naturally appeals to all people are scenes of nature. Look at his Alder Brook: he has preserved a moment when the light was just right and the angle of view conducive to hold it fast forever. His unique rendering of evocative nature scenes may become his greatest legacy. He has given value to the brook, and what greater glory is there than that?

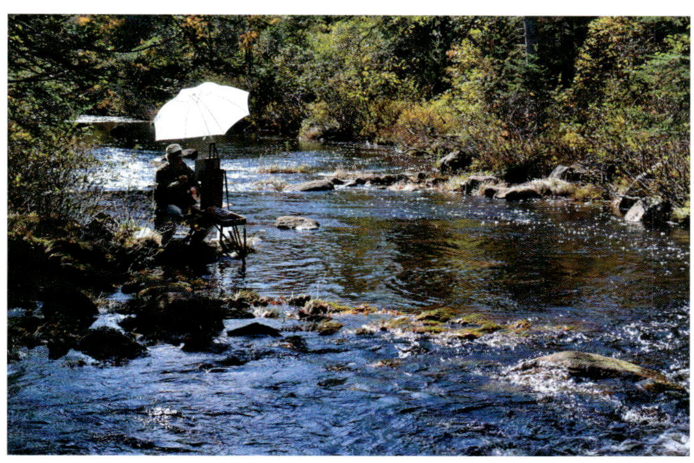

Chronology

1947
Born Waycross, Georgia.

1965
Graduated from high school in Lincoln, Nebraska.

1965–1969
Attended Princeton University, studied with George Ortman and George Segal, received fellowship in Creative Arts Program, awarded B.A. in Art History, 1969.

1969
Spent summer in Munich, Germany, as trainee at Bayerische Vereinsbank and intern at Bavarian National Museum.

1970
Spent seven months in Florence and Rome.

1971–1974
Studied at the School of Museum of Fine Arts, Boston and at Tufts University in Medford, Massachusetts. Awarded M.F.A. degree in 1974.

1974
Taught art for one semester at Tufts University.

1974–1986
Taught courses in painting and drawing for the education department of the Museum of Fine Arts, Boston.

1975
Began building a cabin in Sumner, Maine.

1980
Attended dissections at Boston University School of Medicine.

1981
Married Frannie Mosher.

1981–1988
Lived in Hull, Massachusetts, in winter and Sumner, Maine, in summer.

1988
Moved permanently to Sumner, Maine.

1982–1998
Taught painting in the Museum of Fine Arts, Boston for Harvard University Extension School.

1984
Received commission for a large painting in the lobby of the Charles Hotel in Harvard Square, Cambridge, and a large painting for the lobby of the Cambridge Savings Bank, Harvard Square.

1986–2003
Taught painting at the School of Museum of Fine Arts, Boston one day a week.

1995–1996
Received commission for a painting of the first successful organ transplant. Painting installed in the Countway Medical Library of Harvard Medical School.

2003
Gave up teaching to pursue painting full time.

Solo Exhibitions

2010
Joel Babb: The Process Revealed, Bates College Museum of Art, Lewiston, Maine.

2009
Joel M. Babb: Enlightened Perspectives, Vose Galleries, Boston.

2006
Illuminated: Boston, Maine and Rome, Joel M. Babb, Vose Galleries, Boston.

2002
Intimate Wilderness, Maine Landscapes by Joel Babb, Bates College Museum of Art Lewiston, Maine.

1991
Joel Babb: New Paintings, Gallery on the Green, Lexington, Massachusetts.

1991
Joel Babb: Perspectives, The Art Complex Museum, Duxbury, Massachusetts.

1990
Paintings of Cityscapes and Other New England Scenes, Joel Babb, St. Botolph Club, Boston.

Selected Group Exhibitions

2012
Go Figure, Trudy Labell Fine Art, Naples, Florida.

2010
People, Places & Things: The Art of Alec Soth, Joel Babb, and Ben Aronson, Naples Museum of Art, Naples, Florida.

2010
Reality Check, Trudy Labell Fine Art, Naples, Florida.

2004
Realism Now: Traditions and Departures, Mentors and Protégés, Vose Galleries, Boston.

2003
Maine Seen, Center for Maine Contemporary Art, Rockland, Maine.

2002
Representing Representation V, Arnot Art Museum, Elmira, New York.

2001
Landscapes Seen and Imagined: Sense of Place, DeCordova Museum, Lincoln, Massachusetts.

2000
Eloquent Objects, The Sense and Sensibilities of Still-Life Painting, Bates College Museum of Art, Lewiston, Maine.

1999
Green Woods & Crystal Waters, The American Landscape Tradition, Philbrook Museum of Art, Tulsa, Oklahoma; John and Mabel Ringling Museum, Sarasota, Florida; Davenport Museum of Art, Davenport, Iowa.

1999
Carried Away: The Joy of Collecting Art in Maine, Selections from the Joanna D. and Henry L. McCorkle Collection, Bates College Museum of Art, Lewiston, Maine.

1999
Looking at Katahdin: The Artists' Inspiration, L. C. Bates Museum, Hinckley, Maine.

1998
Notations of Color: Oil Sketching in Maine, Bates College Museum of Art, Lewiston, Maine.

1997
Realism in 20th Century American Painting, Ogunquit Museum of American Art, Ogunquit, Maine.

1996
30th Anniversary, Frost Gulley Gallery, Portland, Maine.

1995
The Urban Landscape, Gerold Wunderlich, New York.

1995
Expedition: Beaches, Seashores and Coastlines, USA, Sherry French Gallery, New York.

1995
An Eye for Maine, Paintings from a Private Collection, Portland Museum of Art, Portland, Maine.

1994
Maine and Other Remote Areas, Sherry French Gallery, New York.

1994
Four Maine Realist Painters, J. S. Ames Fine Arts, Belfast, Maine.

1994
169th Annual Exhibition, National Academy of Design, New York.

1993
Night Light, Barn Gallery, Ogunquit, Maine.

1993
On the Edge: Forty Years of Maine Painting, 1952–1992, Portland Museum of Art, Portland, Maine; Maine Coast Artists, Rockland, Maine; The Reed Art Gallery, University of Maine, Presque Isle, Maine.

1991
Cincinnati Collects: The Corporate View, The Contemporary Arts Center, Cincinnati, Ohio.

1991
Joel Babb, Barbara Sussman, Rush Brown, Hobe Sound Gallery North, Brunswick, Maine.

1989
The Monocular Vision: New England Realist Artists, Fitchburg Art Museum, Fitchburg, Massachusetts.

Selected Bibliography

The Art Collection of Massachusetts Financial Services, A Visual Legacy, Boston, 1992.

Arthur, John, *Green Woods & Crystal Waters: The American Landscape Tradition,* Philbrook Museum of Art, Tulsa, Oklahoma, 2000.

Beem, Edgar Allen, "At Home in Maine," *Down East,* May, 2002, pp. 65–67, 80–82.

_______________, *The Portland Show,* Greenhut Galleries, Portland, Maine, 2002

_______________, "Painting the Town," *Port City Life,* September/October, 2002.

Doran, Robert W., Susan Paine, Karen L. Pfefferle, *Project 25,* Art Department at Wellington Management, Boston, 2004.

Driscoll, John, and Arnold Skolnick, *The Artist and the American Landscape,* First Glance Books, Cobb, California, 1998.

Frenn, Chawky, *100 Boston Painters,* Schiffer Publishing, Atglen, Pennsylvania, 2012.

Jarzombek, Nancy Allyn, *Realism Now: Traditions and Departures, Mentors and Protégés,* introduction by Marcia L. Vose, essay by Trevor Fairbrother, Vose Galleries, Boston, 2003.

Jarzombek, Nancy Allyn, *Illuminated, Boston, Maine and Rome,* Vose Galleries, Boston, 2006.

May, Stephen, "Old Influences, New Approaches," *American Artist,* March, 2004.

McCorkle, Joanna and Henry, *Carried Away, The Joy of Collecting Art in Maine, Selections from the Joanna D. and Henry L. McCorkle Collection,* introduction by Genetta McLean, Bates College Museum of Art, Lewiston, Maine, 1999.

McGregor, James H. S., *Intimate Wilderness, Maine Landscapes by Joel Babb*, introduction by Genetta McLean, Bates College Museum of Art, Lewiston, Maine, 2002.

McLean, Genetta, "Bates College Museum of Art," *American Art Review,* June 2000.

"Mentors and Protégés," *International Artist,* October/November, 2003.

O'Hearn, John D., *Representing Representation V,* Arnot Art Museum, Elmira, New York, 2001.

Vose, Marcia Latimore, *Joel Babb: Enlightened Perspectives,* Vose Galleries, Boston, 2009.

Zevitas, Stephen T., *New American Paintings VII,* The Open Studios Press, Wellesley, Massachusetts., 1996.

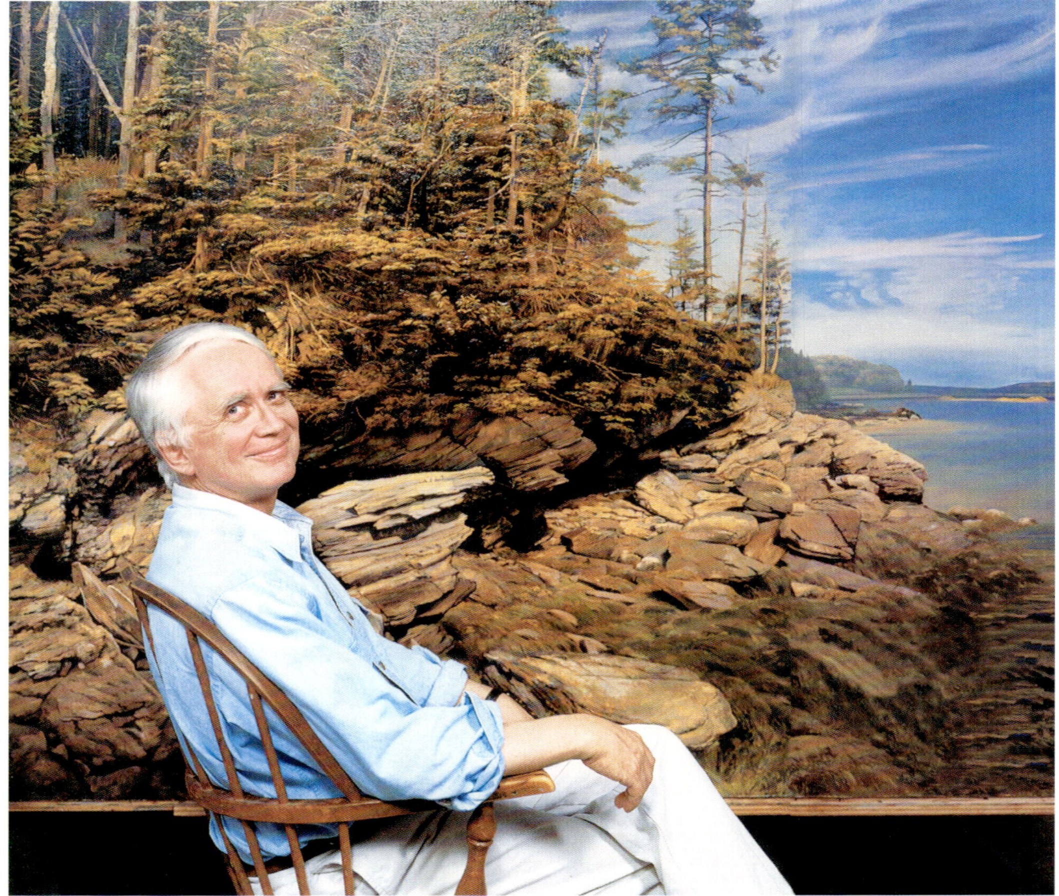

Photo by Amazeen